CW00386451

Looking Again
at the Question of the Liturgy
with Cardinal Ratzinger

Looking Again at the Question of the Liturgy with Cardinal Ratzinger

Proceedings of the July 2001
Fontgombault Liturgical Conference

Edited by
Alcuin Reid OSB

Saint Michael's Abbey Press
MMIII

SAINT MICHAEL'S ABBEY PRESS
Saint Michael's Abbey
Farnborough
Hampshire GU14 7NQ

Telephone +44 (0) 1252 546 105
Facsimile +44 (0) 1252 372 822

www.farnboroughabbey.org
prior@farnboroughabbey.org

Original edition:
Autour de la Question Liturgique
avec le Cardinal Ratzinger
Actes des 'Journées liturgiques de Fontgombault'
22-24 Juillet 2001
Association Petrus a Stella
Abbaye Notre-Dame
Fontgombault
2001

English edition:
© Saint Michael's Abbey, Farnborough, 2003

Cum permissu superiorum

ISBN 0 907077 42 0

A catalogue record for this book is available from the British Library.

Printed and bound by Newton Printing Ltd., London.

Contents

CONTENTS

CONTENTS

Introduction

S OME years ago, whilst a theological student, I submitted a paper to my Professor of Liturgy which quoted at length from Cardinal Ratzinger's work *The Feast of Faith: Approaches to a Theology of the Liturgy*.[1] The paper was not at all well received: "Cardinal Ratzinger is not a liturgist," the Professor retorted, "and we should not use him as an authority on the Liturgy."

Indeed, Cardinal Ratzinger is not a liturgist. But perhaps that is, in fact, one very good reason why one *ought* to turn to him on matters liturgical, for as Father Aidan Nichols OP so aptly put it, "Liturgy is too important to be left to liturgists."[2]

Cardinal Ratzinger is a bishop, a distinguished theologian, Prefect of the Congregation for the Doctrine of the Faith, and a cardinal—more than sufficient credentials to speak intelligently and authoritatively on matters liturgical. And he has certainly spoken and written on the question of the Liturgy frequently. It is probably not too soon to say that, historically, it is in no small way due to his Eminence's public interventions on the state of Catholic Liturgy of the Roman rite since the Second Vatican Council that, in the past two decades, it has been possible publicly to engage in critical assessment of post-conciliar liturgical reforms and practices, and to begin to explore appropriate remedies and paths forward. Such critical examination is necessary because, as the Cardinal himself puts it:

> The Church stands and falls with the Liturgy. When the adoration of the divine Trinity declines, when the faith no longer appears in its fullness in the Liturgy of the Church, when man's words, his thoughts, his intentions are suffocating him, then faith will have lost the place where it is expressed and where it dwells. For that reason, the true celebration of the Sacred Liturgy is the centre of any renewal of the Church whatever.[3]

---

[1] Ignatius Press, San Francisco 1986.

[2] *Looking Again at the Liturgy: A Critical View of its Contemporary Form*, Ignatius Press, San Francisco 1996, p. 9.

[3] Preface to: Franz Breid, ed., *Die heilige Liturgie*, papers from the "Internationale Theologische Sommerakademie 1997" of the Priests' Circle of Linz, Ennsthaler Verlag, Steyr 1997; cited in the paper of Professor de Mattei, below.

But how, today, at the beginning of the third Christian millennium, do we achieve "the true celebration of the Liturgy"? Is the answer a wholesale return to the traditional rites? Is it in accepting a wide diversity of divergent uses — new, old and inculturated — in the Roman rite? Or is it in seeking an official reform of the liturgical reform that followed the Second Vatican Council? These are the issues that were discussed by both liturgists and well qualified non-liturgists alike in the presence of Cardinal Ratzinger at the Abbey of *Notre-Dame de Fontgombault* from 22-24 July 2001.

In making the papers from that meeting available in English translation — papers that inform and challenge — it is hoped to promote wider consideration of the crucial question of the Liturgy in our day, and to underline the necessity and urgency of this task, as Cardinal Ratzinger himself has done so frequently. In this edition, as far as possible, references to English translations of works cited by the authors have been given. In some instances, in order to assist the reader, references not present in the French text have been added.

Saint Michael's Abbey Press gratefully acknowledges the kind permission given by the Right Reverend Dom Antoine Forgeot OSB, Abbot of *Notre-Dame de Fontgombault*, to publish this English edition of the proceedings of the conference, and the generous permission of the individual contributors to translate and publish their papers. We are indebted to the monks of *Notre-Dame de Fontgombault* and to the Society of Saint John, to the Central Catholic Library, Léonie Caldecott, Daniel P.J. Coughlan, Rev'd Dr Peter Joseph, Peter Harden, Christine Parkin, Professor William H.C. Smith, Gregory Taylor, Henry Taylor and Gary Scarrabelotti for their assistance in the preparation of this edition.

Cardinal Ratzinger has stressed — rightly — that there shall be no short-term resolution to the question of the Liturgy. But there can be no resolution at all, there can be no achievement of the true celebration of the Sacred Liturgy for the Church of today, or of tomorrow, if the question of the Liturgy, ignored for too long, is not looked at anew, and without further delay.

Dom Alcuin Reid OSB
Saint Michael's Abbey
Farnborough
29th September 2003

Foreword

The Right Reverend Dom Hervé Courau OSB
Abbot of Triors

T HE idea of a Liturgical Conference at Fontgombault arose from several meetings with Cardinal Ratzinger. His thinking, as his recent book *The Spirit of the Liturgy*[1] shows so well, often centres around the idea of a new Liturgical Movement, or rather of a new "breath" to "reinvigorate" this movement on which so many hopes had legitimately been based. History can not be rewritten and lost opportunities do not come again. The great construction-site of liturgical reform needs to stabilise its foundations. This is not so much wisdom as common sense. The disappointments of the recent past, although they may seem cruel, are not wholly negative, since they provide positive lessons for the future. The Liturgical Movement can only be revived on sound bases, putting greater hope in that special providence which governs the Prayer of the Church: only the Holy Spirit is equipped to enable it to say *Abba – Father*.

The Cardinal did not want a debate in front of crowds of people and, in any event, the environment at Fontgombault would not lend itself to that. At the same time it was essential to provide a representative sample of the participants and, in large part, the choice is that of the Cardinal himself. He wanted those who use the two Roman Missals of 1962 and 1970 to be equally represented.

These conferences took place from 22nd to 24th July 2001. On Sunday 22nd the Cardinal sang Holy Mass (1962 Missal) and preached. At the beginning of the afternoon, after the participants had been welcomed by the Abbot of Fontgombault, Dom Antoine Forgeot, the real work began. Thoughts needed to be channelled in four directions which meant four series of discussions, a lecture followed by more direct applications, i.e., Theology of the Liturgy, anthropological aspects of the Liturgy, Roman rite or Roman rites (or what scope is there for diversity in the Roman Liturgy?). And finally, what are the problems posed by liturgical reform and what lessons can be learned for a new Liturgical Movement?

These various discussions were followed by brief but spirited debates of which a summary appears at the end of this book. Additionally, three

---

[1] Ignatius Press, San Francisco 2000.

laymen made contributions before the Cardinal gave the closing paper. May we all draw from them the light and the courage to work in humility, each one in his appointed place, in the great field of the Prayer of the Church.

Two thoughts from monastic writers from antiquity often came back to me during these conferences. "If you pray, you are a theologian, if you are a theologian, you pray" (St Nilus of Sinai). "The monk (i.e. the Christian) really begins to pray when he is unaware that he is praying" (St Anthony the Great). I link it to the beginning of part four of the Cardinal's book: "Christian faith's great gift: we know what right worship is."[2]

The *devotio moderna* (the first use of the word 'modern'!) brought about a divorce, in about the fifteenth century, between the Liturgy and interior prayer, all too often opening up the latter to the risk of introspection—even if the Carmelite and Jesuit schools were raised up by divine Providence to lessen this danger. In the intellectual movement which came from Dom Guéranger and which was crowned by Vatican II (even if, alas, a great number of its applications are foreign to it), the tenor of this meeting seemed to me to lean towards a *devotio postmoderna,* a renewal with the *devotio antiqua* without calling into question the efforts of the spiritual theology of the second millennium. The aim is to reunite once again the interior Liturgy with that of the Bridal Church, along the lines of the Fathers and without arriving at an *impasse* at the Middle Ages, which knew how to be faithful to it: here St Thomas Aquinas and the Council of Trent are, as the Cardinal has stressed, the irreplaceable points of reference. The third millennium must redress what has been distorted in the preceding one, and that without the reductivist pretension of archaeologism denounced in *Mediator Dei,* the ravages of which have been far from minimal. In particular, unity with the Christian East will be influenced by this reorientation of the Liturgy of the Roman rite which is called on to sample more deeply its authentic sources and to be faithful to them. Its noble simplicity has been too easily confused with an impoverished ritual. The resultant void in sacred art, and the absence of interiority, obscuring that of prayer, are very serious symptoms which above all cry to God that the gift of faith may be abundantly given to souls. That gift renders the Liturgy amenable to the Holy Spirit, the only one who can make us pray in truth, "Abba Father."

Translated by Professor William H.C. Smith

---

[2] Ibid., p. 160.

Mary and Martha

Homily of His Eminence, Joseph Cardinal Ratzinger
Prefect of the Congregation for the Doctrine of the Faith

D EAR brothers and sisters: Saint Luke links the two Gospels—last Sunday's Gospel on the Good Samaritan, and today's on Mary and Martha—by means of a Greek expression which means "to be on the way." The Gospel about the Good Samaritan ends with the word "Go" (*Be on your way*); the other begins with the words: "Jesus was *on his way* towards Jerusalem." We remember the great vision of St Luke, according to which the whole public ministry of Our Lord consists in being "on the way:" *en route* towards Jerusalem, towards the Paschal Mystery, the redemptive mystery of the Cross and the Resurrection. And on this "way," Jesus is looking for our love, our availability, our attention. He prepares us for the mystery of his presence, the gift of his life. After Easter, the same idea occurs, as the Gospel tells us: "Jesus goes before you into Galilee." He is still *en route* towards Galilee, the Galilee of the world in which we must now—with him, through him—proclaim the reign of God, preparing the world for the presence of his reign, for *his* presence. In this sense, the Lord who goes before us into Galilee is with us now on the road towards the new Jerusalem, the heavenly Jerusalem, the world of heaven. Thus in this link between the two Gospels, the Lord also shows us the different dimensions pertaining to the love of our neighbour.

If, in the Gospel on the Samaritan, we perceive especially the exterior aspect of social action, of external material aid for the other person, in the Gospel on Saints Mary and Martha another dimension appears: the dimension of the *presence of Christ's word*—the dimension of meditation, of interiority. Taken together, these two Gospels show us that love of neighbour and love of God are inseparable, indeed that they should interpenetrate one another. In the love of neighbour there must always *also* be the love of God. We must not give the other person material goods only, but also God. Otherwise we are forgetting the essential thing, "the one thing necessary." And correspondingly, in the love of God the love of neighbour must also be present; for in our neighbour it is Jesus himself who comes to us and asks for hospitality.

It seems to me that this is a very important teaching, particularly for the times in which we live. For after the Second Vatican Council, the idea spread that the content of the Gospel consists in social development, and that we should concentrate on doing external, material things. After this we might still, perhaps, have time for God. The consequences of this were all too apparent: even missionaries no longer had the courage to proclaim the Gospel. They felt it was now their primary duty to contribute to the development of the poorer countries. The consequences of forgetting God are terrible: the moral foundations of our societies are being destroyed. This is not "progress." In terrible epidemics, we see all too clearly the consequences of forgetting the essential thing, the necessary thing, God himself. A love of neighbour which forgets God forgets the essential.

But let us return to the Gospel about Mary and Martha. At first sight, it looks like a merely human instruction to do with the essential dimensions of hospitality. The Lord tells us that for a true human hospitality to exist, it is not enough to give food, to give external things. The real host gives more; most especially, he must give his *time*. He must be open to the other, give a little of himself, be attentive to the other in order to be able to respond to his needs. But within this teaching, which at first sight appears to be on a purely human level—for even in a purely human hospitality, we must give more than just external things—we see shining forth a more profound reality: the necessity of being open above all to the *one thing necessary*, to the presence of God who, in his Word, gives us himself.

In this teaching on the necessity of being open to the Lord, of being at the feet of the Lord in order to enter into communion with him, the Lord is also speaking to the Church of today. Because the same problems—let us define them as problems of the correct balance between Mary and Martha— exist most particularly in the Church today. We are truly doing *the work of Martha*. We are busying ourselves with many exterior things: meetings, commissions, synods, discussions, decisions. Many documents are issued, many pastoral programmes are organised; yes, we are doing a great deal. But perhaps, in the course of this ceaseless activity, this permanent service of Martha's, which invests everything in [the success of] pastoral activism, we are forgetting the dimension represented by Mary. We are forgetting that our real availability to the Lord, for the sake of his reign, demands far more from us than simple external actions; we are forgetting that it requires of us, most particularly, our availability to be at the feet of Our Lord, meditating on and listening to his Word, in which he gives us himself.

In a letter from St Thérèse of Lisieux to her sister Céline (19th August 1894), there is a very beautiful passage on this situation in the Church. Meditating on the figures of Mary and Martha, St Thérèse says: "When Mary pours the precious ointment onto the head of the Lord, all the Apostles murmur against her." She continues: "It is the same thing today: even the most fervent Christians, the priests and the bishops, all think that we are exaggerating, that we should serve the Lord like Martha, and not consecrate ourselves to the Lord, not try to console him. Yet nonetheless, from the broken jars of our lives, there arises the precious perfume which purifies the poisoned air of this world."

This thought—that the perfume which purifies the poisoned air of this world comes from the broken jars of people's lives, from this marian dimension—is not only a very profound theology of the contemplative life and of the life of the Church in general, but seems to me to offer a true and very profound theology of the Liturgy. Certainly in the Liturgy we should also give the service of Martha: offering a sacred space to the Lord, offering him our preparations, well-planned ceremonies and the chant, offering him the gifts of the earth, the bread and the wine. All of this is very necessary, and it is equally necessary to do it well. Yet nonetheless, if the marian dimension is not also present in the Liturgy—the contemplative dimension in which we simply sit at the Lord's feet—the most essential thing has gone missing. Similarly, if the Liturgy is truly, in this sense, "marian"—that is to say, if it enables us to sit at the feet of the Lord in order to *hear what he is saying to us,* and to receive the gift of himself—in other words, if the Liturgy is truly contemplative, then it becomes the gesture through which the poisoned air of this world can be purified. I believe that only a really "marian" Liturgy can purify the poisoned air of the world today.

Both in the first reading of today (Gen. 18:1-10), on the apparition of the Trinity to Abraham, and in the Gospel, I find therefore a very profound view of the Liturgy with its two dimensions. In Genesis, it is Abraham who generously offers his hospitality to the Lord, to the Trinity. He offers the calf, the bread, the cheese, he washes the feet of his guests, he gives unreservedly of himself. But in the end it is the Lord who gives the one thing necessary, the essential thing: he gives him a son, and with the son he gives a future, he gives life and hope. The same thing applies in the Gospel: Martha offers good things to the Lord, she offers the gifts of her home, and Mary offers her *listening ear,* her profound availability. But in the end it is the Lord who not only gives his word, but also gives his very self. And this is the essence of the Liturgy: we offer up our poor gifts, and we receive from the hands of the Lord himself *the* gift, the one thing necessary, his Body and Blood; and in his Body and Blood we receive eternal life, the reign of God, Redemption.

Let us pray to the Lord to help us—to help the Church—to celebrate the Liturgy well, to be truly *at the feet of the Lord,* to receive the gift of true life, the essential and necessary reality, for the salvation of all, the salvation of the world. Amen.

Translated by Léonie Caldecott

"Listen, O My Son..."

Welcome by the Right Reverend Dom Antoine Forgeot OSB
Abbot of *Notre-Dame de Fontgombault*

O N behalf of all the Community of Fontgombault, I want to thank you for your presence here which greatly honours us. I am very grateful to the organisers of this meeting, who have chosen our monastery. With all my heart I welcome you to this House of God, of Our Lady, and of St Benedict. I greet you in the name of our Archbishop, Msgr Hubert Barbier, whom I have kept informed about this meeting. Unfortunately, he is at the moment absent from the diocese. The Rector of the Pontifical University of the Holy Cross, in Rome, has also expressed his apologies at being unable to be here. His Excellency, Msgr Fabian Bruskewitz, Bishop of Lincoln, Nebraska, USA, has also assured me of his good wishes and his prayers. His Eminence Cardinal Castrillón Hoyos, Prefect of the Congregation for the Clergy and President of the Pontifical Commission *Ecclesia Dei* "sends all his good wishes for the spiritual, theological and ecclesiastical benefits which will spring forth abundantly from this meeting." Finally, His Eminence Cardinal Medina Estevez, Prefect of the Congregation for Divine Worship, has sent me the following letter:

Rome, 30th May 2001

I am very grateful to you for informing me about the *Journées Liturgiques de Fontgombault* which will take place from the 22nd to the 24th July next, under the presidency of the Rt Rev. Abbot Dom Hervé Courau OSB and in the presence of His Eminence Cardinal Joseph Ratzinger whose recent book on the Liturgy is truly worthy, in all its various topics, of close attention.

Since the Sacred Liturgy is the source and the summit of the Church's life, a deep analysis of its content is always productive and beneficial. For these reasons I congratulate you in anticipation hoping that these conferences will be of great spiritual benefit.

To you, Rt Rev. Fr Abbot, to the monks of the Abbey, and to all the participants in these conferences, I send you, with a full heart, my blessing. Please accept, Rt Rev. Fr Abbot, my most cordial and esteemed wishes in the Lord.

✠Jorge A. Card. Medina Estevez, Prefect

✠Francesco Pio Tamburrino, Secr.

Your Eminence, your presence here is particularly precious to us. We all know the interest that you have taken for some considerable time in the question of the Liturgy, a question so vital for the Church since, according to the Council: "Every liturgical celebration, because it is an action of Christ the priest and of His Body which is the Church, is a sacred action surpassing all others; no other action of the Church can equal its efficacy by the same title and to the same degree."[1]

Your words will guide us in our deliberations and we would wish to receive them with the same docility that St Benedict recommends to his disciple, to whom he says: *Ausculta, o fili, præcepta magistri, et inclina aurem cordis tui...*[2]

May we find, with St Benedict, that disposition which, however simple and naïve it seems, is nevertheless the secret all too little known in our days: to accomplish something worthwhile and lasting. This secret is wholly evangelical and, as such, is of perennial value. In these times requiring difficult discernment this utterly simple meekness, and fidelity to the Church, linked to mutual comprehension and respect for others, can not but help us to work fruitfully.

Allow me here, Eminence, to offer you our fervent and respectful wishes on the occasion of the Jubilee of your fifty years in the priesthood, which you have just celebrated on the Feast of Saints Peter and Paul. The Holy Father paid you a striking testimony, which sprang from his heart as Father and Pastor. We humbly join ourselves with this, thanking you for so much toil, and also no doubt so much pain, in the service of Holy Church. We join in your thanksgiving for the fifty years which have passed and we pray the Lord that He will give you many more, all similarly fruitful.

It is a great joy that we can join our deliberations during these days to the grace of your priesthood. I entrust to Dom Guéranger, author of *L'Année Liturgique* and the *Institutions Liturgiques,* this work which we hope shall be clear and fruitful. It can only be thus if we entrust it to Our Lady, Mother of the Church, saying to her: *Sub tuum præsidium confugimus, sancta Dei Genitrix.*

Translated by Professor William H.C. Smith

---

[1] *Sacrosanctum Concilium*, no 7.

[2] "Hearken, my son, to the precepts of the master, and incline the ear of thy heart..." Prologue of the Rule of Saint Benedict.

The Theology of the Liturgy

Paper by His Eminence, Joseph Cardinal Ratzinger
Prefect of the Congregation for the Doctrine of the Faith

THE Second Vatican Council defined the Liturgy as "the work of Christ the Priest and of His Body which is the Church."[1] The work of Jesus Christ is referred to in the same text as the work of the redemption which Christ accomplished especially by the Paschal Mystery of His Passion, of His Resurrection from the dead and His glorious Ascension.

"By this Mystery, in dying He has destroyed our death, and in rising He has restored life." At first sight, in these two sentences, the phrase "the work of Christ" seems to have been used in two different senses. "The work of Christ" refers first of all to the historical, redemptive actions of Jesus, His Death and His Resurrection; on the other hand, the celebration of the Liturgy is called "the work of Christ."

In reality, the two meanings are inseparably linked: the Death and Resurrection of Christ, the Paschal Mystery, are not just exterior, historic events. In the case of the Resurrection this is very clear. It is joined to and penetrates history, but transcends it in two ways: it is not the action of a man, but an action of God, and in that way carries the risen Jesus beyond history, to that place where He sits at the right hand of the Father. But the Cross is not a merely human action either. The purely human aspect is present in the people who led Jesus to the Cross. For Jesus Himself, the Cross is not primarily an action, but a passion, and a passion which signifies that He is but one with the Divine Will—a union, the dramatic character of which is shown to us in the Garden of Gethsemane. Thus the passive dimension of being put to death is transformed into the active dimension of love: death becomes the abandonment of Himself to the Father for men. In this way, the horizon extends, as it does in the Resurrection, well beyond the purely human aspect and well beyond the fact of having been nailed to a cross and having died. This element additional to the mere historical event is what the language of faith calls a "mystery" and it has condensed into the term "Paschal Mystery" the most innermost core of the redemptive event. If we can say from this that the "Paschal Mystery" constitutes the core of "the work of Jesus," then the connection with the Liturgy is immediately clear: it is precisely this "work of

---

[1] *Sacrosanctum Concilium*, no. 7.

Jesus" which is the real content of the Liturgy. In it, through the faith and the prayer of the Church, the "work of Jesus" is continually brought into contact with history in order to penetrate it. Thus, in the Liturgy, the merely human historical event is transcended over and over again and is part of the divine and human action which is the Redemption. In it, Christ is the true subject/bearer: it is the work of Christ; but in it He draws history to Himself, precisely in this permanent action in which our salvation takes place.

1. Sacrifice Called into Question

If we go back to Vatican II, we find the following description of this relationship: "In the Liturgy, through which, especially in the divine Sacrifice of the Eucharist, 'the work of our Redemption is carried on,' the faithful are most fully led to express and show to others the mystery of Christ and the real nature of the true Church."[2]

All that has become foreign to modern thinking and, only thirty years after the Council, has been brought into question even among Catholic liturgists. Who still talks today about "the divine Sacrifice of the Eucharist"? Discussions about the idea of sacrifice have again become astonishingly lively, as much on the Catholic side as on the Protestant. People realise that an idea which has always preoccupied, under various forms, not only the history of the Church, but the entire history of humanity, must be the expression of something basic which concerns us as well. But, at the same time, the old Enlightenment positions still live on everywhere: accusations of magic and paganism, contrasts drawn between worship and the service of the Word, between rite and ethos, the idea of a Christianity which disengages itself from worship and enters into the profane world, Catholic theologians who have no desire to see themselves accused of anti-modernity. Even if people want, in one way or another, to rediscover the concept of sacrifice, embarrassment and criticism are the end result. Thus, Stefan Orth, in the vast panorama of a bibliography of recent works devoted to the theme of sacrifice, believed he could make the following statement as a summary of his research: "In fact, many Catholics themselves today ratify the verdict and the conclusions of Martin Luther, who says that to speak of sacrifice is "the greatest and most appalling horror" and a "damnable impiety:" this is why we want to refrain from all that smacks of sacrifice, including the whole Canon, and retain only that which is pure and holy." Then Orth adds: "This maxim was also followed in the Catholic Church after Vatican II, or at least tended to be, and led people to think of divine worship chiefly in terms of the feast of the Passover related in the accounts of the Last Supper." Appealing to a work on sacrifice, edited by two modern Catholic liturgists, he then said, in slightly more moderate terms, that it clearly seemed that the notion of the sacrifice of the Mass—even

---

[2] Ibid., no. 2.

more than that of the sacrifice of the Cross—was at best an idea very open to misunderstanding.

I certainly don't need to say that I am not one of the "numerous Catholics" who consider it the most appalling horror and a damnable impiety to speak of the sacrifice of the Mass. It goes without saying that the writer did not mention my book on the spirit of the Liturgy, which analyses the idea of sacrifice in detail. His diagnosis remains dismaying. Is it true? I do not know these numerous Catholics who consider it a damnable impiety to understand the Eucharist as a sacrifice. The second, more circumspect, diagnosis according to which the sacrifice of the Mass is open to misunderstandings is, on the other hand, easily shown to be correct. Even if one leaves to one side the first affirmation of the writer as a rhetorical exaggeration, there remains a troubling problem, to which we should face up. A sizeable party of Catholic liturgists seems to have practically arrived at the conclusion that Luther, rather than Trent, was substantially right in the sixteenth century debate; one can detect much the same position in the post-conciliar discussions on the Priesthood. The great historian of the Council of Trent, Hubert Jedin, pointed this out in 1975, in the preface to the last volume of his history of the Council of Trent: "The attentive reader...in reading this will not be less dismayed than the author, when he realises that many of the things—in fact almost everything—that disturbed the men of the past is being put forward anew today."[3] It is only against this background of the effective denial of the authority of Trent, that the bitterness of the struggle against allowing the celebration of Mass according to the 1962 Missal, after the liturgical reform, can be understood. The possibility of so celebrating constitutes the strongest, and thus (for them) the most intolerable contradiction of the opinion of those who believe that the faith in the Eucharist formulated by Trent has lost its value.

It would be easy to gather proofs to support this statement of the position. I leave aside the extreme liturgical theology of Harald Schützeichel, who departs completely from Catholic dogma and expounds, for example, the bold assertion that it was only in the Middle Ages that the idea of the Real Presence was invented. A modern liturgist such as David N. Power tells us that through the course of history, not only the manner in which a truth is expressed, but also the content of what is expressed, can lose its meaning. He links his theory in concrete terms with the statements of Trent. Theodore Schnitker tells us that an up-to-date liturgy includes both a different expression of the faith and theological changes. Moreover, according to him, there are theologians, at least in the circles of the Roman Church and of her Liturgy, who have not yet grasped the full import of the transformations put forward by the liturgical reform in the area of the doctrine of the faith. R. Meßner's certainly respectable work on the reform of the Mass carried out by

---

[3] Cf. *Geschichte des Konzils von Trient,* vol. 4, Herder, Freiburg 1975.

Martin Luther, and on the Eucharist in the early Church, which contains many interesting ideas, arrives nonetheless at the conclusion that the early Church was better understood by Luther than by the Council of Trent.

The serious nature of these theories comes from the fact that frequently they pass immediately into practice. The thesis according to which it is the community itself which is the subject of the Liturgy, serves as an authorisation to manipulate the Liturgy according to each individual's understanding of it. So-called new discoveries and the forms which follow from them, are diffused with an astonishing rapidity and with a degree of conformity which has long ceased to exist where the norms of ecclesiastical authority are concerned. Theories, in the area of the Liturgy, are transformed very rapidly today into practice, and practice, in turn, creates or destroys ways of behaving and thinking.

Meanwhile the problem has been aggravated by the fact that the most recent movement of 'enlightened' thought goes much further than Luther: where Luther still took literally the accounts of the Institution and made them, as the *norma normans*, the basis of his efforts at reform, the hypotheses of historical criticism have, for a long time, been causing a broad erosion of the texts. The accounts of the Last Supper appear as the product of the liturgical construction of the community; an historical Jesus is sought behind the texts who could not have been thinking of the gift of His Body and Blood, nor understood His Cross as a sacrifice of expiation; we should, rather, imagine a farewell meal which included an eschatological perspective. Not only is the authority of the ecclesiastical Magisterium downgraded in the eyes of many, but Scripture also; in its place are put changing pseudo-historical hypotheses, which are immediately replaced by any arbitrary idea, and place the Liturgy at the mercy of fashion. Where, on the basis of such ideas, the Liturgy is manipulated ever more freely, the faithful feel that, in reality, nothing is celebrated, and it is understandable that they desert the Liturgy, and with it the Church.

2. *The Principles of Theological Research*

Let us return to the fundamental question: is it correct to describe the Liturgy as a divine sacrifice, or is it a damnable impiety? In this discussion, one must first of all establish the principle presuppositions which, in any event, determine the reading of Scripture, and thus the conclusions which one draws from it. For the Catholic Christian, two lines of essential hermeneutic orientation assert themselves here. The first: we trust Scripture and we base ourselves on Scripture, not on hypothetical reconstructions which go behind it and, according to their own taste, reconstruct a history in which the presumptuous idea of our knowing what can or can not be attributed to Jesus plays a key role; which, of course, means attributing to him only what a modern scholar is happy to attribute to a man belonging to a time which the scholar himself has reconstructed.

The second is that we read Scripture in the living community of the Church, and therefore on the basis of the fundamental decisions thanks to which it has become historically efficacious, namely, those which laid the foundations of the Church. One must not separate the text from this living context. In this sense, Scripture and Tradition form an inseparable whole, and it is this that Luther, at the dawn of the awakening of historical awareness, could not see. He believed that a text could only have one meaning, but such univocity does not exist, and modern historiography has long since abandoned the idea. That in the nascent Church, the Eucharist was, from the beginning, understood as a sacrifice, even in a text such as the Didache, which is so difficult and marginal *vis-à-vis* the great Tradition, is an interpretative key of primary importance.

But there is another fundamental hermeneutical aspect in the reading and the interpretation of biblical testimony. The fact that I can, or can not, recognise a sacrifice in the Eucharist as our Lord instituted it, depends most essentially on the question of knowing what I understand by sacrifice, therefore on what is called pre-comprehension. The pre-comprehension of Luther, for example, in particular his conception of the relation between the Old and the New Testaments, his conception of the event and of the historic presence of the Church, was such that the category of sacrifice, as he saw it, could not appear other than as an impiety when applied to the Eucharist and the Church. The debates to which Stefan Orth refers show how confused and muddled is the idea of sacrifice among almost all authors, and clearly shows how much work must be done here. For the believing theologian, it is clear that it is Scripture itself which must teach him the essential definition of sacrifice, and that will come from a "canonical" reading of the Bible, in which the Scripture is read in its unity and its dynamic movement, the different stages of which receive their final meaning from Christ, to Whom this whole movement leads. By this same standard the hermeneutic here presupposed is a hermeneutic of faith, founded on faith's internal logic. Ought not the fact to be obvious? Without faith, Scripture itself is not Scripture, but rather an ill-assorted ensemble of bits of literature which can not claim any normative significance today.

3. Sacrifice and Easter

The task alluded to here far exceeds, obviously, the limits of one lecture; so allow me to refer you to my book *The Spirit of the Liturgy* in which I have sought to give the main outlines of this question. What emerges from it is that, in its course through the history of religions and biblical history, the idea of sacrifice has connotations which go well beyond the area of discussion which we habitually associate with the idea of sacrifice. In fact, it opens the doorway to a global understanding of worship and of the Liturgy: these are the great perspectives which I would like to try to point out here. Also I necessarily have to omit here particular questions of exegesis, in particular the fundamental problem of the accounts of the Institution, on the subject of which, in addition to my book on the Liturgy, I have tried to provide some thoughts in my contribution on "The Eucharist and Mission."[4]

There is, however, a remark which I can not refrain from making. In the bibliographic review mentioned, Stefan Orth says that the fact of having avoided after Vatican II, the idea of sacrifice, has "led people to think of divine worship in terms of the feast of the Passover related in the accounts of the Last Supper." At first sight this wording appears ambiguous: is one to think of divine worship in terms of the Last Supper narratives, or in terms of the Passover, to which those narratives refer in giving a chronological framework, but which they do not otherwise describe. It would be right to say that the Jewish Passover, the institution of which is related in Exodus 12, acquires a new meaning in the New Testament. It is there that is manifested a great historical movement which goes from the beginnings right up to the Last Supper, the Cross and the Resurrection of Jesus. But what is astonishing above all in Orth's presentation is the opposition posited between the idea of sacrifice and the Passover. The Jewish Old Testament deprives Orth's thesis of meaning, because from the law of Deuteronomy on, the slaughtering of lambs is linked to the Temple; and even in the earliest period, when the Passover was still a family feast, the slaughtering of lambs already had a sacrificial character. Thus, precisely through the tradition of the Passover, the idea of sacrifice is carried right up to the words and gestures of the Last Supper, where it is present also on the basis of a second Old Testament passage, Exodus 24, which relates the conclusion of the Covenant at Sinai. There, it is related that the people were sprinkled with the blood of the victims previously brought, and that Moses said on this occasion: "Behold the blood of the covenant which the Lord has made with you in accordance with all these words" (Ex. 24:8). The new Christian Passover is thus expressly interpreted in the accounts of the Last Supper as a sacrificial event, and on the basis of the words of the Last Supper, the nascent Church knew that the Cross was a sacrifice, because the Last Supper would be an empty gesture without the reality of the Cross and of the Resurrection, which is anticipated in it and made accessible for all time in its interior content.

I mention this strange opposition between the Passover and sacrifice, because it represents the architectonic principle of a book recently published by the Society of St Pius X, claiming that a dogmatic rupture exists between

---

4 Cf. "Communion, Community and Mission: On the Connection between the Eucharist, (Parish) Community and Mission in the Church" in Joseph Ratzinger, *Behold the Pierced One*, Ignatius Press, San Francisco 1986.

the new Liturgy of Paul VI and the preceding Catholic liturgical tradition.[5] This rupture is seen precisely in the fact that everything is interpreted henceforth on the basis of the "Paschal Mystery," instead of the redeeming sacrifice of expiation of Christ; the category of the Paschal Mystery is said to be the heart of the liturgical reform, and it is precisely that which appears to be the proof of the rupture with the classical doctrine of the Church. It is clear that there are authors who lay themselves open to such a misunderstanding; but that it is a misunderstanding is completely evident to those who look more closely. In reality, the term "Paschal Mystery" clearly refers to the realities which took place in the days following Holy Thursday up until the morning of Easter Sunday: the Last Supper as the anticipation of the Cross, the drama of Golgotha and the Lord's Resurrection. In the expression "Paschal Mystery" these happenings are seen synthetically as a single, united event, as "the work of Christ," as we heard the Council say at the beginning, which took place historically and at the same time transcends that precise point in time. As this event is, inwardly, an act of worship rendered to God, it could become divine worship, and in that way be present to all times. The paschal theology of the New Testament, upon which we have cast a quick glance, gives us to understand precisely this: the seemingly profane episode of the Crucifixion of Christ is a sacrifice of expiation, a saving act of the reconciling love of God made man. The theology of the Passover is a theology of the redemption, a Liturgy of expiatory sacrifice. The Shepherd has become a Lamb. The vision of the lamb, which appears in the story of Isaac, the lamb which gets entangled in the undergrowth and ransoms the son, has become a reality; the Lord became a Lamb; He allows Himself to be bound and sacrificed, to deliver us.

All this has become very foreign to contemporary thought. Reparation ("expiation") can perhaps mean something within the limits of human conflicts and the settling of guilt which holds sway among human beings, but its transposition to the relationship between God and man can not work. This, surely, is largely the result of the fact that our image of God has grown dim, has come close to deism. One can no longer imagine that human offences can wound God, and even less that they could necessitate an expiation such as that which constitutes the Cross of Christ. The same applies to vicarious substitution: we can hardly still imagine anything in that category — our image of man has become too individualistic for that. Thus the crisis of the Liturgy has its basis in central ideas about man. In order to overcome it, it does not suffice to banalise the Liturgy and transform it into a simple gathering at a fraternal meal. But how can we escape from these disorientations? How can we recover the meaning of this immense thing which is at the heart of the message of the Cross and of the Resurrection? In the final analysis, not through theories and scholarly reflections, but only through conversion, by a radical change of life. It is, however, possible to single out some things which

---

[5] Cf. The Society of Saint Pius X, *The Problem of the Liturgical Reform*, Angelus Press, Kansas City 2001.

open the way to this change of heart, and I would like to put forward some suggestions in that direction, in three stages.

4. Love, the Heart of Sacrifice

The first stage should be a preliminary question on the essential meaning of the word "sacrifice." People commonly consider sacrifice as the destruction of something precious in the eyes of man; in destroying it, man wants to consecrate this reality to God, to recognise His sovereignty. In fact, however, a destruction does not honour God. The slaughtering of animals or whatever else, can not honour God. "If I am hungry, I will not tell you, because the world is mine and all it contains. Am I going to eat the flesh of bulls, shall I drink the blood of goats? Offer to God a sacrifice of thanksgiving, fulfil your vows to the Most High," says God to Israel in Psalm 50 (49):12-14. Of what then does sacrifice consist? Not in destruction, not in this or that thing, but in the transformation of man; in the fact that he becomes himself conformed to God. He becomes conformed to God when he becomes love. "That is why true sacrifice is every work which allows us to unite ourselves to God in a holy fellowship,"[6] as Augustine puts it.

> With this key from the New Testament, Augustine interprets the Old Testament sacrifices as symbols pointing to this sacrifice properly so called, and that is why, he says, worship had to be transformed, the symbol had to disappear in favour of the reality. "All the divine prescriptions of Scripture which concern the sacrifices of the tabernacle or of the Temple, are figures which refer to the love of God and neighbour."[7] But Augustine also knows that love only becomes true when it leads a man to God, and thus directs him to his true end; it alone can likewise bring about unity of men among themselves. Therefore the concept of sacrifice refers to community, and the first definition which Augustine attempted, is broadened by the following statement: "The whole redeemed human community, that is to say the assembly and the community of the saints, is offered to God in sacrifice by the High Priest Who offered Himself."[8] And even more simply: "This sacrifice is ourselves," or again: "Such is the Christian sacrifice: the multitude — a single body in Christ."[9] Sacrifice consists then, we shall say it once more, in a process of transformation, in the conformity of man to God, in His theiosis, as the Fathers would say. It consists, to express it in modern phraseology, in the abolition of difference — in the union between God and man, between God and creation: "God all in all" (1 Cor. 15:28).

> But how does this process which makes us become love and one single body with Christ, which makes us become one with God, take place; how does

---

[6] *City of God*, X, 6.
[7] Ibid., X, 5.
[8] Ibid., X, 6.
[9] Ibid.

this abolition of difference happen? There exists here first of all a clear boundary between the religions founded on the faith of Abraham on one hand, on the other hand the other forms of religion such as we find them particularly in Asia, and also those based, probably, on Asiatic traditions – in the plotinian style of neoplatonism. There, union signifies deliverance as far as finitude (self-awareness) is concerned, which in the final analysis is seen to be a façade, the abolition of myself in the ocean of the completely other which, as compared to our world of façades, is nothingness, which, nonetheless, is the only true being. In the Christian faith, which fulfils the faith of Abraham, union is seen in a completely different way: it is the union of love, in which differences are not destroyed, but are transformed in a higher union of those who love each other, just as it is found, as in an archetype, in the trinitarian union of God. Whereas, for example in Plotinus, finitude is a falling away from unity, and so to speak the kernel of sin and therefore at the same time the kernel of all evil, the Christian faith does not see finitude as a negation but as a creation, the fruit of a divine will which creates a free partner, a creature who does not have to be destroyed, but must be completed, must insert itself into the free act of love. Difference is not abolished, but becomes the means to a higher unity. This philosophy of liberty, which is at the basis of the Christian faith and differentiates it from the Asiatic religions, includes the possibility of the negative. Evil is not a mere falling away from being, but the consequence of a freedom used badly. The way of unity, the way of love, is then a way of conversion, a way of purification: it takes the shape of the Cross, it passes through the Paschal Mystery, through death and resurrection. It needs the Mediator, Who, in His Death and in His Resurrection becomes for us the way, draws us all to Himself and thus fulfils us (Jn. 12: 32).

Let us cast a glance back over what we have said. In his definition: sacrifice equals love, Augustine rightly stresses the saying, which is present in different variations in the Old and in the New Testament, which he sites from Hosea (6:6): "it is love that I want, not sacrifices." [10] But this saying does not merely place an opposition between ethos and worship – then Christianity would be reduced to a moralism. It refers to a process which is more than a moral philosophy – to a process in which God takes the initiative. He alone can arouse man to start out towards love. It is the love with which God loves, which alone makes our love towards Him increase. This fact of being loved is a process of purification and transformation, in which we are not only open to God, but united to each other. The initiative of God has a name: Jesus Christ, the God Who Himself became man and gives Himself to us. That is why Augustine could synthesise all that by saying: "Such is the sacrifice of Christians: the multitude is one single body in Christ. The Church celebrates this mystery by the sacrifice of the Altar, well known to believers, because in it, it is shown to her that in the things which she offers, it is she herself who is

---

[10] Cf. *City of God*, X, 5.

offered."[11] Anyone who has understood this, will no longer be of the opinion that to speak of the sacrifice of the Mass is at least highly ambiguous, and even an appalling horror. On the contrary: if we do not remember this, we lose sight of the grandeur of that which God gives us in the Eucharist.

5. The New Temple

I would now like to mention, again very briefly, two other approaches. An important indication is given, in my opinion, in the scene of the purification of the Temple, in particular in the form handed down by John. John, in fact, relates a phrase of Jesus which does not appear in the Synoptics except in the trial of Jesus, on the lips of false witnesses, and in a distorted way. The reaction of Jesus to the merchants and money changers in the Temple was practically an attack on the immolation of animals, which were offered there, hence an attack on the existing form of worship, and the existing form of sacrifice in general. That is why the competent Jewish authorities asked Him, with good reason, by what sign He justified an action which could only be taken as an attack against the law of Moses and the sacred prescriptions of the Covenant. Thereupon Jesus replies: "Destroy (dissolve) this sanctuary; in three days I will build it up again" (Jn. 2:19). This subtle formula evokes a vision which John himself says the disciples did not understand until after the Resurrection, in remembering what had happened, and which led them to "believe the Scripture and the word of Jesus" (Jn. 2:22). For they now understand that the Temple had been abolished at the moment of the Crucifixion of Jesus: Jesus, according to John, was crucified exactly at the moment when the paschal lambs were immolated in the sanctuary. At the moment when the Son makes Himself the lamb, that is, gives Himself freely to the Father and hence to us, an end is made of the old prescriptions of a worship that could only be a sign of the true realities. The Temple is "destroyed." From now on His resurrected body—He Himself—becomes the true Temple of humanity, in which adoration in spirit and in truth takes place (Jn. 4:23). But spirit and truth are not abstract philosophical concepts—He is Himself the truth, and the spirit is the Holy Spirit Who proceeds from Him. Here too, it thus clearly becomes apparent that worship is not replaced by a moral philosophy, but that the ancient worship comes to an end, with its substitutes and its often tragic misunderstandings, because the reality itself is manifested, the new Temple: the resurrected Christ who draws us, transforms us and unites us to Himself. Again it is clear that the Eucharist of the Church—to use Augustine's term—is the *sacramentum* of the true *sacrificium*—the sacred sign in which that which is signified is effected.

---

[11] Ibid., X, 6.

6. The Spiritual Sacrifice

Finally I would like to point out very briefly a third way in which the passage from the worship of substitution, that of the immolation of animals, to the true sacrifice, the communion with the offering of Christ, progressively becomes clearer. Among the prophets before the exile, there was an extraordinarily harsh criticism of temple worship, which Stephen, to the horror of the doctors and priests of the Temple, resumes in his great discourse, with some citations, notably this verse of Amos: "Did you offer victims and sacrifices to Me, during forty years in the desert, house of Israel? But you have carried the tent of Moloch and the star of the god Rephan, the images which you had made to worship" (Amos 5:25, Acts 7:42). This critique that the Prophets had made, provided the spiritual foundation that enabled Israel to get through the difficult time following the destruction of the Temple, when there was no worship. Israel was obliged at that time to bring to light more deeply and in a new way what constitutes the essence of worship, expiation, sacrifice. In the time of the Hellenistic dictatorship, when Israel was again without temple and without sacrifice, the book of Daniel gives us this prayer: "Lord, see how we are the smallest of all the nations...There is no longer, at this time, leader nor prophet...nor holocaust, sacrifice, oblation, nor incense, no place to offer You the first fruits and find grace close to You. But may a broken soul and a humbled spirit be accepted by You, like holocausts of rams and bulls, like thousands of fattened lambs; thus may our sacrifice be before You today, and may it please You that we may follow You wholeheartedly, because there is no confounding for those who hope in You. And now we put our whole heart into following You, to fearing You and seeking Your Face" (Dan. 3:37-41).

Thus gradually there matured the realisation that prayer, the word, the man at prayer and becoming himself word, is the true sacrifice. The struggle of Israel could here enter into fruitful contact with the search of the Hellenistic world, which itself was looking for a way to leave behind the worship of substitution, of the immolation of animals, in order to arrive at worship properly so called, at true adoration, at true sacrifice. This path led to the idea of *logike thysia* — of the sacrifice [consisting] in the word — which we meet in the New Testament in Romans 12:1, where the Apostle exhorts the believers "to offer themselves as a living sacrifice, holy and pleasing to God:" it is what is described as *logike latreia*, as a divine service according to the word, engaging the reason. We find the same thing, in another form, in Hebrews 13:15: "Through Him — Christ — let us offer ceaselessly a sacrifice of praise, that is· to say the fruit of the lips which confess His name." Numerous examples coming from the Fathers of the Church show how these ideas were extended and became the point of junction between Christology, Eucharistic faith and the putting into existential practice of the Paschal Mystery. I would like to cite, by way of example, just a few lines of Peter Chrysologus; really, one should read the whole sermon in question in its entirety in order to be able to follow this synthesis from one end to the other:

> It is a strange sacrifice, where the body offers itself without the body, the blood without the blood! I beg you—says the Apostle—by the mercy of God, to offer yourselves as a living sacrifice.

> Brothers, this sacrifice is inspired by the example of Christ, who immolated His Body, so that men may live...Become, man, become the sacrifice of God and his priest...God seeks your faith, not your death. He thirsts for your self-surrender, not your blood. He is not appeased by slaughter, but by the offering of your free will.[12]

Here too, it is a question of something quite different from a mere moralism, because man is so caught up in it with the whole of his being: sacrifice [consisting] in words—this, the Greek thinkers had already put in relation to the logos, to the word itself, indicating that the sacrifice of prayer should not be mere speech, but the transmutation of our being into the logos, the union of ourselves with it. Divine worship implies that we ourselves become beings of the word, that we conform ourselves to the creative Intellect. But once more, it is clear that we can not do this of ourselves, and thus everything seems to end again in futility—until the day when the Word comes, the true, the Son, when He becomes flesh and draws us to Himself in the exodus of the Cross. This true sacrifice, which transforms us all into sacrifice, that is to say unites us to God, makes of us beings conformed to God, is indeed fixed and founded on an historical event, but is not situated as a thing in the past behind us; on the contrary, it becomes contemporary and accessible to us in the community of the believing and praying Church, in its sacrament: that is what is meant by the "sacrifice of the Mass."

    The error of Luther lay, I am convinced, in a false idea of historicity, in a poor understanding of unicity. The sacrifice of Christ is not situated behind us as something past. It touches all times and is present to us. The Eucharist is not merely the distribution of what comes from the past, but rather the presence of the Paschal Mystery of Christ, Who transcends and unites all times. If the Roman Canon cites Abel, Abraham and Melchisedech, including them among those who celebrate the Eucharist, it is in the conviction that in them also, the great offerers, Christ was passing through time, or perhaps better, that in their search they were advancing toward a meeting with Christ. The theology of the Fathers such as we find it in the Canon, did not deny the futility and insufficiency of the pre-christian sacrifices; the Canon includes, however, with the figures of Abel and Melchisedech, the "holy pagans" themselves in the mystery of Christ. What is happening is that everything that went before is seen in its insufficiency as a shadow, but also that Christ is

---

[12] Sermon 108; PL 52, 499-500.

drawing all things to Himself, that there is, even in the pagan world, a preparation for the Gospel, that even imperfect elements can lead to Christ, however much they may stand in need of purification.

7. Christ, the Subject of the Liturgy

Which brings me to the conclusion. Theology of the Liturgy means that God acts through Christ in the Liturgy and that we can not act but through Him and with Him. Of ourselves, we can not construct the way to God. This way does not open up unless God Himself becomes the way. And again, the ways of man which do not lead to God are non-ways. Theology of the Liturgy means furthermore that in the Liturgy, the Logos Himself speaks to us; and not only does He speak, He comes with His Body, and His Soul, His Flesh and His Blood, His Divinity and His Humanity, in order to unite us to Himself, to make of us one single "body." In the Christian Liturgy, the whole history of salvation, even more, the whole history of human searching for God is present, assumed and brought to its goal. The Christian Liturgy is a cosmic Liturgy — it embraces the whole of creation which "awaits with impatience the revelation of the sons of God" (Rom. 8:9).

Trent did not make a mistake, it leant for support on the solid foundation of the Tradition of the Church. It remains a trustworthy standard. But we can and should understand it in a more profound way in drawing from the riches of biblical witness and from the faith of the Church of all the ages. There are true signs of hope that this renewed and deepened understanding of Trent can, in particular through the intermediary of the Eastern Churches, be made accessible to Protestant Christians.

One thing should be clear: the Liturgy must not be a terrain for experimenting with theological hypotheses. Too rapidly, in these last decades, the ideas of experts have entered into liturgical practice, often also by-passing ecclesiastical authority, through the channel of commissions which have been able to diffuse at an international level their "consensus of the moment," and practically turn it into laws for liturgical activity. The Liturgy derives its greatness from what it is, not from what we make of it. Our participation is, of course, necessary, but as a means of inserting ourselves humbly into the spirit of the Liturgy, and of serving Him Who is the true subject of the Liturgy: Jesus Christ. The Liturgy is not an expression of the consciousness of a community which, in any case, is diffuse and changing. It is revelation received in faith and prayer, and its measure is consequently the faith of the Church, in which revelation is received. The forms which are given to the Liturgy can vary according to place and time, just as the rites are diverse. What is essential is the link to the Church which for her part, is united by faith in the Lord. The obedience of faith guarantees the unity of the Liturgy, beyond the frontiers of place and time, and so lets us experience the unity of the Church, the Church as the homeland of the heart.

The essence of the Liturgy is, finally, summarised in the prayer which St Paul (1 Cor. 16:22) and the Didache (10:6) have handed down to us: "Maran atha—our Lord is there—Lord, come!" From now on, the Parousia is accomplished in the Liturgy, but that is so precisely because it teaches us to cry: "Come, Lord Jesus," while reaching out towards the Lord who is coming. It always brings us to hear His reply yet again and to experience its truth: "Yes, I am coming soon" (Apoc. 22:17,20).

Translated by Margaret McHugh and Fr John Parsons

The Bishop at the Service of the Liturgy

Intervention of Msgr André Mutien Léonard
Bishop of Namur[1]

I have been asked to speak immediately after His Eminence Cardinal Ratzinger in order to introduce the discussion on his paper which is intended to follow. How does one address all the points raised by our speaker? How does one deal with the disparity between what the Liturgy ought to be and its actual state? How do we find the balance between the precious gains of the Conciliar Constitution *Sacrosanctum Concilium* and the deviations from *Sacrosanctum Concilium* of certain of its interpretations? I presume that if one has asked a bishop to speak immediately after the Prefect of the Congregation of the Doctrine of the Faith it is in order to put forward a more directly pastoral point of view. This task is delicate because I had no foreknowledge of what His Eminence would say.

During my holidays I read the Cardinal's *The Spirit of the Liturgy*. Having read the book I expected that the author would say here what he had written there. This fundamental work examines a number of aspects which are essential to the Liturgy: its cosmic and at the same time historic dimensions; the sacrificial nature of the Mass; the importance of the orientation of the rite; the authentic meaning of the liturgical action; the threat of clericalisation of the eucharistic celebration, etc.

In his opening pages, the author uses an image which, he says himself, is not completely adequate. He compares the Liturgy to a superb fresco which, as the centuries have passed, has been "retouched" as it were, covered with new layers of colour or even whitewashed. Then, centuries later, a competent, artistic group arrives. It cleans the fresco, freeing it from the accumulations of years so well that one finds it again in all its purity and original beauty. But, here it is, suddenly exposed to an environment totally different to its origins. The various layers which covered the fresco certainly hid it, but also protected it against the ill-effects of the surrounding atmosphere, full of pollution

---

[1] Msgr André Mutien Léonard is the youngest of a family of four boys, all of whom became diocesan priests. He studied at the Gregorian University in Rome, then at Louvain where he became Doctor and *maitre agrégé* in Philospophy (with a thesis on Hegel). From 1976 he taught Philosophy at Louvain, and was appointed superior of the seminary of *Louvain-La-Neuve* in 1978. Since 1987 he has been a member of the International Theological Commission. He was appointed Bishop of Namur in February 1991.

unknown at the time of its origin. Exposed to a thousand corrosive agents, the fresco is at risk of being rapidly damaged soon after its rediscovery. So it is with the Liturgy. In the course of its history it became overloaded with additions and repetitions. Then came the Second Vatican Council and its Constitution *Sacrosanctum Concilium*. Freed from unnecessary elements, restored to its original simplicity, but exposed to a new and sometimes deleterious cultural environment, it risks becoming quickly corrupt so that its restoration could well coincide with its loss.

In this context and from the pastoral point of view — which must be mine here — here are the two points which I would like to submit arising from Cardinal Ratzinger's talk and by way of introduction to our discussion.

1. What a Bishop Can Do Immediately to Improve the Liturgy.

By his own manner of celebrating a bishop can himself inspire his people, draw in his priests and his people in a balanced celebration which is at the same time expressive of the mystery and which speaks to the heart of contemporary man. He can do this at the important occasions (the Mass of the Chrism, ordinations, pilgrimages, large gatherings, confirmations with a large number of people), as he can during the regular celebrations in the parishes of his diocese.

In certain of these occasions, such as his pastoral visits, the Bishop can teach about certain aspects of the Liturgy. For example, he can call to mind, from time to time, the meaning of liturgical postures: standing, sitting, kneeling. In certain countries of Northern Europe, a custom has arisen of being almost always seated during the Liturgy, as if St Paul had written: "I fall seated before the Father of our Lord Jesus Christ"! One has to react and explain. The same thing about the manner of receiving Holy Communion. Communion in the hand, very widespread in these countries, can be done with dignity and respect. This is far from being always the case. Sometimes, if not often, the reception is rushed, inattentive and even trivialised. At each celebration of Confirmation, for example, a bishop can remind the people of the two ways of receiving Holy communion, and explain them. Having tried this, I notice that after ten years, some progress has been made. The other teachings given by the Bishop, his contributions in the media, all made with the help of his Diocesan Liturgical Commission, could be an efficacious means of enlightening the faithful and of positively improving the practice of the Liturgy.

Nevertheless, a bishop alone can only do so much because, the liturgical atmosphere is largely conditioned by global factors, disparate tendencies, closely linked to the ambient culture. It is necessary, therefore, to operate at another both wider and deeper level.

2. The Need For a Widespread Campaign

What is most needed in the long run, theologically and pastorally, is a new international Liturgical Movement, keen to promote a better balance through an in-depth *ressourcement*. With reference to the title of Romano Guardini's classic study *The Spirit of the Liturgy*, Cardinal's Raztinger's book of the same title could, together with others, offer a way forward. Such a Liturgical Movement would take time (ten, twenty, or thirty years). In one sense the Church has time, provided that the conception of the Liturgy put forward by such a movement should be the bearer of an authentic future.[2]

Another positive contribution would be to draw up an inventory of the actual gains resulting from the work of the post-conciliar liturgical reform, together with the benefits of the legitimate maintenance of the traditional rite, to make them known and to promote them.

More importantly, would be to see that every Episcopal Conference oversees closely the quality of Professors of the Liturgy in the seminaries, and thus, in a wider manner, the quality of Institutes of Liturgy where these teachers are trained, promoting those who are outstanding.

Finally, the monasteries, the Abbeys and the new communities have, in the long run, a decisive role to play. The faithful who attend these places are not forced by geographical necessity. They attend by choice. That gives these communities a greater freedom of action. Let us suppose, for example, that a parish priest wants to promote the use of Gregorian Chant or to celebrate the Mass according to the ancient eastward orientation. He would run up against criticism and opposition. In a community which is not a parish, on the other hand, one can eventually bring about a more correct celebration of the Liturgy, a little against the prevailing fashion, without fear of shocking the faithful

---

[2] One could argue against this view since, if the Church has the time, families have not, and they need quickly, to find the best liturgical environment for their children. This is correct. The Church needs time to get a worthwhile Liturgical Movement underway. In the short term parents can look for those places most beneficial for the growth of a proper sense of the Liturgy in their children. If, unfortunately, they can not find it in their own parish, they have the right, even the duty, to look elsewhere for celebrations of quality in both the doctrinal and the liturgical sense. It is not a question of running after aesthetically advanced celebrations, but of finding the truth of the Liturgy. It exists in small villages with limited means just as much as in urban centres which are richer in resources.

because we are dealing with a community whose members have chosen to be there. By regular or occasional attendance at such liturgies the faithful can be progressively, and without being shocked, brought to a new and sounder liturgical practice. This could be a tremendous help in its propagation.

Translated by Professor William H.C. Smith

Liturgy and Trinity
Towards an Anthropology of the Liturgy

Paper by Stratford Caldecott
Centre for Faith and Culture, Oxford[1]

B Y the early twentieth century, the battle-lines were drawn up between Rationalists and Romantics, Modernists and defenders of the *ancien régime*. Outside these categories, but at the time — and to some extent even today — insufficiently distinguished from them, the work of *ressourcement* was being carried forward by such figures as Maurice Blondel, Odo Casel, Romano Guardini, Louis Bouyer and Henri de Lubac. These men were trying to escape the nineteenth-century *impasse* by looking further back than the Baroque, further than the Middle Ages, back to the undivided Church of patristic times. In the writings of the Church Fathers they believed they had found a way beyond the opposition of subjectivism and objectivism. The mystery of "participation" would provide the key to a genuine renewal, not merely of the letter but of the *spirit* of the Catholic Liturgy.

According to Blondel and de Lubac, a distortion had crept into Catholic sensibility with the Enlightenment. The distortion amounted to a tendency to separate grace from nature.[2] The Rationalist mentality demanded a world in which natural reason could operate without interference from the theologian. Secure in their knowledge that the supernatural realm would always remain superior to the world of nature, leading Scholastic theologians had permitted this separation, effectively leaving society and cosmos to the interpretation of the new sciences. The Church had lost its grip on the culture, while within the community of believers the supernatural order, deprived of

---

[1] Stratford Caldecott is the European Director of the Chesterton Institute for Faith & Culture in Oxford, the Editor of *Second Spring* and a member of the editorial board of the international review *Communio*. In 1998 he and his wife organised an international conference on the Liturgy and the 'reform of the reform' which resulted in the "Oxford Declaration on the Liturgy." The proceedings of the conference were published as *Beyond the Prosaic*, T&T Clark, Edinburgh 1998. Mr Caldecott has published works of Father Aidan Nichols OP, Professor Spaemann, Jean Borella and others.

[2] See, for example, H. de Lubac SJ, *The Mystery of the Supernatural,* Crossroad, New York 1998. Also Paul McPartlan, *The Eucharist Makes the Church: Henri de Lubac and John Zizioulas in Dialogue,* T&T Clark, Edinburgh 1993.

any intrinsic relationship to the natural, could only be imposed as it were by force—hence the tactics used to suppress Modernism.

The Liturgical Movement associated with the Second Vatican Council was closely related to the *ressourcement.* Yet it was influenced also by Rationalism on the one hand, and certain aspects of nineteenth-century Romanticism on the other. Fr Aidan Nichols described the confluence of these influences as follows:

> If the Enlightenment insinuated into the stream of consciousness of practical liturgists such ambiguous notions as didacticism, naturalism, moral community-building, anti-devotionalism, and the desirability of simplification for its own sake, early Romanticism contributed such baleful notions as piety without dogma, reflecting the idea that man is a *Gefühlswesen* (what really matters is how you feel), a subjectivism different in kind from the Enlightenment's and more voracious, for anything and everything could be made to serve the production of the Romantic ego; an approach to symbolism that was aestheticist rather than genuinely ecclesial; and an enthusiasm for cosmic nature (*Naturschwärmerei*) that would see its final delayed offspring in the 'creation-centred' spirituality of the 1980s.[3]

Aware of the growing gulf between faith and culture, linked to a division within the Church between a passive laity and an active clergy, the Church sought to "raze the bastions" and reach out to the world in the Second Vatican Council. Building on Pius XII's *Mediator Dei* the Council's Constitution on the Sacred Liturgy summed up many of the insights of the Liturgical Movement, most especially the fact that in the divine sacrifice of the Eucharist "the work of our redemption is accomplished" (no. 2), implying the realism of the mystery of salvation in every Mass. This included an acknowledgement at the very outset that action should be subordinated to contemplation, the visible to the invisible. However, the Constitution gave particular prominence to the theme of "active participation" (*participatio actuosa*): "Mother Church earnestly desires that all the faithful should be led to that full, conscious and active participation in liturgical celebrations which is demanded by the very nature of the Liturgy" (no. 14). To encourage this participation, the Constitution recommended simplification of the rites (no. 34) on the one hand, and careful attention to the people's responses (acclamations, gestures, etc.) on the other (no. 30).

The true meaning of the *actio* in which the Council Fathers intended the faithful to participate has been explained by Cardinal Ratzinger, most recently in his book *The Spirit of the Liturgy*.[4] It is essentially an act of prayer. The Council was reacting against the view that prayer was something the

---

[3] A. Nichols OP, *Looking at the Liturgy: A Critical View of its Contemporary Form,* Ignatius Press, San Francisco 1996, p. 36.

[4] Ignatius Press, San Francisco 2000, pp. 171-7.

faithful did *on their own* while the Mass was being celebrated by the priest. Nevertheless, the emphasis that the Council laid on the priest's responsibility to ensure this active participation on the part of the faithful in the Liturgy *as prayer* did in practice give a great deal of weight to outward and vocal activity, which was observable, as distinct from the more important inner *actio* which this activity was supposed to promote.

It seems that those who were charged with the task of carrying out the reform in the name of the Council, far from transcending Rationalism and Romanticism, managed to perpetuate the worst elements of both. The functionalism and activism of the Rationalist tendency was married with a Romantic over-emphasis on community and feeling. The dualism of nature and grace was attacked, but not at its root. Clericalism was not overcome, but simply adopted another form. Intimations of transcendence — indeed, references to the soul — were minimised. Within the churches, walls were whitewashed and relics dumped in the name of "noble simplicity" (no. 34). Unlike the much earlier Cistercian rebellion against artistic extravagances at Cluny, this modern campaign for simplicity was not coupled with the asceticism and devotion that might alone have rendered it spiritually "noble." It fell easy victim to the prevailing culture of comfort and prosperity. [5]

1. Loss of the Vertical Dimension

The misjudgments to which I am referring, and which have been extensively analysed elsewhere,[6] were not able to affect the liturgical act itself or its validity, but they were serious enough to be accounted by many a disaster, and to provoke a schism. How did this disaster come about? A great part of the explanation must lie with the cultural moment. All earlier liturgies, Fr

---

[5] At the height of this movement, in 1967, the American writer Robert W. Jenson wrote an article entitled "God, Space and Architecture" (see *Essays in the Theology of Culture,* Eerdmans, Grand Rapids 1995, pp. 12-13), in which he rejects the idea in Church architecture of a "common focus for all present" and any evocation of an "absolute and changeless Presence," which he terms the "God of religion," not the "God of the Gospel." Instead, its forms should "broken, restless, even nervous.... We should not find a church soothing. The forms of church buildings should be ready to fall, or to take wing. They should have the dynamics of the temporary." They should also be small, since according to Jenson large congregations are obviously a thing of the past. The comparison here is with the theatre of audience-participation that was so popular at the time. The fragmentation of ordered narrative is of a piece with postmodernism. These views and others like them were common at the time. Jenson's architecturally un-soothing, nervous churches did take shape, but since they were overheated and lined with soft carpets, the aesthetic discomfort they induced was soon forgotten.

[6] See e.g. James Hitchcock, *Recovery of the Sacred: Reforming the Reformed Liturgy,* Ignatius Press, San Francisco 1995; S. Caldecott (ed.), *Beyond the Prosaic: Reviving the Liturgical Movement,* T&T Clark, Edinburgh 1998; David Torevell, *Losing the Sacred: Ritual, Modernity and Liturgical Reform,* T&T Clark, Edinburgh 2000.

Nichols points out, "formed part of a culture *itself ritual in character.*"[7] The prevailing culture that began to emerge after the Second World War, far from being "ritual in character," was one in which ritual, hierarchy, reverence and custom were regarded with suspicion. Human freedom and creativity depend upon such rules and frameworks, not on liberation from them. A leading anthropologist writing at the end of the 1960s, Mary Douglas, argued that the contempt for ritual forms leads to the privatisation of religious experience and thereby to secular humanism. The reformers were blithely unaware of such contemporary reappraisals of Liturgy.[8]

The very act of undertaking a far-reaching reform in these circumstances (however necessary a reform may have been) was bound to encourage an activist mentality that would regard itself as the master of the Liturgy. Humble receptivity, so essential in matters of worship, was "put on hold" during the time it would take to make the desired changes. But a virtue once suspended is hard to revive. The reformist attitude showed itself in three particular ways. Firstly, having escaped from the kind of theological Rationalism that was associated with the old Scholastic manuals, they fell into the trap of *historicist* Rationalism.[9] Pope Pius XII had warned against "archaeologism" in *Mediator Dei*, but the committees responsible for implementing *Sacrosanctum Concilium* appear to have chopped and trimmed, manipulated and manhandled the Liturgy as though trying to reconstruct a primitive liturgy.[10]

Secondly, as Casel, Bouyer, Guardini and others had insisted, the liturgical act is not only a prayer (for at least that much had been generally recognised) but also a *mystery*, in which something is done to us which we can

---

[7] A. Nichols OP, *Looking at the Liturgy*, p. 85 (my italic).

[8] See *Looking at the Liturgy*, p. 69, and K. Flanagan, *Sociology and Liturgy*, Macmillan, London, 1991. Also cf. K. Flanagan, *The Enchantment of Sociology*, Macmillan, London 1996/99.

[9] See J. Borella's analysis in *The Sense of the Supernatural* (Edinburgh: T&T Clark, 1998), Part I. Robert Sokolowski, in *Eucharistic Presence*, CUAP Washington 1994, speaks of a "theology of disclosure," complementary to the ontological theology of the Scholastics but also to positive theology, defending the latter against the danger of historicism. Instead of reducing the Gospel to the level of historical fact alone, it enables us to see how the events of history disclose the God who chooses to reveal himself in this way.

[10] Louis Bouyer had written in 1954: "we may well wonder occasionally what would remain for future generations of the faithful if some modern promoters of a 'living' liturgy were allowed complete freedom to remodel the Church's Liturgy according to their own ideas" *Liturgical Piety*, University of Notre Dame Press, 1955, p. 8. The point was to return to the sources in which the authentic nature of the Liturgy could be rediscovered without committing what Bouyer called the "fatal mistake" of trying to remodel the external aspects of the Church on the externals of any previous period. Paulos Mar Gregorios puts it well in *The Joy of Freedom: Eastern Worship and Modern Man*, Christian Literature Society, Madras 1986, p. 29: "The purpose of historical research into liturgies is not to restore a so-called primitive liturgy in its pristine purity and correct form, but rather to find a form of worship in which the past generations feel just as much at home as the present."

not fully understand, and which we must consent to and receive. The emphasis had swung towards didacticism, the endless preaching and explaining of the action of the Liturgy. Over-simplified (and often patronising) vernacular translations were intended to facilitate this. But in reality a sense of the sacred is essential to the act of worship, and is always inseparable from a sense of transcendence. Worship demands repentance and receptivity. Correctly understood, "active participation" in the Liturgy is therefore no merely external activity, but rather an intensely *active receptivity*: the receiving and giving of the self in prayer.

Thirdly, the reformers' Modernistic rebellion against any kind of ordered, harmonious space separating sacred and profane was in fact a rebellion against the symbolism of space, and ultimately against all symbolism in the true sense. Symbols were to be reduced to the status of visual aids, in the service of a purely didactic rather than a sacramental ideal of Liturgy. This was a rejection of sacred cosmology.[11] With the loss of cosmic symbolism it was as though the vertical dimension of the Liturgy had become inaccessible, and everything was concentrated on the horizontal plane, with an emphasis upon the cultivation of warm feelings among the congregation.

A fourth tendency has been mentioned by Cardinal Ratzinger on several occasions, namely the failure to understand the Liturgy as a *sacrifice* – not as a separate sacrifice in addition to that of Calvary, or a "reconstruction" of the Passion, but as the self-same act performed once and for all, making present the sacrifice of the Cross "in an unbloody manner" throughout the Church, in diverse times and places. Thus the Mass was reduced to one of its aspects: that of a sacred meal, a celebratory feast.

The result of all these tendencies was a loss of liturgical beauty. Not that beauty *per se* is sacred: that would be the error of the aesthete. The deepest sense of beauty is the splendour of God's glory, perceived by the spiritual senses. Hans Urs von Balthasar has elucidated this in the first volume of his series *The Glory of the Lord*. Thus in *New Elucidations* he writes:

> God's glory, the majesty of his splendour, comes with its most precious gifts to us who are to 'praise the glory of his grace' (Eph. 1:6). This last summons constitutes the norm and criterion for planning our liturgical services. It would be ridiculous and blasphemous to want to respond to the glory of God's grace with a counter-glory produced from our own creaturely reserves, in contrast to the heavenly Liturgy that is portrayed for us in the Book of Revelation as completely dominated and shaped by God's glory. Whatever form the response of our Liturgy takes, it can only be the expression of the most pure and selfless reception possible of the divine majesty of his grace; although reception, far from signifying something

---

[11] Cf. J. Ratzinger, *The Spirit of the Liturgy*.

passive, is much rather that most active thing of which a creature is capable.[12]

With the loss of the transcendent reference of the Liturgy understood as a response to the divine glory, beauty is reduced to a purely subjective quality—a matter of personal taste—which is then easily swept aside in the interests of a more seemingly objective content: the moral lesson to be conveyed by the ritual. Thus, once again, we see the act of worship becoming didactic, moralising, sentimental.

If the frustration of the reform was due in large measure to errors such as these, it can be understood and counteracted today only by attaining a deeper understanding of the true nature of the Catholic Liturgy. The lesson of the liturgical reform is that the Liturgy must ultimately be understood not in isolation, not in purely historical terms, not aesthetically, not sociologically, but *ontologically*, that is to say, in its full metaphysical and meta-anthropological depth.

2. Search for an Adequate Anthropology of the Liturgy

It was Pope John Paul II who set the Church on the road to an adequate anthropology, for example in his famous Wednesday catecheses on the book of Genesis, behind which lay earlier, more philosophical works such as *The Acting Person* and *Love and Responsibility*. This anthropology has most often been discussed in connection with the moral theology of the family. I will summarise it briefly, before trying to relate it to the Liturgy.[13]

The first point to make is that human will or free choice lies at the centre of the Pope's conception of man. This freedom, however, is founded on truth. To choose freely is "to make a decision according to the principle of truth."[14] Truth is not something imposed arbitrarily from outside by the divine will, as it became for the Nominalists of the fourteenth century. It is normative precisely because it is intrinsic to the person, who must learn to choose *in accordance with reality* in order to achieve self-fulfilment. Thus the

---

[12] H.U. von Balthasar, *New Elucidations*, Ignatius Press, San Francisco 1986, p. 130. See also Balthasar, *The Glory of the Lord*, vol. I, "Seeing the Form" Ignatius Press and T&T Clark, San Francisco and Edinburgh 1982, especially pp. 79-127, 571-583.

[13] The following discussion of the Pope's anthropology is based upon Mary Shivanandan, *Crossing the Threshold of Love*, T&T Clark, Edinburgh 1999; Rocco Buttiglione, *Karol Wojtyla: The Thought of the Man Who Became Pope John Paul II*, Eerdmans, Grand Rapids 1997; Kenneth L. Schmitz, *At the Centre of the Human Drama*, CUAP, Washington 1993; David L. Schindler, *Heart of the World, Centre of the Church*, Eerdmans and T&T Clark, Edinburgh and Grand Rapids 1996, Introduction.

[14] *Crossing the Threshold of Love*, p. 61. For Balthasar, too, human action and freedom reveal the structure of truth, unveiling being itself: "There is no other anthropology but the dramatic;" H.U. von Balthasar, *Theo-Drama*, Ignatius Press, San Francisco, 1988-98, vol. II, p. 335. The truth of existence is acted out or "performed."

order of values or moral norms transcends the separation of subjective and objective which is characteristic of modern philosophy, because these norms are "personalistic:" that is, intrinsic to the person. *The Acting Person* coins the term "reflexive" to describe our awareness of ourselves as the source of our actions. Reflexive consciousness is the condition of freedom. It is not the cognitive grasping of the self as object by the mediation of an idea, but the lived experience of being an acting person.[15]

Secondly, the Pope recognises that the particular nature of human action is that of an *embodied* creature rather than a pure spirit. The human person is a unity of soul and body, so that the truth which must be chosen is one that includes the reality of the body. Here the reflections of the philosopher Wojtyla are deepened by the Pope's meditation on Holy Scripture. The human creature is formed in what he calls "original solitude," a solitude that distinguishes him from all the other animals. This state of isolation is connected with the fact that man is only able to achieve fulfilment "through a sincere gift of himself." The aptitude for self-gift is what makes it impossible for Adam to find a suitable "helper" or companion among the animals. It isolates him, but at the same time it potentially opens him — to the Other, to the Woman, whom he greets with a cry of joy when she is brought to him for the first time. It is also this capacity for community, for *communio,* that constitutes his likeness to the trinitarian God. The self-giving of man, the fact that his heart is made to be *given into the keeping of another*, is an image of the divine processions: the generation of the Son, and his unity with the Father in the Holy Spirit who is "spirated" by both.

Thus the Pope recognises our likeness to the Trinity not merely in the possession of freedom, but in "nuptiality" — in the *physical difference of man and woman*. The image of God is certainly in the soul, which images God as spirit. But the image of God *as Trinity* is found first and foremost in the nature of man as "male and female," and precisely in the nuptial relationship described in the second chapter of Genesis. And what is characteristic of the relationship of male to female, when compared with all other physical differences that exist between individuals, is that it is a difference that is specifically ordered towards the reproduction of life. Gender complementarity exists for the sake of procreation. Marriage partners are not merely turned towards one another: they are also oriented towards a *potential third*, towards the child which expresses the unity of both in one flesh. It is therefore an open relationship, not a closed or dualistic one. Angelo Scola describes the structure of this relationship as one of "asymmetrical reciprocity."[16] Sexual difference is not

---

[15] See *At the Centre of the Human Drama*, pp. 75-6. This describes the break Wojtyla made in the name of realism from other forms of phenomenology which start from intentionality and lead to idealism, through the construction of an "absolute subject."

[16] A. Scola, "The Nuptial Mystery," in *Communio*, Winter 1998. The reciprocity of this relationship could be said to be asymmetrical also in a "vertical" sense: a certain priority rests with the one who engenders love by loving. This priority may not imply inequality,

overcome or cancelled out in the unity of marriage, because each spouse does not simply complete the other: he or she opens up new depths, new possibilities within the other. It is precisely in this respect that marriage mirrors the "dynamism" of the eternal *perichoresis*.

The anthropology that emerges through the writings of John Paul II is therefore marked by a nuptial and a trinitarian structure. The Pope's "Christian non-dualism" is not a denial of the legitimacy of Christian dualism, but it *preserves dualism* within a trinitarian dynamic. It is premised on the fact that all merely dualistic relationships are inherently unstable, and thus have a tendency to collapse into some form of monism. The sexual relationship, for example, if it is not open to new life, collapses into a form of narcissism. Connected with this is a strong sense of what is wrong with the act of contraception. To contracept is wrong because by acting against the being of the child *who might otherwise come to exist* through the act, it turns the relationship back into a dualistic one, no longer "asymmetrical" and no longer open to a mysterious "third person." It is to act (however unknowingly) not just against the potential child but against the presence within the marriage of the Holy Spirit, who is the Giver of Life.

Now we can turn back to the Liturgy. What makes the connection is the fact that the mystery of the Mass has the same root as marriage, that nuptial mystery which is written into the essence of human nature. The marriage partners in this case are Christ the Bridegroom and his Bride the Church. The union between them is a covenant in the Holy Spirit. The Liturgy enacts the marriage of the Lamb, combining the wedding banquet of the Last Supper with the redemptive act of the Passion. (On all of this one may read the seventh chapter of *Mulieris Dignitatem*, by Pope John Paul II.) Furthermore the trinitarian character of the Mass makes it "asymmetrical" in the same way that marriage is asymmetrical (cf. Ephesians 5:31-2). The "offspring" of this union are Christian souls, indwelt by the Holy Spirit.[17]

3. Symbolic Realism and the Intelligence of the Heart

Resistance to the Pope's nuptial anthropology is deeply rooted. Rationalism can not be overcome by mere intensity of sentiment. Romanticism can not be overcome by more careful planning and calculation. We are caught in the dichotomy characteristic of Western thought since Descartes: the radical division between cold objectivity ("clear and distinct ideas") and unintelligent subjectivity. According to Christian "non-dualism," if two realities are to be

---

but it does imply difference. It derives from the fundamental fact of creaturely being, namely that it exists at all only in relation: its identity lies in the activity of receiving— receiving also, with its being, the capacity to give (cf. *Mulieris Dignitatem*, 29).

[17] Seen in this light, of course, the maleness of the priest who mediates Christ becomes highly significant. It becomes much easier to see why it would not be appropriate to ordain women to the priesthood.

united without losing their distinctiveness, they must find their unity in a third. If this is applied not to the relationship *between* persons, but to the human faculties *within* the individual, it suggests that reason and intuition, thought and feeling, may find their unity and fulfilment in a third faculty, the "intelligence of the heart" without which soul and body would not cohere to form a single hypostasis (and without which, therefore, the Incarnation itself would be impossible).

In his essay on "Tripartite Anthropology" in the collection *Theology in History*,[18] Henri de Lubac traces the rise and fall in Christian tradition of the idea that man is composed not simply of body and soul, but of body, soul and spirit (1 Thess. 5:23). Of course, in much of the tradition the soul and spirit are treated as one, yet traces of the distinction remain, whether in St Teresa's reference to the "spirit of the soul" or (arguably) in St Thomas's *intellectus agens*. It is certainly present in *The Philokalia*, where the Eastern Fathers contrast the *nous* dwelling in the depths of the soul with the *dianoia* or discursive reason.[19] Jean Borella also writes of this topic of the "human ternary," making clear its roots in the Old Testament.[20] For the philosopher who became John Paul II, the "third" in question seems to be that "reflexive" consciousness by which we experience the drama of human existence as acting persons.

The spirit is the "place" within us where we receive the kiss of life from our Creator (Gen. 2:7), and where God makes his throne in the saints. Thus when St Paul appeals to the Romans (Rom. 12:1-2) to present their bodies as a living sacrifice in "spiritual worship" (*logike latreia*), he immediately continues: "Do not be conformed to this world but be transformed by the renewal of your mind [*nous*], that you may prove what is the will of God, what is good and well-pleasing and perfect." Paul implies that the "logic" of Christian worship—a logic of self-sacrifice that conforms us to the will of God—corresponds to a *new intelligence*. Discussions of the Liturgy in the immediate postconciliar period may not have taken enough account of this fact—with the results we have already noted.

As a natural faculty, even before it is "supernaturalised" by the indwelling of God's Holy Spirit at baptism, the spiritual intellect or *apex mentis* is the organ of metaphysics. It is recognised in all religious traditions, and the knowledge of universals which it gives (however distorted and confused after the Fall) is part of the common heritage of humanity. This is the faculty which perceives all things as symbolic in their very nature; that is, as expressing the attributes of God. The existence of God can be known from the things that are made; and the "book" of nature can be "read" according to the multiple

---

[18] H. de Lubac, *Theology in History*, Ignatius Press, San Francisco 1996.

[19] *The Philokalia: The Complete Text*, compiled by St Nikodimos and St Makarios, Faber & Faber, London 1979- .

[20] *The Secret of the Christian Way*, ed G. John Champoux, SUNY Press, 2001, esp. pp. 75-88, 103-14.

aspects of the divine Wisdom present throughout creation. Thus Balthasar writes:

> The whole world of images that surrounds us is a single field of significations. Every flower we see is an expression, every landscape has its significance, every human or animal face speaks its wordless language. It would be utterly futile to attempt a transposition of this language into concepts. Though we might try to circumscribe, even to describe, the content these things express, we would never succeed in rendering it adequately. This expressive language is addressed primarily, not to conceptual thought, but to the kind of intelligence that perceptively reads the *gestalt* of things.[21]

Whatever name we give it ("intellect," "imagination" or "heart"), what Balthasar has in mind here is a faculty that transcends yet at the same time unifies feeling and thought, body and soul, sensation and rationality. It is the kind of intelligence that sees the meaning in things, that reads them as symbols — symbols, not of something else, but of *themselves as they stand in God*. Thus in the spiritual intelligence of man, being is unveiled in its true nature as a gift bearing within it the love of the Giver. Ultimately things — just as truly as persons — can be truly known only through love. In other words, a thing can be known only when it draws us out of ourselves, when we grasp it in its otherness from ourselves, in the meaning which it possesses as beauty, uniting truth and goodness.[22] This kind of knowledge is justly called *sobria ebrietas* ("drunken" sobriety) because it is ecstatic, rapturous, although at the same time measured, ordered, dignified. It is an encounter with the Other which takes the heart out of itself and places it in another centre, which is ultimately the very centre of being, where all things are received from God.[23]

All of this is implicit in the Liturgy, the school where we learn this drunken sobriety, this intelligence of the heart.[24] Its ABC is the language of

---

[21] *Theo-Logic*, vol. I, "The Truth of the World," Ignatius Press, San Francisco 2000, p. 140.

[22] Again, it was Nominalism that severed the link between the order of being (the true) and the order of value (the good). On the "circumincession of the transcendentals," see the important dissertation by David Christopher Schindler, "The Dramatic Structure of Truth, in Dialogue with Hans Urs von Balthasar and Continental Philosophy from Kant to Heidegger," Washington DC 2001.

[23] *Læti bibamus sobriam ebrietatem Spiritus:* "Let us joyfully taste of the sober drunkenness of the Spirit..." This quotation from the Breviary is cited from Romano Guardini *The Spirit of the Liturgy*, Sheed & Ward, London: 1930, ch. 1. No doubt the phrase derives from St Anselm's influential commentary on the first Pentecost, when men who were filled with the Holy Spirit and sent out to evangelise the world were at first mistaken for drunkards (Acts 2:13).

[24] "We need to be led from the form to the content. In other words, we need an education which will help us to grow into an inner appropriation of the Church's common Liturgy:" J. Cardinal Ratzinger, *The Feast of Faith*, Ignatius Press, San Francisco 1986, p. 71. The same approach would help to heal the breach between Liturgy and dogma (ibid., p. 36). On the

natural symbols, such as water, light, oil and the gestures of the body, which the Liturgy employs to speak of the sacramental mysteries unfolding within it. But symbols are far from being mere "visual aids," designed by the experts of the Church to communicate an idea or moral lesson that might more easily be conveyed in concepts to educated people. The Orthodox theologian Alexander Schmemann explains that the symbol is not merely an "illustration" but rather a genuine "manifestation:" "We might say that the symbol does not so much 'resemble' the reality that it symbolises as it *participates* in it, and therefore is capable of communicating it in reality." According to Schmemann also: "a sacrament is primarily a revelation of the [potential?] *sacramentality* of creation itself, for the world was created and given to man for conversion of creaturely life into participation in divine life."[25]

4. Living the Liturgy

In the preceding two sections I have been suggesting that the "watermark" of the Trinity is found throughout all of creation at every level, wherever the identities of two things are preserved (and deepened) by uniting them in a third. Human and divine natures are united in the Person of the Son (Chalcedon). God and humanity are united in the sacrament of the Church (Vatican II). Man and woman are united in the "one flesh" of marriage. Reason and feeling are united in the intelligence of the heart.

Contrasted with this is the *dualism* which can only unite two things by absorbing one of them into the other. Dualism of this type afflicts the relationship of Church and world, priest and people, grace and nature, faith and culture, man and woman. It is the root both of clericalism and of secularism. The obvious conclusion from this analysis is that many seemingly unrelated problems in the Church have a common cause. The crisis over sexuality, brought into the open by the reaction to *Humanæ Vitæ* in 1968, stems from the mentality that fails to understand the true nature of the "asymmetric" relationship between man and woman. This is the same mentality that fails to understand the relationship between priest and people in the Liturgy. This failure may express itself either in a clerical domination of the laity, or in a reversal of that relationship that eliminates all sense of the transcendent. On the one side, we find a poisonous cocktail of clericalism, aestheticism and misogyny. On the other, we observe "politically correct"

---

need for a renewal of "mystagogic" catechesis see S. Caldecott, "The Secret Path: A Catholic Response to the New Age," *The Chesterton Review*, November 2001.

[25] A. Schmemann, *The Eucharist: Sacrament of the Kingdom*, St Vladimir's Seminary Press, Crestwood, NY 1987, pp. 38 and 33-4. See also *For the Life of the World*, SVS Press, Crestwood, NY 2000, Appendices. An important defence of "symbolic realism" is given by the Western writer Jean Borella in the following books: *The Secret of the Christian Way* (op. cit.); *La Crise du Symbolisme Réligieux*, L'Age d'Homme, Lausanne 1990; *Le Mystère du Signe*, Maisonneuve & Larose, Paris 1989.

liturgies devoted to the themes of justice and peace: everyone sitting in a circle, praying for the homeless and passing the consecrated chalice from hand to hand, with the priest improvising parts of the eucharistic prayer in order to make it more relevant and friendly.

Social charity can not be reduced to a dualistic relationship without becoming either sentimental or domineering. During the eighteenth and nineteenth centuries, the Liturgy gradually became separated from any living concern with social justice—or at least, it seems to have become hard to see the connection.[26] Naturally, Christians were expected to go out from the Liturgy and live virtuous lives, and thus have a transformative effect on society, but they did this by crossing from sacred space into secular space, rather than by discovering a deeper relationship between the two. This could be described as a profanisation of charity; a secularisation of solidarity. The post-conciliar reaction was to emphasise the horizontal dimension of the Liturgy (social concern) over the vertical (the act of worship), or even to confuse the two. Whole religious orders went into steep decline as the communitarian aspect of their mission took precedence over the liturgical, the love of neighbour over the love of God. The problem of liberation theology was therefore a product not of the 1960s, but of the dualism of an earlier era.

Social solidarity is more securely grounded on right worship than on common feelings: the love of neighbour is founded on the love of God. This is in fact one of the clear implications, not only of the Ten Commandments themselves (the first three of which are devoted to the worship of God), but of the new Christian anthropology. The human person is by its very nature "trans-centric," or other-centred. We love God, and this opens us to the life of the other in our neighbour; we love our neighbour, and this opens us to the love of God. We do not simply go out to do good to another in the world, inspired by our worship of God in the church. Rather, the love of God sends us out to do good, because it reveals who we are and who is our neighbour. We are not (only) imitating the love of God that we see demonstrated in the Liturgy, but *living the Liturgy out in the world*.[27] The Liturgy is not (merely) separate in a horizontal sense from what goes on outside, but separate in the sense of being "interior," or revealing the inner meaning and purpose of what lies outside. Sacred space, sacred time and sacred art are distinctive, not (just) as belonging to a parallel world, but as defining the centre of *this* world: the world in which we live and work.

The secure possession of an authentic Christian anthropology thus reveals itself in the close involvement of the Church—whether as parish, as diocese, as religious order, as secular institute or as ecclesial movement—in

---

[26] See Michael J. Baxter, "Reintroducing Virgil Michel," *Communio*, Fall 1997.

[27] This point is beautifully developed in two books by Michael L. Gaudoin-Parker: *Hymn of Freedom: Celebrating and Living the Eucharist*, T&T Clark, Edinburgh 1997, and *Heart in Pilgrimage: Meditating Christian Spirituality in the Light of the Eucharistic Prayer*, Alba House, NY 1994.

forms of social action to relieve distress and to build a "culture of life." But it also reveals itself in more subtle ways: in the spirit with which the priest addresses the congregation, and the respect with which he is treated by them.[28] He must lavish the same quality of attentiveness and devotion on the least of his brethren as he does on his rubrics and vestments on the one hand, and on the parish stalwarts on the other. Simone Weil once said that "prayer is attention," and we can make her words our own. The living prayer which is kindled in the Liturgy — as it were from the Paschal candle at Eastertide — and without which the Liturgy becomes an empty shell, involves a quality of loving attention which is directed towards that Other whom God has placed in our path, the Other who is a sign of the uniting Third, the Holy Spirit.

5. Conclusion

My intention in this paper was to steer a course between the clashing rocks of Rationalism and Romanticism. The modern temptation is to think that the Liturgy is something we can analyse "scientifically," with a view to controlling and perhaps improving it. Alternatively, we may think it nothing more than a collective celebration of togetherness to generate a strong community spirit. Here the rational and romantic approaches bring out the worst in each other. But with the awakening of the heart's intelligence, both approaches are transformed. The Liturgy is understood from within, organically rather than mechanically. It is no longer a machine to be tinkered with, but a garden to be tended. The romantic tendency is also transformed. Feelings are rightly ordered towards the God who is our true centre because he is transcendent, and who is the giver of unity because he is other than ourselves.

Understood in this way the Liturgy reveals us to ourselves, because it reveals "the mystery of the Father and his love" (in the famous words of *Gaudium et Spes*, 22). The Father's love is not a *thing*, not an object to be known and researched, but an act, a deed, an event, which may be known only through participation. In the Son, in the reception of his Gift which is the Holy Spirit and Redemption, we are broken open and poured out for the world, mingling our lives with his in the communion of the Church. Such talk makes no sense if the heart is not able to see the whole in the parts, the symbols as sacrament. But if the eye of the heart is opened, the world's true centre and purpose are unveiled. Our own identity as children of God, our "most high calling," is brought to light.

---

[28] Here Pope John Paul II stands out as a living icon of true priestly holiness.

The Practical Application
of Anthropological Principles

Intervention of Father François Clément[1]

I̵N the west, since the end of the Middle Ages, with the arrival on the scene
of Nominalism and the other philosophies which derived from it, man is at
the centre of the intellectual world. He is indeed, for neo-philosophers
such as Luc Ferry,[2] the only "transcendent element" still accepted within the
intellectual horizon of post-modernism, which has made its own the "death of
God" and patricide. Simply recalling this tells us to what extent the whole of
religious reality today is necessarily subordinate to the conception of man (a
western conception, it is true); and yet we believe, with the Catholic Tradition,
that man is *capax Dei*, and that he is by nature turned towards his creator.[3] The
Tridentine reform, with its strong emphasis on centralisation, had the
advantage of transmitting intact to us this heritage which had been born in a
quite different context, and had been crystallised, so far as concerns the
essential elements, after the Carolingian period, and had the disadvantage of
establishing a sort of division, for practical purposes, between the untouchable
and monolithic deposit, and the "clothing" which was looked on as being
capable of being modified in accordance with the tastes of the day; it also led
to very great attention being paid to validity (which was certainly
understandable, when faced with people who denied even the substantial
nature of the mystery), which was detrimental to any kind of living synthesis,

---

[1] Father François Clément is a priest of the diocese of Freiburg (Switzerland). Before his
ordination in 1981, he had spent some time as a monk (Clervaux in Luxemburg, and
Solesmes), and his experience of choral singing during that time lent a further breadth to
the liturgical studies toward which he was inclined. He was awarded his Master's degree in
theology for a dissertation concerning the Missals of Cluny and Cîteaux. He serves those
centres of worship in his diocese which have been licensed for celebrations using the 1962
Missal (in Lausanne, Geneva, and Neuchâtel). His influence in the matter of vocations
(especially for his own diocese) gives him a practical understanding of the part played by
the Liturgy in spiritual life.
[2] Luc Ferry, *L'Homme-Dieu, ou le sens de la vie* [The Divine Man, or the Meaning of Life]
Grasset, Paris 1996.
[3] Saint Thomas, *Summa Theologica, Prima*, questions 90-102: this question is to be found
towards the end of the treatise on the Trinity, like a kind of hinge opening out onto the
treatise on the creation; see also *Prima*, qu. 43, 5, ad 2, and *Prima Secundæ*, qu. 4, 3 and qu. 5,
5; *Lumen Gentium* nos. 12-14.

of knowing how to unite a respectful understanding with the kind of intuition which enables us to enter into the mysteries at a level beyond that of words or of concepts; after passing through all that, here we are at a turning-point in the history of the Liturgy. We should not underestimate the influence of the "Enlightenment," of which there have been representatives, who may be more or less intransigent, since the eighteenth century; they prefer a liturgy in which the main emphasis is laid either upon the didactic aspect, or upon that of pure worship offered to God; what is at stake, therefore, for them and for their successors, is a fully rounded concept of man, or on the other hand one that is reductionist and truncated. Devotions, interior and exterior participation, the degree of display in ceremonial, the place of the priest and that of the congregation are all problems relating to this question. Romanticism would then raise the same questions, but with different answers and differing risks: aestheticism, man being dominated by sentiment, a cosmological vision which was inclined towards paganism, naturalism, and so on.

Since the period of the years just before the Second Vatican Council, following the Liturgical Movement which made an effort towards better understanding of the sacred rites, and towards putting them into practice in a more convincing fashion (the two watch-words were *ressourcement* and *aggiornamento*), we are seeing today a dissolution which puts into question even the concept of "Roman Liturgy." We must ask ourselves what, apart from a few supposedly immutable elements, a mere outline, stripped to basics rather than "dusted off," do we actually have in common with our predecessors? Should we, then, repudiate *en bloc* the ideas which have motivated (or, depending on one's point of view, disturbed) the Church for the past half-century, so as to return to a state of things we have subsequently decided was, after all, better? Ordinary common sense tells us that is impossible (we are in fact living thirty-five years after the Council), but it is not impossible, and may be desirable to draw a few lessons from this, and to try to encourage a more balanced approach in the future.

The Liturgy establishes a connection between two worlds: God's heaven and the world He has created. Since first he developed a consciousness, man tried to give this expression in ways which might be more or less adequate. Its authority and status derive from the Incarnation: Christ is the Mediator *par excellence*, God and man; He sends his Spirit to bring us into the mystery of Trinitarian Love. Christian Liturgy can not be anything other than the reflection of these realities of faith. But if faith is immutable in its content and in its object, its expression down the centuries, as translated into the public prayer of the Church, has certainly changed, and has produced an "organic unfolding," very much in the style of doctrine: *legem credendi statua; lex supplicandi*, as the well-known axiom has it.[4] God "has no need of our

---

[4] Denzinger-Schönmetzer, *Enchiridion Symbolorum Definitionum et Declarationum*, (Ed XXXVI emendata), Herder, Freiburg, Barecelona & Rome, 1976, no. 246.

praise,"[5] but it is of the first importance for us, that what Christ the Son of God willed for the sake of his glory and for our salvation, continues to be faithfully transmitted and profoundly experienced, and that it should be the vehicle of grace for all generations.

In accordance with the brief summary of facts we have just made, we need to have the courage to be clear about things. If the reforms the Church desired have any sense today, it can only be in continuity with the great Tradition: handing down, means allowing life to pass on. It is, of course, only as concerns the expression of faith and morals that a reversal of evolution is impossible, but in that perceptible continuity with those forms handed down from the past, there is rooted a very sure sense – which has no need to be explained nor demonstrated – of the immutability of faith. It is often people who are, to all appearance, very far from faith and from the Church, who are surprised to see how such a heritage, the wealth of which many people recognise as being quite exceptional, is being abandoned. Perhaps, after forty years, we are already in a better position to see some analyses made, and a few possible courses of action sketched out, with the benefit of a certain degree of tranquillity.

1. Left Brain and Right Brain

Experimental psychology gives these terms to the distinctive and complementary functions, in man, of our intellect: left brain is rational thinking, intellectual rigour, the activities of judgement and classification; it sets limits which prevent us from wandering, from getting lost. The right brain is the seat of everything that can not be shut in: dreams, intuitions, symbols, poetry. The former protects us against fear and gives us security, the second boosts our confidence. Now;

> Western society has increasingly concentrated more or less exclusively on making use of the left side of the brain...Mediaeval mysticism has given way to a disciplined way of thinking which, little by little, has given its colouring to the whole ambience of society...Unfortunately, this gives preference to the object rather than the subject of thinking...Yet the imbalance is no less dramatic for that. Those steps on which spiritual life is built up are rooted in trust and openness, and derive from the right side of the brain. Thus the increasingly one-dimensional evolution of our society has turned away from religions, which have themselves been caught up in this movement...*Consuming* sacraments or spiritual nourishment does not satisfy a fully-rounded person. The latter needs to co-ordinate objectivity

---

[5] Common Preface to Eucharistic Prayer IV in the Missal of Paul VI.

and realism with a different atmosphere, with another dimension, with a *Communion* of the inmost heart of his being with Life, with the Spirit.[6]

The balance between transcendence and proximity, between intellectual and intuitive, word and silence, symbolic and notional: it is easy, one would suppose, to list off those binary categories which seem to be forever irreducible…But it is exactly doing that, which would mean giving way to simplistic habits of analysis, the origins of which we know only too well. Liturgy essentially belongs in the category of "doing" (cf. the etymology of the word: *ergon* = work), and not that of "knowing." We have to find a way of doing it, in practice, which does not make these concepts contradictory, but fruitful; not dualist, but trinitarian. Thus, for instance, symbols always remain to some extent opaque: it is in that very quality that they are showing themselves to be transcendent in relation to reason. They are part of those "non-verbal signs" which often shape our being at a far deeper level than ideas.[7]

2. "'For Ever' Lasts a Long Time"

This evocative title comes from the pen of a monk who died in 1975. In the fine book to which he gave this title, he talks about the inimitable consciousness of time as opening upon eternity, which is found in our dear monasteries. One of the favourite words of the Liturgy is *Hodie*. It brings together in an eschatological *kairos* what the death-dealing *chronos* can never destroy. We must at all costs rediscover a silence which is not empty, but is fullness; a time which does not weary because it is true and filled with beauty, beyond those fractures which everyone perceives and at the same time allows to pass on: a fixed rigidity, or an endless creativity which knows no measure. Continuity should be demonstrated in the gestures of faith and of piety, in our musical heritage, in a natural way in a ceremonial which can not be improvised. The contrary of this is a disdain for ritual forms which reduces religious experience to a purely personal dimension. True liberty can never dispense with established rules. What Scripture calls the "heart" of man is both a workshop and a sanctuary, wherein this harmonisation and this synthesis are gradually brought into being. If the Liturgy does not encourage the habits of peaceful prayer and of spontaneous adoration, then has it not failed in its essential task?

---

[6] Claude Piron, *Le bonheur clés en main* [The Keys to Happiness in Your Hand], Saint Maurice, 1998, pp. 283 f.

[7] See A. Nichols OP, *Looking at the Liturgy*, Ignatius Press, San Francisco 1997, p. 72f [French edition, *Regard sur la liturgie et la modernité*, Geneva 1996, pp. 79f.].

3. Tradition, Modernism and Post-Modernism

There was a time when the argument from tradition was final and conclusive. Which is in any case not as stupid as it sounds; when something endures through the centuries, outlasting civilisations, it is because it holds within it values which have some universal, timeless quality. Contemporary mentality no longer functions in this mode: it claims to be able to do without roots, so as to be able to re-invent the world every morning, at its own pleasure and for its own profit. For a long time, a triumphant positivism, the myth of progress, and scientific empiricism have led us to believe in wonderful evenings to come. But this euphoria has repeatedly been succeeded by disillusionment, by which our society is tinged with depression and which strikes our contemporaries each time with full force. There are no intellectual landmarks, nor anything which by way of symbolic channels might be able to restore some meaning to existence. The modern age was wallowing in an aggressive anticlericalism and an atheism with which Vatican II was concerned,[8] and to which the Council tried to respond with some kind of dialogue. But, as has been written, not without a certain very British humour: "Despite the wonderful erudition liturgical scholars brought to the remaking of the rites, liturgists…'managed to back modernity as a winning ticket, just at the point when it became converted into post-modernism.'"[9] The man to whom they were trying to direct their efforts then—was he as real as was claimed? And were they not too inclined to regard the Liturgy as raw material which could be reshaped according to one's wishes, given that they had fallen for those presuppositions which in turn fed upon such a procedure?[10] Some people nowadays are saying that the Liturgy is much too serious a matter to be just left to the specialists…Many of our contemporaries feel something like vertigo at the spiritual emptiness, and they are ready to accept absolutely any esoteric spirituality so as to fill it. It is probable that the liturgical reform would have been able to have a more peaceful aspect, a more respectful attitude towards its heritage, if it had happened thirty years later. It seems as if the haste with which some changes were made did not contribute to their quality; a general sense of "cultural revolution" did not help in upholding a visible continuity; and the proof of that, even today, may be seen in the more or less virulent ostracism of certain things and people.

A lack of credibility is far less to be feared, today, from the fact that we can not explain everything. Our contemporaries are not, in general, put off by ritual bearing the stamp of *sobria ebrietas*. Encouraging people to be patient in learning about the Liturgy gives them an idea of its value: something that can

---

[8] In *Lumen Gentium* nos. 19-21, for instance.

[9] Quotation of K. Flanagan by A. Nichols OP, *Looking at the Liturgy*, pp. 81-82; [French edition, p. 89].

[10] Cf. the 'Thesaurus' proposed by the Benedictine Confederation, which was intended to replace the Antiphonary—but this proved unworkable in practice…

be immediately consumed does not carry the same weight in the domain of religion, as in the rest of life. Because they were seeking at all costs to "make the rites speak in the language of our time,"[11] people thought they must mercilessly eliminate every single archaism (unless it helped the purpose they were aiming for), must avoid repetitions, encourage a mathematical-type logic, and so on. In doing so, they forgot that the language of the Liturgy embodies an accumulated wisdom which is not tied down to any particular context, being equidistant from all the ages. It is addressed to the eternal man.

4. Man, a Social Animal

Many people perceive a certain kind of existentialism as forming the background to contemporary man's approach to everything. It makes him particularly sensitive to the dignity of the human person, to its unique worth; with the corollary, sometimes negative, of a subjective approach which prevents communication at any depth or with any reality. A sense of ecclesial communion rectifies this disadvantage; it sends its roots deep into trinitarian love.[12]

Never, there can be no doubt, has so much been talked about the "communal" dimension of the Liturgy, to the point at which it becomes a celebration of itself, at which the "president" imposes his own personality, his tastes, his passing fancies, the whole weight of his subjective attitudes, generally without being conscious of it, and with the best intentions in the world...The essential thing is not a matter of technique, but of supernatural charity and of spiritual communion. It is most necessary to recover a *sensus Ecclesiæ*, in which everyone receives their unique and particular place, for the glory of God and for the good of all, as we hear in the admirable hymn of the feast of the dedication of a church: *Urbs Jerusalem beata...quæ construitur in cælis vivis ex lapidibus...Tunsionibus, pressuris expoliti lapides, suis coaptantur locis per manus artificis, disponuntur permansuri sacris ædificiis.*[13] Rather than doing anything, it is a matter of allowing things to be done.

---

[11] This expression, which has become famous, was coined by Archbishop A. Bugnini CM.

[12] Cf. Cardinal Joseph Ratzinger, *Principles of Catholic Theology: Building Stones for a Fundamental Theology*, Ignatius Press, San Francisco 1987, pp. 15-17; [*Theologische Prinzipienlehre. Bausteine zur Fundamentaltheologie* (Munich, 1982) pp. 15-27]; and likewise: A Nichols OP, *The Theology of Joseph Ratzinger*, Edinburgh 1988, pp. 110-132. It is also the idea of late romantic theologians of the 'Gesamtkirche,' 'Église totale,' or 'Whole Church,' which formed a prelude to the theology of the Mystical Body: the Liturgy is the supreme medium for the mediation of the Church, which did not by any means imply a complete revision of the liturgical books, but simply a few modifications in detail: cf. A. Nichols' quotation of Monsignor Sailer in *Looking at the Liturgy*, pp. 39-40.

[13] Blessed city, Jerusalem...who of living stones are built and who art the joy of heaven above...Many a blow and biting sculpture polished well those stones elect, in their places now compacted by the heavenly Architect, Who therewith hath willed forever that His palace should be decked.

5. Perceptible Continuity or Subtle Revolution?

What people call "the man of today" is no doubt fairly similar to the one of yesterday and to the one of tomorrow. Amid the various streams which find expression in the Liturgy, one thing is increasingly obvious: the turning-point of the seventies marked a definite break. The allergies of this group of people and of those are curiously focussed on the same things (liturgical language, ornaments, incense, Gregorian chant...) and the watershed date of October 11th 1962 means for one group the end of everything, and for the others the beginning of freedom. For the younger generation, all that is history, and they are sometimes dismayed by these rearguard actions, whilst they often suffer on account of a fairly widespread mediocrity. They certainly do need solid teaching, but they also need mystery, sacredness, beauty, and a serious approach. When they find these, the difference can very soon be seen, but sometimes there is also present a certain spirit of consumerism, which leads to liturgical tourism. The remark is often passed that one has the impression of a more or less total black-out on what came before the liturgical reform. Just as in other spheres relating to doctrine or to morality, the old formulas have been made more flexible: it is not a matter of new content, which would be heterodox; nor the new presentation of an identical content, which would hardly be of interest; but the novelty of the form and presentation becomes, in some sense, in itself a motive for credibility. All the processes of adaptation and of inculturation—which constitute one of the special gifts peculiar to the Catholic Church—are rooted in this; but adapting to what, and for how long? The philosophy now predominating more often results in a virtual reality which is soon out of fashion, than in a universality which will last.

The Liturgy should be directed to every man of good will, and toward man in all his dimensions. It is as vast as the Heart of Christ. When it is humble and authentic, celebrated in the faith which brings it into contact with the living God, then it rings out down the ages, a language with many forms which does not age with time. It is fashioned in the image of the Man-God who is its centre and its only Mediator, in fruitful tension between heaven and earth. May this third millennium renew it from within, guided by the Spirit who leads us into all truth.

COMPLEMENTARY NOTES

1) As concerns the slow process of sedimentary deposit in the Liturgy in the West, it would, it seems to me, be possible to make a positive study which would start, for instance, from the sacramentaries and the *Ordines Romani* and would show how a certain skimming-off process was at work, setting aside

everything which was too much shaped by historical contingencies, so as to leave only what transcends time and space; and would also show what were the "moments of grace," which were the occasions of an important process of crystallisation: the work of Saint Gregory the Great, spread right across his empire by Charlemagne; the role of the great monasteries such as Cluny; the whole culture developed and transmitted by the cathedral schools; and so on.

2) The "Liturgical Movement" which people have as appearing at the beginning of the twentieth century was not a creation *ex nihilo*. It is in any case all too often known to people only in its final phase, which started after the second world war, and is called the "political stage" in the sense that people were by then starting to cut into the living substance, and beginning to want to put into practice the "technicians' revolution" which had up till then been going on behind closed doors. We have to do proper justice to figures such as Dom Guéranger, whom people have often frivolously accused of being no more than the representative of a certain romanticising of the past, a sort of liturgical Viollet-le-Duc. He is far more widely known for his *Année Liturgique* [*The Liturgical Year*] than for his *Institutions Liturgiques*,[14] which is the book we might consider as outlining the way ahead. He is certainly sensitive to the beauty of the Liturgy; he draws inspiration from the Middle Ages, as much as from the Early Church; and yet his restoration of monasticism and his love of learning come together with the Liturgy in a keen awareness of the Church, the only factor capable of uniting a society in which everything had been overturned and disordered for decades, or equally of counteracting the sentimental individualism particular to Romanticism. For him, the prayer of the Church is something shared among the family, and by its spiritual beauty and the transcendence of its language it is a power for evangelisation. Thus it is that he has a certain sacred respect for this venerable aspect of the Liturgy, which keeps him clear of any exaggeration, even of an "ultramontane" kind. There would be a great deal to be gained by turning back again to this un-polemical figure, who takes everything as it comes, quite humbly, so as to enter into them and make them his own in a spirit of filial obedience—a spirit which was quite clearly lacking in some specialists working "in the name of the Church."

3) In the sphere of dogmatic theology, we talk about apophatic and kataphatic theology; in view of the rule *Lex orandi, lex credendi*, these categories may be applied to liturgical studies. In this balance (which, obviously, could not be of a purely quantitative nature) and in an attention to this way that one complements the other, many apparent oppositions can be more clearly perceived; we can see, superimposed one upon the other, the *sobria ebrietas*, the invisible and the visible, Cîteaux and Cluny, and so on. What is eternal and

---

[14] Vols. I - IV, Palmé, Paris et Bruxelles 1878, 1880, 1883 & 1885.

ineffable passes through the channels of what is human and incarnate: we must at one and the same time both speak and keep silence, both sing and pray silently. Many concepts would be better comprehended in this light: participation, simplicity, intelligibility, community. It is in any case damaging to favour only one alternative: you generally end up, in such cases, by having the worse of the two, and sometimes one that is worse in both respects. Thus, an artificially constructed Liturgy may be loquacious and boring, with a poverty of content and of expression, wrapped-up in exaggerated fashion in the immanent dimension, and falsely spiritual. Now, balance comes from a greater elevation and from a greater distance: if we believe in this, because experience has shown it to us, we are more naturally convincing and less preoccupied with connecting up with the spirit of the world...

4) Some misunderstandings arise from a failure, on a practical level, to recognise their origins: the frequently bitter conflicts which erupt concerning the mystery of the Liturgy certainly show how the emotional aspect grips people at a far deeper level than do ideas. We always respond, of course, on a rational level, and find ourselves on the wrong floor. Is this not due to a certain spiritual pride, and generally accompanied by a profound disdain for "non-specialists"? A fairly typical example is the response offered those who say that the reformed rite of Mass does not take sufficient account of the aspect of sacrifice: to which people reply, "Oh, yes it does—look, you find the word here, and here..."—without admitting that many gestures, manners of representing things, silences, which formerly expressed this, seem to have been pitilessly eliminated.

5) What we ask of those who exercise a liturgical ministry, and especially of the celebrant, is all too often superhuman, and not supernatural: a constant preoccupation with what you have to say, what comment to offer, what to choose, adapting things to the congregation actually *in front of you*, whence originates a concentration on accessory elements, and the constant search for something "better," which is never satisfactory, for some novelty, since temporary forms are soon worn-out. The space for an inward dimension is devoured by the accessory elements, and, finally, we are far less free than within a coherent structure polished by centuries of use. The inclination of our poor human nature is always sloping downward towards the least possible effort, towards mediocrity, and that produces in most people feelings of discouragement, fatigue, or even disgust and indifference.

Translated by Henry Taylor

Roman Rite or Roman Rites?

Paper by Dom Cassian Folsom OSB[1]

T HIS paper is different from the two preceding talks in that it is concerned more with practice than with theory. The theological and anthropological foundations of the Liturgy are of fundamental importance, but once they have been established, one must build on them: the Liturgy must be celebrated in all of its nitty-gritty concreteness. This conference will examine liturgical practices of the past — in order to suggest certain attitudes toward liturgical practices of the present.

The original title of this conference was formulated as a question: "Roman rite (singular) or Roman rites (plural)?" I would like to re-formulate the topic as a statement, as a thesis to be demonstrated. The new title is this: "Within the unity of the Roman rite, there is room for the legitimate diversity of different usages." This affirmation is very simple, almost banal, but sometimes a re-statement of simple things can be useful. First I will define the terms used in this statement. Secondly, I will try to demonstrate the thesis from the point of view of the history of the Liturgy.

I. Definition of Terms

A. Rite

1. The first term to be defined is "rite," a word of polyvalent meaning. For the anthropologist, "rite" is described as a series of practices, collective or individual, repetitive in nature, which have to do with social attitudes, relations between individuals and groups, relations between the world of men and the world of the gods — which practices are manifested in cultic actions and ceremonies. We will not be using the word in this general sense.

2. The word "rite" is also used to denote a liturgical family, a way of celebrating the Christian mysteries which is peculiar to an ethnic, linguistic or

---

[1] Dom Cassian Folsom is a Benedictine monk who entered St Meinrad Archabbey in Indiana, USA, where he was professed in 1980. He studied at *Sant Anselmo*, the Pontifical Institute of Liturgy in Rome. He developed a career as a professor of Liturgy in Rome and for three academic years (1997-2000) he was the director of *Sant Anselmo*,. He has been the superior of a new monastic community *Maria Sedes Sapientiæ* for two years, firstly in Rome and then in Norcia, the birthplace of St Benedict.

cultural group, manifested by a complex of well-defined liturgical practices and customs. These ritual traditions have their own liturgical books, their own calendar, their own arrangement of the liturgical year, their own ways of celebrating the sacraments. Concerning the Eucharist, each rite has its own euchological tradition, its own lectionary, its own chants, its own order of Mass. "Rite" used in this sense can also indicate the particular doctrine or theological emphasis of a church, as distinct from other churches; it includes an entire historical and political tradition; it can indicate the language and culture of an entire people, which has often been deeply influenced by the liturgical tradition itself. It is in this large, general sense that we speak of the various Western and Eastern rites. Perhaps it would be useful to list the major ones here, so as to give an idea of the enormous diversity of the liturgical families which exist in the Church.

Originating in Antioch, the West-Syrian tradition:
— the Jacobite or Syrian orthodox (a portion of which entered into communion with Rome in 1783, called the Antiochene Syrians)
— the Maronites of Lebanon (in communion with Rome since 1182[2])
— the Malankar rite (a Syrian tradition of India which joined the Jacobites of Antioch in 1653; in 1930 a group entered into communion with Rome)

Also originating in Antioch: the East-Syrian tradition:
— the Nestorians[3] (a portion of which entered into communion with Rome in 1555,[4] called the Chaldeans)
— the Malabar rite: the Syrian tradition as it developed in India (which entered into communion with Rome under the influence of Portuguese missionaries in 1599)

Originating in Alexandria:
— the Coptic tradition (with a small group in communion with Rome since 1895)[5]
— the Ethiopian rite (with a small group in communion with Rome since the same period)[6]

---

[2] This is a common misconception. The Maronites have always been in communion with Rome. Communication, but not communion, was lost during centuries of difficulties under Moslem rule. The Maronites always accepted Chalcedon and the authority of Pope Leo acclaimed at that Council, and the successors of Leo. Cf. Bishop P. Dib, *History of the Maronite Church* (French orig., Beirut 1962, Eng. trans. by Rev. S. Beggiani) Detroit 1971, pp. 9-41; Idem., *D.T.C.*, vol. X, col. 1-142; L'Abbé Y. Moubarac, *Pentalogie Maronite*, Vol. I, Cénacle Libanais, Beirut 1984, pp. 133-93 [Ed.].
[3] Today they are called the Assyrian Church of the East. They do not hold the heresy known as Nestorianism [Ed.].
[4] 1553 is the correct year. This Catholic group are called the Chaldeans [Ed.]
[5] 1895 was the year of the re-establishment of their Patriarchate, but earlier, namely in 1741, and 1824 (first erection of the Patriarchate), groups of Copts became Catholic [Ed].

Originating in Armenia:
—founded in 3rd century (the Armenian Christians just celebrated their 1700th anniversary; there has been a Catholic branch of this rite since 1742).

Originating in Georgia:
—founded in 3rd-4th centuries

Originating in Constantinople:
—the Byzantine tradition, making up the largest group of Eastern Christians. For this rite, there are national groupings in Greece, Russia and territories of the former Soviet Union, Serbia, Rumania, Bulgaria, Georgia, Cyprus, the Czech Republic, Poland, Finland and the Diaspora. In addition, there are the so-called "uniate Churches,"[7] in communion with Rome: Ukranian, Croatian, Ruthenian (the Carpathian mountain region between former Czechoslovakia and the Ukraine) and Rumanian.
—The Melkites (Christians of West Syria and of Egypt who remained faithful to the Council of Chalcedon and gradually accepted the Byzantine rite).

As can be seen, even to identify the various Eastern rites is a challenge, because of their extraordinary diversity.

The West has also known a great deal of liturgical pluralism. The non-Roman western rites include:
    —the Ambrosian or Milanese rite
    —the Spanish or Mozarabic rite
    —the Gallican rite
    —the ritual tradition of North Africa
    —the Celtic rite

Each of these liturgical traditions of the west has its own specific character and identity. The Ambrosian rite and the Mozarabic rite are still being celebrated today.

And then, of course, there is the Roman rite! The interesting thing about the Roman rite is that since it embraces countless numbers of countries, ethnic groups, cultures and languages, it is universal in scope. This universality does not preclude local expressions, however, which may be more or less developed according to the circumstances of history. Local peculiarities in liturgical practice within the Roman rite, when they form a coherent system, are more properly called "usages."

---

[6] Formal union of the Ethiopians with Rome was proclaimed in 1626. This and the other dates given in the Editor's notes are taken from *The Eastern Christian Churches: A Brief Survey* by R. G. Roberson, CSP (Oriental Institute, Rome, 4th edition, 1993) [Ed].

[7] This term is no longer used, except by the Orthodox. These Churches are always called in official documents, "Eastern Catholic Churches" [Ed].

3. This brings us to the third definition of the word "rite:" a sub-set of a given liturgical tradition, more properly called a "use" or "usage." These usages may exist at the level of nations or kingdoms (England for example, as in the "Sarum use"), at the diocesan level (Aquileia, Ravenna, Benevento, Lyon, Braga), at the level of the monastic or religious family (Cluniacs, Cistercians, Carthusians, Dominicans, Franciscans, Praemonstratentions, Carmelites). All of these so-called "rites" are heavily dependent on the Roman tradition, and can arguably be called different "usages" of the Roman rite.

4. And finally, the word "rite" can mean a specific unit of liturgical action, such as the offertory rite, the communion rite, and so forth.

Now the point of all this is to show that when it comes to liturgical practice, the treasury of the Church contains a veritable embarrassment of riches. There is enormous diversity in the one symphony of praise which the faithful offer continuously to the thrice-holy God.

B. Unity of the Roman rite

Let us return to the thesis again, to refresh our memory. "Within the unity of the Roman rite, there is room for the legitimate diversity of different usages." We have described the words "rite" and "usage;" let me say a word now about unity. The phrase "the unity of the Roman rite" comes from *Sacrosanctum Concilium* no. 38 in the section on adaptation: "Provided that the substantial unity of the Roman rite is maintained, the revision of liturgical books should allow for legitimate variations..." The context makes it clear that the substantial unity of the Roman rite is guaranteed by the liturgical books themselves. Hence paragraph 39 talks about "the limits set by the typical editions of the liturgical books." We can thus understand the extreme importance of the Latin typical editions and their accurate translation into the vernacular languages. Paragraph 22 of *Sacrosanctum Concilium* states that the unity of which we speak is guaranteed by the competent authority, that is the Apostolic See, and then, as laws may determine, by the bishop. This is also a very important point: liturgical unity depends not only on the liturgical books, but also on the competent ecclesiastical authority.

C. Legitimate diversity

In a similar way, "legitimate diversity" is also a question of the competent authority, which approves or legitimates certain practices that may be peculiar to certain places or circumstances. The principle of diversity is clearly stated in paragraph 37 of *Sacrosanctum Concilium*: "Even in the Liturgy, the Church has no wish to impose a rigid uniformity in matters which do not involve the faith or the good of the whole community." Unity without diversity can degenerate into sterile uniformity; diversity without unity degenerates into chaos and anarchy. The authority of the Church is the custodian of both unity and diversity.

II. Demonstration of the Thesis from the Point of View of the History of the Liturgy

Having given a brief definition of terms, we can now turn to a demonstration of the thesis I have proposed (Within the unity of the Roman rite, there is room for the legitimate diversity of different usages). To do so, I will limit myself to the area of the Eucharistic celebration. Since this is too broad a topic for a short presentation such as this, I must impose another limit: I will speak only of the *Ordo Missæ* — not the euchology, not the lectionary, not the chants, not the calendar — just the *Ordo Missæ*. Once again, the topic is too vast, so I will further limit myself to the offertory rites of the *Ordo Missæ* — not the entrance rites, nor the communion rites, but just the offertory rites. My reason for this choice is two-fold: first, there is a certain amount of controversy over the offertory rites in the *Novus Ordo*, and I thought that a closer look at this section of the *Ordo Missæ* might be helpful; secondly, I just happened to have more documentation on hand for the offertory rites, which made my work a bit easier.

A. Before looking at specific texts, a brief introduction to the *Ordo Missæ* is necessary.[8] The *Ordo Missæ*, as a specific literary genre, is a collection of private prayers for the use of the priest, to help him to manifest his devotion during the celebration of the Mass. Bonifaas Luykx, in a ground-breaking study published in 1954,[9] distinguished three types of *Ordo Missæ*: the apology type, the frankish type and the rhenish type.

1. The apology type

In the earliest stages, various private prayers which the celebrant recited *ad libitum* formed the nucleus of this genre. Collections of these devotional prayers (to foster the piety of both priests and laity) are found in the carolingian *Libelli Precum*. Soon three groups of apology prayers formed around three specific moments of the Mass: prayers *ad communionem, ad munus offerendum, ante altare*. Luykx proposes that these private prayers helped to make the objective celebration of the Mass into a subjective experience of prayer for the priest.

---

[8] I am indebted to the useful summary of this topic found in the study of B. Baroffio and F. Dell'Oro, "L'*Ordo Missæ* di Warmondo d'Ivrea," *Studi Medievali* 16 (1975/II) pp. 795-823. Cf. especially pp. 801-806.

[9] B. Luykx, *De oorsprong van het gewone der Mis*, De Eredienst der Kerk 3, Utrecht-Antwerpen 1954. The German translation is more readily available: *Der Ursprung der gleichbleibenden Teile der heiligen Messe (Ordinarium Missæ), Priesterum und Monchtum* (=Liturgie und Monchtum 29), Maria Laach, 1961, pp. 72-119.

2. The frankish type

In a second stage of development, the collections of prayers loosely corresponding to these three moments of the Mass came to be connected with specific ritual gestures. The insertion of rubrical directives made the link between prayer and gesture more clear. The oldest example extant of this type is found in the Gregorian Sacramentary of Amiens (10th century). Other examples are from the 11th century, when this type reached its peak of development, before declining in the shadow of the rhenish Ordo. However, in south-central France (for example, in the Lyon area), this form of the *Ordo Missæ* remained in use.

3. The rhenish type

Parallel to the division of the Carolingian empire into two parts after the death of Charlemagne, parallel to the separate development of liturgical chant repertoires along the same dividing lines, parallel to the corresponding linguistic diversification (French and German), the *Ordo Missæ* likewise develops along two different lines according to the same geographic-linguistic-political divisions: the frankish type in the west and the rhenish type in the east (the germanic part). To be more precise, the *Ordo Missæ* of this third type originated in the abbey of Sankt Gallen in Switzerland, and spread throughout the entire area of the Rhine river, extending to the important imperial monastery of St Alban in Mainz. When the Romano-Germanic Pontifical (coming from the same scriptorium in Mainz) made its way down the Italian peninsula in the second half of the 10th century, the rhenish *Ordo Missæ* came with it. This is the direct model for a more complete description of the Mass, the *Ordinarium Missæ*, which was spread widely throughout all of Europe by the franciscan-roman liturgical books, and finally sanctioned by the *Missale Romanum* of Pius V.

In the second part of this presentation, I would like to take a look at the offertory rites of selected *Ordines Missæ*, from the earliest stages of development up to various usages of the 13th century. The earliest extensive description of the Mass is the *Ordo Romanus I* of the 7th century. From this single trunk of the tree, two major branches develop, corresponding roughly to the division of the Carolingian empire mentioned earlier. I will take one example from the frankish or gallican tradition, and one example from the rhenish or germanic tradition. With the passing of time, these two branches put forth a great profusion of leaves and shoots, which developed into distinct liturgical usages within the Roman rite. I will look at two of them: the Cistercan use and the Roman-Franciscan use, the latter of which is the basis for the later development of the *Ordo Missæ* in the Roman rite. All in all, we will look at five texts. I would like to examine each text according to the following categories:

    a.   brief introduction to the document
    b.   the structure of the liturgical action
    c.   the agents: who is acting?
    d.   the gestures performed
    e.   the words used
    f.   the theological or spiritual emphasis of the text

B. Analysis of the offertory rites of five *Ordines Missæ*

1. *Ordo Romanus I*[10]

a. Introduction: *Ordo Romanus I*, dating from the first half of the 8th century, is the first extensive description of the Mass of the Roman rite that we have. It is amazing that before 750, we have only fragmentary descriptions of the Mass, bits and pieces here and there. We would like to know how the Eucharist was celebrated before this time, but like archeologists, we can only propose theories to explain the very scanty evidence available. Even the *Ordo Romanus I* does not have as its primary intention a description of the Eucharistic celebration *per se*. It is rather a text written by a papal master of ceremonies, who is primarily concerned with ordering the ceremonial so that proper court etiquette be maintained. Nonetheless, it is a text of fundamental importance in the history of the Eucharistic celebration of the Roman rite.

b. Structure of the liturgical action: The offertory rite of the papal Liturgy begins with "Oremus," already disconnected from any particular prayer (#63). The collecting of the offerings is divided into three categories: the offerings of the people, the offerings of the clergy and those of the pontiff himself.

    The offerings of the people are collected with diplomatic nicety and grand hierarchical style, while the various people involved perform their tasks with choreographical precision. The pontiff first receives the gifts of the leading men of the nobility (*principes*) (#69), then he goes to the centre of the *confessio* to receive the gifts of certain public officials (#74), finally he goes to the women's side to receive their offerings (#75).

Offerings of bread

Because of the quantity of offerings to be collected, the work is divided as follows. The pontiff receives the offerings of bread from a certain number of the nobility, and hands them to the regional subdeacon. This subdeacon passes the offerings to another subdeacon following close behind him, who

---

[10] Michel Andrieu, *Les "Ordines Romani" du Haut Moyen Age, vol II: Les Textes (Ordines I-XIII)*, Spicilegium Sacrum Lovaniense 23, Louvain 1948, réimpression anastatique 1971, pp. 1-112 (hereafter cited as Andrieu, vol. II). I am indebted to the excellent study by Johannes Nebel: *Die Entwicklung des romischen Messritus im ersten Jahrtausend anhand der Ordines Romani: eine synoptische Darstellung*, diss. Pontifio Istituto Liturgico di Sant'Anselmo, Roma 2000.

places the bread in a linen cloth held by two acolytes. Following behind the pontiff is the hebdomadarian bishop, who receives the offerings which the pontiff is not able to take personally; the bishop himself places these offerings in the linen cloth, without going through the subdeacon intermediaries.

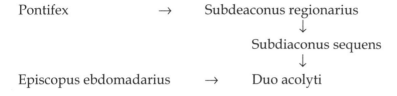

Offerings of wine

The wine is receives by a different set of personnel. The archdeacon receives the flasks of wine from the same nobles, which he pours into a large chalice held by another regional subdeacon. When the chalice is full, the subdeacon empties it out into a larger vessel, carried by an acolyte who is following close behind. Just as the pontiff could not receive all the offerings of bread personally, so also the archdeacon can not receive all the offerings of wine. He is assisted, therefore, by a deacon (whose function is parallel to that of the hebdomadarian bishop), who empties the flasks directly into the larger vessel of the acolyte, without passing through the intermediary of the regional subdeacon's chalice.

This same procedure is repeated for receiving the gifts on the men's side, at the confessio, and on the women's side. Once the gifts have been collected, the archdeacon then washes his hands (#77) and begins the elaborate preparation of the gifts on the altar. He first receives the flask of wine offered by the pope himself, then the flasks of the deacons, and water from the archcantor for mixing with the wine. The water is poured into the chalice in the form of a cross (#80).

While everyone takes their positions, the pontiff rises from his chair and comes to the altar. He makes a sign of reverence to the altar (*salutat altare*) (#82), and then receives the gifts of bread from the hebdomadarian priest and from the deacons. The archdeacon receives the pontiff's offering of bread and gives it to him (#83); the pontiff then places it on the altar (#84). The archdeacon then takes the chalice from the subdeacon and places it on the altar next to the offerings of bread. It is interesting to note that the chalice has handles, and that the archdeacon, as a sign of reverence, uses a cloth called the *offertorium* whenever he needs to touch the chalice. At this point all is ready, and the pontiff, *inclinans se paululum ad altare*, gives a nod to the schola to conclude the offertory chant (#85). It is not clear whether the phrase *inclinans se* refers to a gesture of prayer, or is part of the sign given to the choirmaster.

c. Agents: The large number of participants and the diversity of their roles is perhaps the most significant characteristic of the offertory rite in *Ordo Romanus I*.

- pontifex
- episcopus ebdomadarius[11]
- presbyter ebdomadarius
- archidiaconus
- diaconus
- subdiaconus regionarius[12]
- subdiaconus sequens
- subdiaconus oblationarius[13]
- acolyti
- archiparafonista[14]
- primicerius notariorum[15]
- secundicerius notariorum
- primicerius defensorum[16]
- secundicerius defensorum

d. Gestures: There are no indications of any gestures of offering. The pontif makes some kind of gesture of reverence to the altar when he arrives there from his chair (*salutat altare*). The phrase *inclinans se paululum ad altare* at the end of the preparation of the gifts may indicate a gesture of prayer, but the evidence in unclear.

e. Words: There are no indications for any kind of verbal prayer, although the *super oblata* can be presumed.

---

[11] The bishop and priest who serve in this capacity fulfil their duties a week at a time.

[12] The *regio* is one of the seven ecclesiastical districts of the city of Rome.

[13] The *oblationarius* has the task of taking care of the lamps and the candles, and insuring the supply of bread and wine for the Eucharist. Cf. Andrieu, vol. II, p. 45.

[14] Head cantor of choirmaster.

[15] *Primicerius* simply means the head or chief of his group or college. The *primicerius notariorum* is the head of the notaries, who served in the papal chancery. The *secundicerius* is his second-in-command.

[16] The *defensor* exercised some sort role in the field of law (for example as judge, advocate, lawyer). In the stational Liturgy, he would be mounted on horseback, and would precede the pope as he made his way to the stational church. During the Liturgy, the *defensore* would be vested and would have a specific place in the sanctuary. Gregory the Great chose seven *defensores* from the larger college to form a special group with the title of *regionari*. Cf. Andrieu, vol. II, pp. 41-42.

f. Theological/Spiritual emphasis: Since the literary genre is that of a papal *ceremoniale*, the primary preoccupation is to maintain the court ceremonial and the elaborate etiquette of papal liturgies. While the involvement of various levels of society in the offering of the gifts is noteworthy, there is very little attention given to the Eucharist *per se*. What will happen in the subsequent development of the liturgical tradition is that the elaborate ceremonial will be greatly simplified while the paucity of gesture and verbal prayer will be amplified to correspond to a different sense of priestly piety.

Time restrictions do not permit us to describe the subsequent development of *Ordo Romanus I* in any detail, so a thumb-nail sketch will have to suffice. When this text arrived north of the Alps, it became the basis for two recensions: a short recension which circulated in Gaul before the Carolingian liturgical reforms, and a long recension which was influential in the germanic section of the empire (the Rhineland in particular) after Charlemagne's reform.[17] Both recensions are attempts to adapt the papal Liturgy to the needs of the Church in franco-germanic lands.

In terms of the development of the offertory rite, each recension adds a further element or two showing increased attention to gestures of offering and including some kind of prayer associated with those gestures; whether the prayer is verbal or not, however, remains unclear. *Ordo Romanus XV* (end of 8th century), representing the tradition of the shorter version in frankish lands, adds the following information. When the pontiff has received all the offerings, and goes to the altar, he takes the two altar-breads that he personally is offering, raises his eyes and his hands to heaven, and prays to God privately:

> *Ipse vero pontifex novissime suas probrias [oblationes] duas accipiens in manu sua, elevans oculis et manibus cum ipsis ad celum, orat ad Deum segrete et, conpleta oratione, ponet eas super altare.*[18]

Andrieu observes that this gesture is only adopted in Rome with the arrival of the Romano-Germanic synthesis in the 10th century.[19] After the preparation of the chalice, for which no particular gesture of offering is indicated, the pontiff says the *super oblata* silently, maintaining a profound bow all the while, saying out loud only the conclusion of the prayer:

---

[17] Cf. the authoritative study of Johannes Nebel cited earlier.

[18] *Ordo Romanus XV*, 33 in Michel Andrieu, *Les "Ordines Romani" du Haut Moyen Age, vol III: Les Textes (suite) (Ordines XIV-XXXIV)*, Spicilegium Sacrum Lovaniense 24, Louvain 1951, réimpression anastatique 1974, p. 102 (hereafter cited as Andrieu, vol. III).

[19] Andrieu, vol. III, p. 71, n. 1.

Tunc pontifex, inclinato vultu in terra, dicit orationem super oblationes, ita ut nullus præter Deum et ipsum audiat, nisi tantum Per omnia sæcula sæculorum.[20]

Ordo Romanus V, representing the tradition of the longer recension, coming from the Rhineland around the end of the 9th century, adds two small elements. After the gifts have been prepared, when the pontiff goes to the altar he not only makes some sign of reverence as in *OR I* (*salutat altare*), but he also prays. The text says: "*Tunc surgens pontifex a sede...descendit ad altare et orat et salutat altare...*"[21] The nature of this prayer is not specified. The *super oblata* which was assumed in *OR I* but not mentioned explicitly, is referred to here as an oration which is said secretly: "*...dicta oratione super oblationes secreta et episcopo alta voce incipiente:* Per omnia sæcula sæculorum...*"[22]

In these two examples, the gestures of offering are still quite limited, and there is as yet no indication of any verbal prayer beyond the *super oblata*. According to the thesis of Luykx, it was the franco-germanic genius which began to fill in these moments of the Liturgy with prayers and gestures expressing the personal piety of the priest. The first step in this process was the use of apology-type prayers, as mentioned earlier. The second stage of development was the linking of certain prayers with specific moments of the Mass. The oldest example available to us of this frankish type *Ordo Missæ* is found in the Sacramentary of Amiens.

2. The Sacramentary of Amiens (frankish type), 9th century[23]

a. Introduction: The manuscript of Amiens, a Gregorian sacramentary, dates from the second half of the 9th century.[24] In the *Ordo Missæ* are inserted any number of private prayers of the priest, both apologetic (confessing his own sins and unworthiness) and intercessory (praying for the needs of various groups of people).

b. Structure of liturgical action: The rubrical direction is very brief: *Cum vero panem et vinum posuerit super altare dicat*. And again: *Quando ponitur oblata super altare*. There are six prayers given in the text, but they are simply listed one after the other, probably *ad libitum*. It is not yet clear at this stage of development what the relationship is between text and gesture. After the six

---

[20] *Ordo Romanus XV*, 35 in Andrieu, vol. III, p. 102.

[21] *Ordo Romanus V*, 53 in Andrieu, vol. II, p. 220.

[22] *Ordo Romanus V*, 58 in Andrieu, vol. II, p. 221.

[23] For the text of the *Ordo Missæ*, cf. Victor Leroquais, *L'Ordo Missæ du sacramentaire d'Amiens* in *Ephemerides Liturgicæ* 41 (1927) pp. 435-445 (hereafter cited as "Leroquais Amiens").

[24] I have not been able to determine to which family of Gregorian sacramentaries this manuscript belongs. Leroquais' presentation of the *Ordo Missæ* of this sacramentary does not go into the question.

prayers the priest turns to the people with his request for their intercession: *Orate fratres*. The people respond with their prayer for him: *Sit Dominus in corde tuo...*

c. Agents: The *Ordo Missæ* is meant for the *sacerdos*. The rubric allows the possibility for a deacon: *Si diaconus legerit [evangelium]...* The people are mentioned (*populus*) as responding to the *Orate fratres*.

d. Gestures: The series of prayers are intended for the moment when the priest places the gifts of bread and wine on the altar. No further information is given.

e. Words: Here for the first time we find the words of these private prayers of the priest.   This is the specific contribution of the *Ordo Missæ* of the Sacramentary of Amiens.

f. Theological/Spiritual emphasis: The prayers ask God to accept the oblation, they intercede for the living and the dead, they beg for the forgiveness of sins and the reward of eternal life. Five of the six prayers begin with the invocation *Suscipe, sancta Trinitas*. The second prayer makes memory of the mysteries of the Lord's incarnation, life, death and resurrection and asks for the intercession of all the saints. The overriding concern here is priestly intercession.

3. The manuscript Sangallensis 338 (rhenish type), mid-11th century[25]

a. Introduction: In the third stage of development of the *Ordo Missæ*, prayers are not only grouped together in one of the three moments of the Mass where priestly piety can have greater personal expression (communion, offertory and entrance), but the individual prayers are connected to specific ritual gestures; this is indicated by expanded rubrical directives. The *Ordo Missæ* of this third type seems to have originated in the famous monastery of Sankt Gallen in Switzerland, and through its inclusion in the Roman-Germanic Pontifical of the 10th century, becomes the basis for the subsequent development of the *Ordo Missæ* in the Roman rite. One of the most representative examples of this type is the manuscript Sangallensis 338. The manuscript itself seems to have been copied in the 11th century, although the content may well go back a century earlier.

b. Structure of liturgical action: The priest receives the gifts from some unidentified person and gives him a blessing. There is a prayer for acceptance which the priest recites at that moment, although exactly where he is or what

---

[25] Michael G. Witczak, *St Gall Mass Orders (I): Ms. Sangallensis 338: Searching for the Origins of the "Rhenish Mass Order"* in *Ecclesia Orans* 16 (1999) pp. 393-410.

gestures he performs remains unclear. Returning to the altar, the priest says an apology prayer before proceeding further.

There are three prayers listed for the offering of the oblatio (bread). The first one was seen also in the Sacramentary of Amiens (*Suscipe sancta Trinitas hanc oblationem quam tibi offero in memoriam incarnationis...*). The prayer of intercession for the dead has some similarity to the parallel prayer in the Sacramentary of Amiens, although the ending is different. There are two prayers for the offering of the chalice.

Then, with raised hand, the priest blesses both the oblation and the chalice. There follows the incensing of the gifts and of the people, accompanied by specific prayers. Afterwards, the priest turns to the *circumstantes* and says: *Orate pro me peccatore.* The response is not indicated in this manuscript.

c. Agents: The *Ordo Missæ* is intended for the priest: the words *presbiter* and *sacerdos* are used interchangeably. The deacon is mentioned in connection with the reading of the Gospel. Some unidentified server hands the priest the gifts of bread and wine. After the incensing of the gifts, various people (again unidentified) are incensed individually. The *circumstantes* mentioned are not described: does this refer to the deacon and clerics in the sanctuary or to the assembled faithful?

d. Gestures: There is brief mention of a series of actions: receiving the oblation, going to the altar, offering the oblation, offering the chalice, blessing the gifts with upraised hand, placing the incense in the thurible, swinging the thurible toward individual people, turning toward the *circumstantes*. While the rubrical directions are rather sparse, the specific contribution of this type of *Ordo Missæ* is that there is a rubric which links each prayer to a specific liturgical gesture.

e. Words: The prayers contain the same major themes we saw in the Sacramentary of Amiens: plea for acceptance of the gifts being offered, request for forgiveness, intercession. Since there are not as many prayers as in the Amiens manuscript, however, this thematic content is more streamlined. There are two new elements in respect to the texts we have seen thus far. One is the series of prayers to accompany the incensing (#51-55).[26] The second is a number of prayers in view of the consecration yet to come:

> #43: *Sanctifica quæsumus domine hanc oblationem, ut nobis unigeniti filii tui domini nostri Iesu Christi corpus fiat. Per.*
> #47: *Oblatum tibi domine calicem sanctifica, et concede, ut nobis unigeniti filii tui domini nostri Iesu Christi sanguis fiat. Per Christum.*

---

[26] The psalm verse *Dirigatur oratio mea sicut incensum in conspectu tuo, Domine* used by the Saint Gall text for the offertory (Sangallensis #51) is used by the Amiens Sacramentary for the offering of incense before the Gospel (Leroquais, *Amiens*, p.441).

#49: *In nomine domini nostri Iesu Christi, sit signatum, ordinatum, et benedictum, et sanctificatum, hoc sacrificium. Per Christum dominum.*

f. Theological/Spiritual emphasis: At this stage of development of the *Ordo Missæ*, there is already a rather sophisticated integration of the objective liturgical action with subjective priestly piety. Themes derived from the Roman canon (prayers that the sacrifice be accepted, confirmed, ratified and changed into the body and blood of Christ) combine with prayers for pardon and intercessory petitions.

4. The Cistercian use, 12th century[27]

a. Introduction: A monk of Solesmes, Paul Tirot (†1998), in his study entitled: *Un "Ordo Missæ" monastique: Cluny, Citeaux, La Chartreuse*[28] has argued that contrary to popular belief, the Cistercian *Ordo Missæ* was not taken from the local diocese (Chalon-sur-Saon), but rather from the monastery of Cluny. It belongs neither to the Frankish nor the Rhenish tradition, but is an original composition of Cluny, based upon *Ordo Romanus I*, with the intention of adapting the Roman tradition to the needs of monastic simplicity. The Cistercian rite and the Carthusian rite are based upon the Cluniac tradition.

b. Structure of liturgical action: The offertory rite is truly a common effort between the priest and deacon, with the carefully co-ordinated involvement of various other members of the monastic community.

    After the priest sings *Dominus vobiscum* and *Oremus*, the deacon begins to prepare the altar. The priest takes the chalice and paten from the deacon and places them on the right side of the corporal; then he moves to the left side of the altar to receive the incense. Meanwhile the deacon continues the preparation of the gifts. The incensation is done in two parts: the first by the priest, after which he has his fingers washed in preparation for the sacrifice. (It is interesting to note that the fingers are kept together from this point on: not just from the consecration as in the later development of the Roman rite). Then the priest makes a profound bow and prays: *In spiritu humilitatis*. While this is going on, the deacon carries out part two of the incensing. When the priest is ready, he turns to the choir (note the involvement of the monastic community)

---

[27] The *Ordo Missæ* of the Cistercian use can be found in Chapter 53 (*Quomodo se agat sacerdos et ministri ad Missas festivas*) of *Ecclesiastica officia*. The best edition is by D. Choisselet—P. Vernet, edd., *Les Ecclesiastica officia cisterciens du XIIème siècle*, Abbaye d'Oelenberg, Reiningue 1989, pp. 156-168. Prayers of the *Ordo Missæ* taken from the missal of Dijon 114 (82) can be found on pp. 364-368 of the same edition. I am indebted to Fr. Maciej Zachara MIC, for his work on this topic.

[28] P. Tirot, *Un "Ordo Missæ" monastique: Cluny, Citeaux, La Chartreuse*, BEL Subsidia 21, Roma 1981. Cf. the conclusions on pp. 113-118.

and says: *Orate fratres*. It is not clear who says the response. After this come the secret (or several secret prayers, as the case may be).

c. Agents: The monastic community is directly involved in the liturgical action, with responsibilities shared by the following: Sacerdos, Abbas, Fratres (monks), Diaconus, Subdiaconus, Minister (thurifer).

d. Gestures: This monastic *Ordo Missæ* contains a number of expressive gestures: the use of the *offertorium* (which we saw also in *OR I*), covering the chalice and host with the corporal, kissing the hand of the priest when handing him any sacred object, the sober manner of incensing the offerings, the hand washing of the priest and his keeping his fingers together thereafter in honour of the sacred host which he desires to touch with pure hands.

e. Words: There is only one private prayer of the priest: *In spiritu humilitatis* along with the *Orate fratres* with its response. The texts are only slightly different than those which have come down to us to this day. The response to the *Orate fratres* uses biblical expressions to describe the prayer of the priest rising as a remembrance into the presence of God.

f. Theological/Spiritual emphasis: The offertory rites of the Cistercian use are indeed streamlined and succinct, carried out in an atmosphere of monastic sobriety. The fact that gesture is emphasised much more than word is entirely in keeping with the monastic spirit of silence. While it is for the priest to offer the gifts, the deacon also has a considerable role to play, carried out in harmony with other ministers and with the whole monastic community.

5. The Roman-Franciscan use[29]

a. Introduction: It is well known that the Franciscans adopted the Liturgy of the papal court as their own: this wedding of the Roman and Franciscan geniuses and the extremely rapid expansion of the Franciscan order led to the widespread diffusion of this particular liturgical synthesis. The Missal of Honorius III was adopted by the Franciscans in 1230, and soon became known as the *Regula Missal*. This was revised at the papal court in the 1240's to bring it in line with the more developed Breviary. The Franciscan minister general, Haymo of Faversham undertook a revision of the rubrics in 1243-44. The *Ordo Missæ* thus revised is known as the *Indutus Planeta*, from the opening words of the document. It is of fundamental importance for the history of the *Ordo Missæ* of the Roman rite, since it forms a bridge between the *Paratus Ordo Missæ* of the Roman Curia (1227) and the later stages of development of the

---

[29] *Indutus Planeta* (1243) as found in S.J.P. Van Dijk, *Sources of the Modern Roman Liturgy*, vol 2: Texts, Studia et Documenta Franciscana II, Leiden 1963, pp. 3-14. Hereafter cited as Van Dijk.

Missale Romanum, from the *editio princeps* of 1474, to the Ordo of Johannes Burckard of 1502, culminating in the 1570 Missal of Pope Pius V. It is useful for our purposes in that it is an example of a particular usage of a religious order within the Roman rite, standing in continuity with the rhenish *Ordo Missæ* tradition of the 10th –11th centuries. Note that this in an *ordo* for private Mass and for the weekday conventual Mass: *Incipit ordo agendorum et dicendorum a sacerdote in missa privata et feriali iuxta consuetudinem ecclesie romane.*[30]

b. Structure of liturgical action: The offertory rite shows a neat series of doublets; almost without exception each gesture is accompanied by its corresponding prayer:

Gesture:　　Offering of host
Prayer:　　*Suscipe, sancte Pater*

Gesture:　　Blessing of water, pouring the water into the chalice
Prayer:　　*Deus, qui humanæ substantiæ dignitatem*

Gesture:　　Offering of chalice
Prayer:　　*Offerimus tibi, Domine*

Gesture:　　Covering of chalice
Prayer:　　*In spiritu humilitatis*

Gesture:　　Signing the gifts with the sign of the cross
Prayer:　　*Veni sanctificator*

Gesture:　　Hand washing, for which there is no corresponding prayer

Gesture:　　Bowing profoundly at the centre of the altar
Prayer:　　*Suscipe, sancta Trinitas, hanc oblationem*

Gesture:　　Turning to the people for the *Orate Fratres*
Prayer of circumstantes: *Suscipiat Dominus sacrificium*

Then follows the secret prayer or prayers, leading into the preface.

c. Agents: Since this is an *ordo* for private Mass, there is no reference to deacon and subdeacon. There is the *sacerdos*, a *minister*, the people (*populus*) and *circumstantes* (referring to those in the sanctuary?).

d. Gestures: The gestures are clearly described by the rubrics, each gesture accompanied by a prayer, as already mentioned.

---

[30] Van Dijk, p. 3.

e. Words: The direct source for the prayers is the *Indutus Planeta Ordo Missæ* of the Roman Curia (1227), which in turn is in direct line with the Rhenish *Ordines Missæ* of the Sankt Gallen tradition. The prayers are an amalgam of apologies, intercessions, requests for acceptance, classical collects from the ancient sacramentaries, and biblically inspired petitions.

f. Theological/Spiritual emphasis: One of the most significant aspects of this particular *Ordo Missæ* is that it is meant for the private Mass of the priest. Thus the long process of change is completed: from the pontifical Mass of pope or bishop with the myriad of assisting clergy and laity exemplified by *Ordo Romanus I*, to the private Mass of priest and server in the *Indutus Planeta* of the Roman-Franciscan synthesis.

This rapid survey of selected *Ordines Missæ* examined five examples out of a myriad of possibilities. These examples are taken from the Roman rite itself, from various points along the spectrum of its historical development, and from various usages within the Roman rite. They show a progressive development from few gestures of offering unaccompanied by any kind of verbal prayer to a carefully elaborated system of interwoven gestures and prayers. Differences (which can be considerable) are due primarily to time (historical period of development) and space (variations according to geographical region).

Conclusion

These examples show that within the Roman rite, the liturgical tradition has known considerable variety. When the competent ecclesiastical authority today must make decisions about unity and diversity in the Liturgy, it must weigh carefully political,[31] canonical and specifically liturgical factors. Political and canonical issues may be complex. From the liturgical point of view, however, the question is extremely simple: within the unity of the Roman rite, there is room for the legitimate diversity of different usages.

APPENDIX 1: ORDO ROMANUS PRIMUS[32]

69. Pontifex autem <postquam dicit *Oremus*, statim> descendit ad senatorium, tenente manum eius dexteram primicerio notariorum et primicerio defensorum sinistram, et suscipit oblationes principum per ordinem archium.

---

[31] Cardinal Ratzinger pointed out that "pastoral" is perhaps a better word than "political" here.

[32] Michel Andrieu, Les "Ordines Romani" du Haut Moyen Age, vol.II : Les Textes (Ordines I-XIII), Spicilegium Sacrum Lovaniense 23 (Louvain : 1948), réimpression anastatique 1971, pp. 1-112.

70. Archidiaconus post eum suscipit amulas et refundit in calice maiore, tenente eum subdiacono regionario, quem sequitur cum sciffo super planetam acolytus, in quo calix impletus refunditur.

71. Oblationes a pontifice suscipit subdiaconus regionarius et porrigit subdiacono sequenti et subdiaconus sequens ponit in sindone quam tenent duo acolyti.

72. Reliquas oblationes post pontificem suscipit episcopus ebdomadarius, ut ipse manu sua mittat eas in sindone qui eum sequitur.

73. Post quem diaconus, qui sequitur post archidiaconem, suscipit <amulas> et manu sua refundit in sciffum.

74. Pontifex vero, antequam transeat in partem mulierum, descendit ante confessionem et suscipit oblatas primicerii et secundicerii et primicerii defensorum ; nam in diebus festis post diacones ad altare offerunt.

75. Similiter ascendens pontifex in parte feminarum

G	Omnes codd., præter G
et complet superscriptum ordinem.	ordine quo supra omnia explet.

GA	omnes codd., præter GA
76. Similiter et presbiteri si necesse fuerit post eum vel in presbiterio faciunt. Post hoc pontifex, tenente ei manum primicerio et secundicerio, reddit ad sedem suam, abluit manus suas.	76. Tunc, tenentibus primicerio et secundicerio manus eius, redit in sedem.

77. Archidiaconus stans ante altare, expleta susceptione, lavat manus <suas>; deinde respicit in faciem pontificis, <at ille> annuit ei et ille resalutato accedit ad altare.

78. Tunc subdiaconi regionarii, levantes oblatas de manu subdiaconi sequentis <super brachia sua>, porrigunt archidiacono et ille componit altare; nam subdiaconi hinc inde porrigunt.

79. Ornato vero altare, <tunc> archidiaconus sumit amulam pontificis de subdiacono oblationario et refundit super colum in calicem, deinde diaconorum <et in die festo primicerii, secundicerii, primicerii defensorum>.

80. Deinde descendit subdiaconus sequens in scola, accipit fontem de manu archiparafonistæ et defert archidiacono et ille infundit, faciens crucem, in calicem.

81. Tunc ascendunt diaconi ad pontificem; quos videntes primicerius, secundicerius et primicerius defensorum regionariorum et notarii regionarii et defensores regionarii descendunt de aciebus, ut stent in loco suo.

82. Tunc surgit pontifex a sede, descendit ad altare et salutat altare <et> suscipit oblatas de manu presbiteri ebdomadarii et diaconorum.

83. Deinde archidiaconus suscipit oblatas pontificis de oblationario et dat pontifici.

84. Quas dum posuerit pontifex in altare, levat archidiaconus calicem de manu subdiaconi regionarii et ponit eum super altare iuxta oblatam pontificis <ad dextris>, involutis ansis cum offerturio, quem ponit in cornu altaris, et stat post pontificem.

85. Et pontifex, inclinans se paululum ad altare, respicit scolam et annuit ut sileant.

86. Tunc, finito offertorio, episcopi sunt stantes post pontificem, primus in medio, deinde per ordinem, et archidiaconus a dextris episcoporum, secundus diaconus a sinistris et ceteri per ordinem disposita acie.

87. Et subdiaconi regionarii, finito offertorio, vadunt retro altare, aspicientes ad pontificem,

GA	Omnes alii codd.
ut quando dixerit *Per omnia secula,* aut *Dominus vobiscum,* aut *Sursum corda,* aut *Gratias agamus,* ipsi sint parati ad respondendum,	

stantes erecti usquedum incipiant dicere hymnum angelicum, id est *Sanctus, Sanctus, Sanctus.*

G	Omnes codd., præter G
88. Ut autem expleverint, surgit pontifex solus	Quem dum

GW	Omnes codd., præter GW
in canone;	et intrat in canonem;

APPENDIX 2: THE SACRAMENTARY OF AMIENS[33]

Cum vero panem et vinum posuerit super altare dicat: Hanc oblationem, quesumus, omnipotens Deus, placatus accipe, et omnium offerentium et eorum pro quibus tibi offertur peccata indulge. Et in spiritu humilitatis et in animo contrito suscipiamur, Domine, a te, et sic fiat sacrificium nostrum ut a te suscipiatur hodie et placeat tibi Domine Deus.

---

[33] Victor Leroquais, *L'Ordo Missæ du sacramentaire d'Amiens* in *Ephemerides Liturgicæ* 41 (1927) pp. 435-445.

Quando ponitur oblata super altare: Suscipe, sancta Trinitas, hanc oblationem quam tibi offero in memoriam incarnationis, nativitatis, passionis, resurrectionis, ascensionisque Domini nostri Ihesu Christi, et in honore omnium sanctorum tuorum qui tibi placuerunt ab initio mundi, et eorum quorum hodie festivitas celebratur, et quorum hic nomina et reliquie habentur, ut illis proficiat ad honorem, nobis autem ad salutem, ut illi omnes pro nobis intercedere dignentur in celis quorum memoriam facimus in terris.

Alia quando profert oblata: Suscipe, sancta Trinitas, hanc oblationem quam tibi offero pro omni populo christiano, pro fratribus et sororibus nostris, et pro his qui nostri memoriam in suis continue habent orationibus, ut in presenti sæculo remissionem peccatorum recipiant et in futuro præmia consequi mereantur æterna. Per.

Memoria imperatoris et totius populi christiani: Suscipe, sancta Trinitas, hanc oblationem quam tibi offero pro rege nostro et sua venerabile prole et statu regni Francorum, pro omni populo christiano, et pro elemosinariis nostris et pro his qui nostri memoriam in suis continuis habent orationibus ut hic veniam recipiant peccatorum et in futuro premia consequi mereantur æterna.

Memoria sacerdotis: Suscipe, sancta Trinitas, hanc oblationem quam tibi offero pro me peccatore miserrimo omnium hominum, pro meis peccatis innumerabilibus quibus peccavi coram te in dictis, in factis, in cogitationibus, ut præterita mihi dimittas et de futuris me custodias, pro sanitate corporis et anime meæ, pro gratiarum actione de tuis bonis quibus cotidie utor. Quid retribuam Domino pro omnibus que mihi retribuit? Calicem salutaris accipiam et nomen Domini invocabo. Laudans invocabo Dominum et ab inimicis meis salvus ero.

Memoria defunctorum: Suscipe, sancta Trinitas, hanc oblationem quam tibi offero pro animabus famulorum famularumque tuarum *ill.* ut requiem æternam dones eis inter tuo sanctos electos, ut in illorum consorcio vita perfruantur æterna.

Inde vertat se ad populum dicens: Orate, fratres, ut vestrum pariter et nostrum sacrificum acceptabile fiat Deo.

Et respondet populus: Sit Dominus in corde tuo et in labiis tuis, et recipiat sacrificum sibi acceptum de ore tuo et de manibus tuis pro nostrorum omnium salute.

APPENDIX 3: MS. SANGALLENSIS 338[34]

36. *Et oblationem accipiendo dicat:*

37. Acceptabilis sit deo omnipotenti oblatio tua.

38. Suscipe sancta trinitas hanc oblationem quam tibi offert famulus tuus, et præsta ut in conspectum tuum tibi placens ascendat.

39. *Tunc rediens sacerdos ad altare antequam secretam dicat accuset se ipsum dicens:*

40. Domine deus omnipotens fac me peccatorem hodie secundum magnam misericordiam tuam, accedere ad sanctum altare tuum et præsta, ut non sit mihi hoc sacrificium reatus ad pœnam, sed ablutio salutaris ad ueniam. Per dominum.

41. *Ad offerendam oblationem.*

42. Suscipe sancta trinitas hanc oblationem quam tibi offero in memoriam incarnationis, nativitatis, passionis, resurrectionis, ascensionis domini nostri Iesu Christi, et in honore omnium sanctorum tuorum qui tibi placuerunt ab initio mundi, et eorum omnium quorum hodie festa celebrantur, et quorum hic nomina et reliquiæ habentur, ut illis proficiat ad honorem, nobis autem ad salutem, ut illi omnes pro nobis intercedere dignentur in cælis, quorum memoriam facimus in terra.

43. *Alia.* Sanctifica quæsumus domine hanc oblationem, ut nobis unigeniti filii tui domini nostri Iesu Christi corpus fiat. Per.

44. *Pro defunctis.* Suscipe sancta trinitas hanc oblationem, quam tibi offero pro anima^{bus} famuli^{orum} tui^{orum}, ut per hoc salutare sacrificium purgate, sanctorum tuorum consortio mereatur^{ntur} adunari. Per Christum dominum nostrum.

45. *Ad offerendum calicem.*

46. Offerimus tibi calicem salutaris, et deprecamur clementiam tuam, ut in conspectum diuinæ maiestatis tuæ cum odore suauitatis ascendat. Amen. Per Christum.

47. *Item.* Oremus. Oblatum tibi domine calicem sanctifica, et concede, ut nobis unigeniti filii tui domini nostri Iesu Christi sanguis fiat. Per Christum.

48. *Tunc eleuata manu benedicat utrosque dicens:*

49. In nomine domini nostri Iesu Christi, sit signatum, ordinatum et benedictum, et sanctificatum, hoc sacrificium. Per Christum dominum.

50. *Postea incensum accipiens et ponat in turibulum dicens:*

51. Dirigatur oratio mea sicut incensum in conspectu tuo, domine.

---

[34] Michael G. Witczak, *St. Gall Mass orders (I): Ms. Sangallensis 338: Searching for the origins of the "Rhenish Mass Order"* in *Ecclesia orans* 16 (1999), pp. 393-410.

52. *Item.* Incensum istud a te benedictum ascendat ad te, domine, et descendat super nos misericordia tua.

53. *Quando odor eiusdem incensi uniquique porrigitur dicat:*

54. Acendat in nobis dominus ignem sui amoris et flammam æternæ caritatis.

55. *Item.* Illo nos igne quæsumus domine spiritus sanctus inflammet quem dominus noster Iesus Christus misit in terram et uoluit uehementer accendi.

56. *Tunc conuertat se sacerdos ad circumstantes et dicat:*

57. Orate pro me peccatore.

APPENDIX 4: THE CISTERCIAN USAGE[35]

Diaconus autem post Evangelium displicet corporale habens tres plicatus in latum et quattuor in longum, medium latitudinis ponens in medio altaris. Et statim post *Oremus* opertis manibus de offertorio, tenens sinistra manu pedem calicis, dextra autem patenam, offerat sacerdoti simul utrumque, manum eius semel osculans. Sacerdos simul utrumque assumens deponat iuxta corporale ad dexteram partem, reliquiens ea diacono preparanda, et postea trahat se ad sinistrum cornu altaris, ibidem consistens donec recipiat thuribulum ad thurificandum calicem. Diaconus vero positus offertorio super altare, ponat calicem super corporale in secundo plicatu anterioris et sinistre dextreque partis, et panem ante calicem, revolvens super eum corporale. Quod si plures hostiæ: fuerint, unam separatim, alias insimul mittat. Deinde reportet patenam et offertorium super ministerium. Interim dum hæc aguntur a sacerdote et diacono, unus ministrorum cuius officium est, teneat thuribulum ante abbatem vel ante sacerdotem si abbas deest, subdiacono incensum tenente. Posito itaque incenso in thuribulo: qui thuribulum tenet offerat illud sacerdoti, osculans ei manum. Quod sacerdos accipiens : thurificet calicem isto modo. Semel volvat illud circa calicem, semel thurificet dexteram partem altaris desuper, semel et sinistram, semel quoque anteriorem. Quod dum fecerit, diaconus ponat manum suam sub ascella ipsius tenens ei casulam: ut expeditius possit agere. Quo facto reddat thuribulum diacono. Deinde ablutis digitis aqua sibi a subdiacono de ampulla data, et in pelvi ad hoc preparata recepta, et tersis ad linteum ad hoc deputatum: incurvus ante altare faciat orationem.

In spiritu humilitatis et in animo contrito suscipiamur, Domine a te, et sic fiat sacrificium nostrum ut a te suscipiatur hodie et placeat tibi, Domine Deus.

Diaconus autem thurificet prius dexteram partem ipsius altaris bis deforis. Deinde elevans manum thurificet bis crucem, et inde transiens per retro altare

---

[35] D. Choisselet – P. Vernet, edd. *Les* Ecclesiastica officia *cisterciens du XII*ᵉ *siècle*, Abbaye d'Oelenberg, Reiningue 1989, pp. 156-168; 364-368. Capitulum 53: *Quomodo se agat sacerdos et ministri ad Missas festivas.*

ad sinistram partem thurificet eam similiter et crucem. Deinde reddat thuribulum subdiacono, qui ponat ubi poni solet. Ipse vero retro redeat sub gradu altaris in dextera parte, ut cum sacerdos se verterit ad chorum dicens *Orate fratres:* trahat ei deorsum medium casulæ.

Orate, fratres, pro me peccatore, ut meum pariter ac vestrum in conspectu Domini acceptabile fiat sacrificium.

Dominus sit in corde tuo et in labiis tuis, suscipiatque de manibus tuis sacrificium istud, et orationes tuæ ascendat in memoriam ante Dominum pro nostra et totius populi salute.

Deinde supplicans ei secedat in locum suum, ubi stet donec sacerdos dicat *per omnia sæcula sæculorum.* Qui sacerdos dicto *Orate fratres* mediocriter ut possint audiri, reducat vultum ad altare eadem parte qua se vertit ad chorum. Postea trahat se ad librum qui est in sinistro cornu, dicens sub silentio *Oremus* ad primam secretam et ad secundam, si una vel plures sequuntur. Interim autem minister ille qui thuribulum obtulit sacerdoti, deferat diacono et subdiacono aquam ad lavandum manus suas. Sacerdos vero provideat ne disiungat illos digitos quibus debet tractare Corpus Domini, postquam eos aqua abluerit: nisi dum fecerit cruces super hostiam et calicem, vel quando se signaverit.

APPENDIX 5: THE FRANCISCAN USAGE — *Indutus Planeta* (1243)[36]

Sacerdos accipit patenam cum hostia duabus manibus mediocriter elevatis, et dicit:

Suscipe, sancte Pater, omnipotens æterne Deus, hanc immaculatam hostiam, quam ego indignus famulus tuus offero tibi Deo meo, vivo et vero, pro innumerabilibus peccatis et offensionibus et negligentiis meis, et pro omnibus circumstantibus, sed et pro omnibus fidelibus christianis vivis atque defunctis: ut mihi et illis proficiat ad salutem in vitam æternam. Amen.

Interim vero sacerdos benedicens ampullam cum aqua, quam minister ad dexteram sacerdotis assistens offert, infundit calici dicens:

Deus, qui humanæ substantiæ dignitatem mirabiliter condidisti et mirabilius reformasti: da nobis per hujus aquæ et vini mysterium, ejus divinitatis esse consortes, qui humanitatis nostræ fieri dignatus est particeps, Jesus Christus Filius tuus, qui tecum vivit et regnat in unitate Spiritus Sancti Deus, per omnia sæcula sæculorum. Amen.

Deinde accipiens calicem cum duabus manibus mediocriter elevatis, offert eum dicens:

---

[36] S.J.P. Van Dijk, *Sources of the Modern Roman Liturgy*, vol. 2: Studia et Documenta Franciscana II, Leiden 1963, 3-14.

Offerimus tibi, Domine, calicem salutaris, tuam deprecantes clementiam: ut in conspectu divinæ majestatis tuæ, pro nostra et totius mundi salute, cum odore suavitatis ascendat. Amen.

Collocatur vero hostia ad sinistram, calix vero ad dexteram. Deinde corporali simplici plicato, cooperitur calix quod superponitur calici cum hac oratione:

In spiritu humilitatis et in animo contrito suscipiamur, Domine, a te: et sic fiat sacrificium nostrum in conspectu tuo hodie, ut placeat tibi, Domine Deus.

Postea fit signum crucis super hostiam et calicem cum oratione:

Veni, sanctificator omnipotens æterne Deus *(ita quod primo ducatur manus super hostiam, secundo super utrumque)*, et bene+dic hoc sacrificum, tuo sancto nomini præparatum.

De benedictione vero incensi et incensatione et aliis quæ pertinent ad solemnitatem habebitur in "Ordinationibus."

Et parum inclinatus super altare et manibus junctis, vadit ad abluendum manus suas.

Deinde rediens ad medium altaris, profunde inclinatus, junctis manibus, dicit:

Suscipe, sancta Trinitas, hanc oblationem, quam tibi offerimus ob memoriam passionis, resurrectionis, ascensionis Jesu Christi Domini nostri: et in honore beatæ Mariæ semper Virginis, et beati Joannis Baptistæ, et sanctorum Apostolorum Petri et Pauli, et istorum et omnium Sanctorum: ut illis proficiat ad honorem, nobis autem ad salutem: et illi pro nobis intercedere dignentur in cælis, quorum memoriam facimus in terris. Per.

Qua finita, erigens se osculatur altare, et vertens se ad poulum, parum inclinatus dicit:

Orate fratres, ut meum ac vestrum sacrificum acceptabile fiat apud Deum omnipotentem.

Circumstantes vero respondeant:

Suscipiat Dominus sacrificum de manibus tuis ad laudem et gloriam nominis sui, ad utilitatem quoque nostram totiusque Ecclesiæ suæ sanctæ.

Deinde, regirans se ex parte dextera, stans contra medium altaris dicit secretam vel secretas; jungit manus dicens ultimum Per Dominum nostrum. *Quibus completis, elevatis et extensis manibus dicit:* Per omnia sæcula sæculorum.

Towards a Legitimate Diversity

Intervention of Dom Daniel Field OSB[1]

D OM Cassian Folsom has showed us, with remarkable precision, how "within the unity of the Roman rite, there is room for a legitimate diversity of different liturgical customs;" he has illustrated with particular local examples, taken from the history of mediaeval liturgy, the rule which the Council's Constitution on the Liturgy gave for the work of revising the liturgical books: "Provisions shall also be made…for legitimate variations and adaptations to different groups…provided that the substantial unity of the Roman rite is preserved."

Now, what is the current situation?

1) It is (only) thirty years since we left behind the era when the Roman rite was uniformly determined for all the Churches who had no rite of their own.

It has now been recognised, thanks to quite specific historical studies[2] dedicated to this subject, that the liturgical uniformity of the post-Tridentine period was not the result of the activity of the Holy See, but of requests made by the diocesan bishops.

At the Council of Trent, it was the bishops who took the initiative in demanding a uniform liturgy which would be universally obligatory.

At the time of promulgating the Missal, Pope Saint Pius V allowed those dioceses which had had liturgical books proper to them for over two hundred years the freedom to retain them: well, all the dioceses sooner or later adopted the Missal of Saint Pius V, except for a few great Churches like Milan.

In France, in the course of the seventeenth century, a movement began to emerge of "fabricating" diocesan Missals and Breviaries: the well-known neo-gallican liturgies, which Dom Guéranger so vigorously opposed in the nineteenth century. Yet the Holy See did not react to these events.

---

[1] Dom Daniel Field is a monk of Randol, where he is the cellarer, having entered Fontgombault in 1969. He acquired a love for the Sacred Liturgy even before entering monastic life, through his contact with the canons of Notre-Dame at Paris. He has, on several occasions, contributed to CIEL's annual Colloquium.

[2] See the doctoral thesis of Lino Pizzi, presented at the Pontifical Institute in 1988: *Unificazione della liturgia in Occidente: Frutto della azione del Papato?* of which an 'Excerptum' was published (Rome, 1988).

Thus, if it is true that Saint Pius V's intervention, by his bulls promulgating the Breviary and the Missal, deprived the diocesan bishops of their traditional powers in liturgical matters, withdrawing the liturgy of particular churches from the realm of custom, or from peculiar legislation, so as to bring it within the realm of universal legislation,[3] it certainly seems, nevertheless, that the Holy See itself did not, for a long time, have the intention of drawing all the possible conclusions from this new canonical situation. As late as the nineteenth century, Dom Guéranger encountered difficulties on the part of Rome concerning the return of the French dioceses to the Roman Liturgy!

2) It was the explicit will of the Second Vatican Council that "Provisions shall also be made, when revising the liturgical books, for legitimate variations and adaptations to different groups, regions, and peoples, especially in mission lands,"[4] the competent authorities for "deciding on the adaptations" being the bishops' conferences.[5]

And indeed, in publishing the liturgical books in their various translations, the bishops' conferences certainly did make a number of choices from amongst the possibilities provided for in the Latin 'typical' editions, and did make some adaptations: but as a whole this was no great matter, and certainly did not open up any possibilities in the direction of the old liturgical books.

Thus we can only note that, where the bishops themselves, in the Council, had demanded and provided for "legitimate differences," and where the Roman 'typical' editions had allowed the opportunity for them, the bishops imposed an interpretation of the reform tending towards uniformity.

This is, it is true, no longer the uniformity of the era of "rubricism" as it is called, with a strongly pejorative connotation. It is a uniformity of tendency, of direction, we might say a "dynamic" uniformity.

Within the use that is made of "the free range which the new *Ordo Missæ* gives to creativity," this uniformity excludes any borrowing from any aspect whatever of the post-Tridentine Liturgy. And what is more, as we hear upon all sides, simply using the Missal published in 1969, strictly as it is, with several pieces in Latin and in Gregorian plainchant, on an altar where the priest is not facing towards the faithful, he risks being stigmatised as "fundamentalist" or having it said that what he does is not in line with the Council.

The bishops have often spoken of "bi-ritualism" — something they reject absolutely — as being opposed to this uniformity. It seems to them, that if the authorisation were freely made available for celebrating according to the Missal of 1962, this would create a second diocesan community, that of the old

---

[3] Which was confirmed by canon 1257 of the 1917 Code of Canon Law.

[4] *Sacrosanctum Concilium*, no. 38.

[5] Ibid., no. 39.

rite, by the side of the diocesan new rite community, and that the two communities would be in danger of not being able to communicate on the liturgical level—in the same way as a community of oriental rite Catholics might exist within a Latin diocese.

Quite to the contrary, this would be a proper part of "legitimate differences," and of the diversity of liturgical customs within the substantial unity of the Roman rite, not to create a "bi-ritualist" situation, but simply a liturgical diversity appropriate to the diversity of congregations.

3) Cardinal Ratzinger, in the paper he read on the 24th October 1998,[6] remarked indeed that the diversity one can find existing between the various ways of celebrating with the new Missal is often greater than would exist between an old liturgy and a new liturgy, if both were celebrated according to the directions in the liturgical books.

That brings us back to Dom Cassian's suggestion. If, in fact, the competent authority is perfectly prepared to admit that "the free range which the new *Ordo Missæ* gives to creativity is sometimes extended beyond reasonable bounds," as Cardinal Ratzinger was deploring at this very same conference in 1998, there should consequently be no difficulty in admitting that celebrating in accordance with the post-Tridentine books is equally one of the forms of "legitimate diversity" within the "substantial unity of the Roman rite."

This will be all the more so, since creativity in liturgical matters was quite specifically disapproved of by the Council: "Therefore no other person [that is, other than "the Apostolic See and, as laws may determine, on the bishop," or "various kinds of competent territorial bodies of bishops legitimately established," i.e. the bishops' conferences], even if he be a priest, may add, remove, or change anything in the Liturgy on his own authority."[7]

The type or model of the Roman rite is, quite obviously, that which the Roman Pontiff personally celebrates.

This model is "exported" into all the Churches which do not enjoy their own proper rite, or which are not connected with a Church which has its own proper rite. It is at this juncture, as Dom Cassian has shown us, that the diversity of liturgical custom develops: whilst conserving the liturgical pattern of the Roman rite, the various Churches adapt this in some way or other, in accordance with their own particular traditions.

Is it not the Missal which, in the course of a process lasting centuries, has shaped the Catholic mind of the faithful who accepted it, which represents *par excellence* the usage best adapted for those who draw therefrom the life of grace in abundance? That, there is no doubt, is the profound motivation which

---

[6] Cf. "Ten Years of the Motu Proprio *Ecclesia Dei*" in *The Latin Mass*, vol. 8, no. 2 (Spring 1999), pp. 15-18.

[7] *Sacrosanctum Concilium*, para. 22, § 3; cf. §§ 1, 2.

inspired the Holy Father to write those well-known words in his Motu Proprio *Ecclesia Dei.*

What has thus been said of the Roman Missal published by Saint Pius V could also be said of the Missals of the great religious orders, that of Cluny for example—from which, let us recall, the Cistercian and Carthusian Missals are derived—or equally that of the Carmelites, of the Premonstratensians, the Dominicans, and so on. All of these derive from the Roman rite, but from a Roman rite which had not undergone the same development as that of the secular Churches, which issued in the Missal of Saint Pius V: these are differing liturgical usages, yet still perfectly legitimate ones, within the substantial unity of the Roman rite.

Conclusion

The Holy Father has a good many times pointed out how these differing usages might be established: on the one hand, by the Pontifical Commission *Ecclesia Dei*; on the other hand, through initiatives on the part of diocesan bishops in their respective dioceses.

Many people, however, have been worried about the limited effect of what may be undertaken by these two authorities, and that was the subject of difficulties raised in various groups in recent years.

It is no doubt necessary to perceive, on the one hand, that the Holy See, if it declares differing liturgical usages legitimate, has in mind especially ecclesial communities, and not, normally, individual priests as such. Previous legislation, it is true, laid upon all Dominican priests the obligation to celebrate, always and everywhere, according to the Dominican Rite:[8] that was the legal situation at a given time, and is not an absolute requirement, ecclesially speaking. It is all the more the case that the Holy See could not possibly permit any priests, in order to demand that they be allowed always to use the old Missal, should throw suspicion on the Liturgy that the Holy Father himself celebrates.

On the other hand, it is indispensable that a conversion of the heart should come about, a change in mentality, as Cardinal Ratzinger himself has several times said with emphasis. The realm of the Liturgy is not just any ordinary realm of administration in the Churches: it is the realm in which the faithful of Christ, bishops, priests and lay people, enter into the mystery of the

---

[8] See the article by Father L.-M. de Blignières, *"Actes fondatuers et gestes de communion"* ('Foundational Acts and actions of Communion'], in *Sedes Sapientiæ*, no. 68 (summer, 1999).

Death and the Resurrection of the Saviour, as celebrated in the wonderful sacrament of the Eucharist.

Translated by Henry Taylor

Problems of the Liturgical Reform

Paper by Canon André Rose[1]

M Y paper is divided into three parts: 1. The Constitution *Sacrosanctum Concilium* of Vatican II; 2. The implementation of the post-conciliar reform in the official, "typical" liturgical books; 3. The introduction of the Liturgy on a practical level in French (according to the official liturgical books: the Missal and lectionaries). We will mainly be turning our attention to the *Mass* (the *Ordo Missæ*).

It is important to distinguish the three stages quite clearly, and not to confuse one with another in the critical consideration we may give them.

1. The Constitution 'Sacrosanctum Concilium' of Vatican II.

Let us just recall a few points of the teaching of the conciliar Constitution:

a) Paragraphs numbers 5 & 6 present the basic doctrine on the "work of salvation accomplished by Christ" (para. 5). The document recalls the profound unity of Christ's Paschal Mystery, of his Passion and Resurrection. Thus it is that, in the vision of the Liturgy and the early tradition, that of the Old Testament and the Fathers, the Cross is the source of life; it is just this inseparable union of the Cross and the Resurrection which gives us the Spirit, that we may live in the expectation of the Lord's coming again in glory in the course of our own lifetime. That is especially mentioned in paragraph five: "The work of Christ the Lord in redeeming mankind and giving perfect glory to God...achieved...by the Paschal Mystery of His blessed Passion, His Resurrection from the dead, and the glorious Ascension, whereby 'dying, he

---

[1] Canon André Rose was ordained priest in Namur, his own diocese, in 1943. He has been a titular canon of the cathedral since 1957. We have many articles by him on the Christian understanding of certain Psalms, on the basis of a traditional text (Septuagint, Vulgate, Vetus Latina). He has also written about the New Testament, the Fathers, and eastern (Byzantine and Coptic) and western Liturgies. He is the author of *Psaumes et Prière chrétienne* [The Psalms and Christian Prayer] (1965), and *Les psaumes, voix du Christ* [The Voice of Christ in the Psalms] (1982). In 1967 he was appointed as an expert to the Liturgy *Consilium*, in which post he remained until 1972, as secretary to the Commission responsible for determining the course of Psalms in the Daily Office and the biblical readings for the Office and for the Mass, and for the collects and Prefaces of the Mass. He has since continued to publish various studies (on Scripture in the liturgical tradition).

destroyed our death and, rising, he restored our life' (Easter Preface)." At the end of paragraph five, there is a little detail that is interesting, even from the ecumenical point of view: the evocation of Christ, unconscious on the Cross, giving water and blood, Baptism and the Eucharist, "the wondrous sacrament of the whole Church."

Next, paragraph six shows how this work begun by Christ is carried forward by the Church in the Liturgy: "He sent the apostles, filled with the Holy Spirit. This He did that, by preaching the gospel to every creature (14), they might proclaim that the Son of God, by His Death and Resurrection, had freed us from the power of Satan (15) and from death, and brought us into the kingdom of His Father. His purpose also was that they might accomplish the work of salvation which they had proclaimed, by means of sacrifice and sacraments, around which the entire liturgical life revolves."

b) Paragraph seven evokes the presence of Christ in the Liturgy, particularly in the sacrifice of the Mass. We understand, of course, that this presence is at the same time the sign of his Resurrection, and of the Spirit which he sends upon us. It is thus in this sacrament in particular that we are in contact with him, filled with his Spirit and ever turned towards the day of our meeting, as we await his coming in glory.

c) Paragraph ten affirms that "the Liturgy is the summit toward which the activity of the Church is directed" and "the font from which all her power flows." "From the Liturgy, therefore, and especially from the Eucharist, as from a font, grace is poured forth upon us; and the sanctification of men in Christ and the glorification of God, to which all other activities of the Church are directed as toward their end, is achieved in the most efficacious possible way."

d) Paragraph twenty-three reminds us that "there must be no innovations unless the good of the Church genuinely and certainly requires them; and care must be taken that any new forms adopted should in some way grow organically from forms already existing." This is obviously most important for the liturgical reform.

e) In number forty-seven and the following paragraphs, concerning the eucharistic mystery, it is recalled that the Mass perpetuates — it makes mysteriously present — the sacrifice of the Cross — the source of life — and that it is the memorial of the Death and the Resurrection of Christ. This is the very heart of the eucharistic celebration. The text likewise insists on the relationship between the two parts of the Mass: "The two parts which, in a certain sense, go to make up the Mass, namely, the Liturgy of the word and the eucharistic Liturgy, are so closely connected with each other that they form but one single act of worship" (para. 56). It is therefore necessary to get the faithful "to take their part in the entire Mass, especially on Sundays and feasts of obligation" (ibid.).

f) In paragraph 102, concerning the liturgical year, the conciliar text insists on Sunday, the "Lord's day," on which the Church commemorates the Resurrection of Christ, and the whole of his Paschal Mystery, since the Resurrection comes out of the Cross. For our eastern brethren (I am thinking especially of the Byzantine rite), each Sunday involves a series of tropes — we would say, of greater antiphons — which glorify the Cross and the Resurrection inseparably, setting them in relation to the *Theotokion*, that is, the evocation of the Virgin; we find that in all the eight musical modes of Sundays. This emphasis on the Cross-Resurrection is of course connected with the Incarnation: it is because he is the Son of God incarnate, that he can give his life in dying for us. That same paragraph 102 evokes the two great cycles of the liturgical year: Lent and Easter on one hand, and Advent-Christmas-Epiphany on the other. The subsequent paragraphs stress the important place of the Virgin and of the saints.

g) In paragraph 116, Gregorian chant is recognised as being "specially suited to the Roman Liturgy: therefore, other things being equal, it should be given pride of place in liturgical services." I see nothing, up to the present, which might replace this great Gregorian tradition, which is such an aid to contemplation...

Let us simply keep this wise directive in mind: "The rites should be distinguished by a noble simplicity; they should be short, clear, and unencumbered by useless repetitions" (para. 34). Repetition is not an evil in itself, it helps us to inwardly assimilate something: I am thinking of the "Lord, I am not worthy...," which we repeat three times so as to be more inwardly aware of it: that is not a pointless repetition.

2. The Official ("typical") Liturgical Reform

- The Mass

a) On the positive side, we must recognise that we now have a greater wealth of *readings*: the four Gospels are read in the course of a year; many passages from the Epistles, from the Apocalypse and from the Old Testament which are — on Sundays — related to the Gospel. The special times of year keep their traditions: thus, for example, the Gospel of John is read from mid-Lent up to Pentecost (the Roman tradition); and similarly the reading of the Acts of the Apostles during the Easter season has, most felicitously, been kept on (whereas some people wanted to put these readings after Pentecost — which is historicism...); the season of Easter is the time when the Spirit, emanating from the glorified Christ, is spread abroad in the Church, it is the season of the Church. Of course, the Holy Spirit was given at Pentecost, but the season of Easter is the time when Christ rises from the dead, when he is glorified (as the Gospel says) and spreads the Spirit.

b) There are more *Prefaces*, and there are four *Eucharistic Prayers*:

The first Eucharistic Prayer being the traditional Roman Canon (an ancient and most venerable Canon, which unfortunately is no longer said in certain parishes; it is true that it does not yet have the parts on the Holy Spirit which the fourth and fifth centuries will see develop, even though the *omni benedictione cælesti et gratia repleamur* is an allusion to the Spirit).

Eucharistic Prayer II is the *adaptation* of a prayer of the *Apostolic Tradition* attributed to Hippolytus (third century). It is very difficult to know who composed this anaphora. In the Apostolic Tradition we have the whole of this Canon.

"We give thanks to you, through your beloved Child Jesus Christ:" Christ is the Child, so said the Fathers; the same Greek word, παις, had been used in Isaiah in the sense of servant, but here it expresses a more intimate relationship; Christ is "sent...as Saviour, Redeemer, the Messenger of the divine will...he who is your inseparable Word." I do not know why the word *inseparabilem* has not been retained, as this demonstrated the unity of the Father and the Son "through whom you have created all things."

"This Son became incarnate and was made manifest, being conceived of the Holy Spirit by the Virgin;...to win for you a holy people, he stretched out his hands, in the great gesture of his Passion, to deliver from suffering all who believe in You."

It is then recalled — but the text as a whole was not retained in the new prayer — that "the Son of his own will gave himself up to suffering, so as to destroy death and to break the bonds of the devil and trample hell under his feet, giving light to the just" who were waiting in the underworld. But these allusions to hell, to the underworld, have been removed; only the reference to the Resurrection was kept. It is a pity that the original text, containing a greater wealth of allusion, was not adhered to here. All of that can be found in the great icon of the Resurrection which is the traditional one in the East, in which Christ, having destroyed hell, reaches his hand to Adam; he has already destroyed death, and is thus shown manifesting and effecting the resurrection.

The *Memores* recalls the Institution; *igitur*, we are therefore obeying the command of Christ — which is most important, because this is a living memorial — not dead — of the Death and Resurrection. Then "we offer you *bread...and cup*," but this bread and this cup are mysteriously transformed into Christ; and then we return to the original thanksgiving. It is at this point that we find, for the first time in the liturgical tradition, the invocation of the Spirit.

The Third Eucharistic Prayer is a new composition within the lines of the traditional framework. Father Bugnini did a great deal of work at Rome, on the development of this third Eucharistic Prayer. We should note the allusion in it to Malachi 1:11, *a solis ortu usque ad occasum oblatio munda*, which foretold the Eucharist, but which was — unfortunately — not included in the translated versions.

The Fourth Eucharistic Prayer is a new composition, with a Preface incorporated into it which evoked the whole history of salvation, as in the oriental rites.

- The Calendar

Sunday has been emphasised, as have the special seasons of Advent and Easter: each day has been provided with its proper formularies, with a greater variety of texts, which help us to enter more fully into the mystery: this is a helpful and significant aspect.

However;

a) The choice to allow Episcopal Conferences to decide the location of the Ember Days has in practice resulted in their suppression. The lovely formularies of the old Missal (for example: the autumn Ember Days, which evoked the Jewish feasts of the Atonement and of Tabernacles) have thus completely disappeared. Furthermore, in their place we are recommend to choose from among a number of votive Masses! The Rogations have practically disappeared, for the same reason, at the same time as the lovely *Exaudivit* Mass, with its formulary emphasising the importance of prayer.

b) Why do away with the pre-Lenten (Septuagesima) season? Because of this, the faithful find themselves, as it were, "parachuted" straight into Lent on Ash Wednesday, with no preparation whatever. Yet we ought to be prepared for this. By all means, we could have made a new adaptation of this season, but why do away with it? In some places, there used to be a procession at that time to bury the *Alleluia* until Easter; there is a whole mystical understanding of the *Alleluia* which we are going to sing to eternity.

c) If the readings for the First and Second Sundays in Lent have been retained (Temptation and Transfiguration), the lectionary has not specified for use every year the three traditional readings from the Roman Liturgy (the Samaritan woman, the man born blind, the resurrection of Lazarus), which a first draft had nonetheless planned to use every year. The figures of Moses and Elijah, relating to fasting and prayer, are no longer recalled together in the course of the first week, as used to happen.

d) Why do away with the reading, during Holy Week, of those Passion narratives other than the one set for Palm Sunday? There was nothing to prevent their being retained on Monday and Tuesday in Holy Week. The texts for Wednesday in Holy Week and for Good Friday are all changed round, no doubt for "pastoral" reasons, whereas the choice of readings in the old Missal formed a most coherent whole.

e) For the Easter Vigil, it would have been quite in order to retain the old readings, whilst specifying the readings about the creation, the Sacrifice of Isaac and that of the paschal lamb (this latter now appears on Maundy Thursday, where it is less appropriate than on Good Friday—since the Friday is the day when the true Paschal Lamb was sacrificed), and that of the crossing of the Red Sea, as the required readings, together with some prophetic readings. The reading from Daniel, which was common to all the eastern and western rites, has completely disappeared. The traditional canticles have not been kept, except for the first (*Cantemus Domino*). Above all, it is quite contrary to the entire tradition to set the Baptism *after* the Gospel. All the Liturgies place it after the last of the Old Testament readings.

f) If the Season of Easter has been retained, there remains the problem of Pentecost. By all means, it is a good thing to have insisted on ending the season on the fiftieth day. But could we not have kept two days for commemorating the Holy Spirit? To tell the truth, the historically late placing of the Ember Days within the octave of this feast is not a happy development; how can one reconcile fasting with the season of Easter? On this point the formularies of the old Missal seem inadequate; and in any case they are late material (there is an article by Father Jungmann which makes the hybrid character of this octave quite clear[2]).

g) As for the *sanctoral*, if it is a good idea to retain the four classes of feasts (solemnities, feasts, obligatory commemorations, and optional commemorations—formerly feasts of the first, second, third and fourth classes), the mechanical application of this rule is not a good idea. The "feasts" (the second class) no longer have a first Vespers; thereby, the traditional notion of the liturgical day starting the previous evening disappears. This Office is only retained for Sundays and solemnities. If it was a good idea to give due emphasis to the Lord's Day, could we not, as was done hitherto, translate to the next day any feast which fell on the Sunday? Thus it comes about that some feasts of the Blessed Virgin (for example, her Nativity, on the 8th September), or those of the Apostles, sometimes completely disappear. On the same subject, the rule about one single collect seems somewhat drastic: if, for example, a sacrament or sacramental is being conferred on a solemnity or a feast day, why not allow for a second collect?

For the Mass:

a) It is a good thing to have emphasised the reading of the Old Testament. But was it necessary to set these readings for every Sunday, given that they are sometimes really difficult for the faithful? It certainly ought to be laid down that one of the first two readings may be omitted. What should we say about

---

[2] "The Octave of Pentecost and Public Penance in the Roman Liturgy" in J. Jungmann SJ, *Pastoral Liturgy*, Challoner, London 1962, pp. 239-251.

those weekday readings from the Old Testament, such as for example the story of Jephthah sacrificing his own daughter (Judges 11: 29-39a), set for the Thursday of the twentieth week in ordinary time (year 1)? In the old lectionaries, it was only on certain great solemnities that there was a third reading.

b) Doing away with many of the priest's private prayers is not a good idea. There was no reason why Psalm 42, *Judica me Deus*, could not have been kept, and also the Last Gospel, which the priest could have said in an undertone, as a personal act of thanksgiving.

c) Let us come to the problem, a most controversial one, of the offertory prayers. Behind this reform we must recognise the influence of Dom Bernard Capelle; he was afraid that the faithful might think of the offertory as a human offering, distinct from that of Christ, and suggested an offertory procession (with an offertory hymn), as there had been in the seventh and eighth centuries at Rome, followed immediately by the prayer over the gifts.

Pope Paul VI did not agree to this suggestion, as he wanted some prayers for the priest to say. Various texts were suggested, as for example, for the bread, a text taken from the *Didache* (9:4): "As this broken bread was scattered upon the mountains, but was brought together and became one, so let thy Church be gathered together from the ends of the earth into thy kingdom;" and an analogous text for the wine. The texts finally chosen were those in use today, of the "blessings:" "Blessed art Thou . . ."

Jungmann explains the fairly late origin of the offertory prayers of the *Ordo missæ* of Saint Pius V: *Suscipe sancte Pater*...etc. In fact these prayers have in view the eucharistic offering itself: they can only be understood as an anticipation of the Canon.

Similar material can be found in the "Liturgy of Saint John Chrysostom," where the *Proskomidia* (the actions for preparing the sacred bread, accompanied by the private prayers of the priest before the beginning of the Holy Liturgy and the Great Entrance) anticipates the Eucharistic Prayer: "We, who mystically represent the cherubim...set aside all earthly preoccupations...so as to welcome the Lord of the universe..."

The fact is, perhaps, that we have become allergic to all symbolism.

As for the ritual, the reform tried to avoid any repetition, and to reduce the number of certain signs: fewer signs of the cross, for example. Nonetheless, the repetition of certain formulæ used to give the faithful time to interiorise the prayer: let us think of the *Dominus, non sum dignus*, for example, which was formerly repeated three times before Communion.

A Remark: our analysis has only been applied to the reform of the Missal: in that of the daily office there are many positive points, such as the use in the office of readings (formerly called Matins) of extracts from the Fathers or from the Saint of that day, the reduction in the amount of psalmody, or again the introduction of New Testament canticles into Vespers, which help the faithful to join in more easily. This brings us to the question of translations: I will only talk about those used in the *French* language.

3. The Problem of the French Translations[3]

We find ourselves confronting a serious problem here: that of the official translations. These should in principle offer a faithful version of the 'typical' Latin text. Yet the result is quite different. It will be enough to give a few striking examples.

a) The Translations of the Bible

1) We can start with the *Psalms*, read in particular at the Mass, as responsorial psalms. In translating them, faithfulness to the Hebrew text was kept in view, without any consideration of the Christian tradition, whereas in that tradition the choice of psalms was always made in relation to the mystery being celebrated. A few examples of strange translations:

— *Minuisti eum paulo minus ab Angelis*: "Thou hast made him but a little lower than the angels" (Ps. 8:5), applied to Christ and his Passion in Hebrews 2:6-9, becomes : "You wanted him to be a little less than a god".

— *Non derelinques animam meam in inferno*: "Thou wilt not leave my soul to the dwelling of the dead" (Ps. 15:10, quoted in Acts 13:35), becomes: "You can not abandon me unto death;" there is no longer any mention of the *soul*, nor of the *dwelling of the dead*, and henceforward it is hard to apply this passage to the Resurrection.

— *Super aquas quietis eduxit me, animam meam refecit*: "He leadeth me beside the waters of rest, he restoreth my soul" (Ps. 22:2-3). In Revelation 7:17 we can read: "[the Lamb] shall guide them unto fountains of waters of life." The text becomes: "He leads me near to peaceful waters and revives me." There is no longer any mention of "rest."

— *Quare tristis es, anima mea*: "Why are you cast down, O my soul" (Ps. 41:6), to which a reference is implied in Matt. 26:38: "My soul is very sorrowful," becomes: "Why be so sad, my soul." One can no longer connect this psalm with the Passion.

---

[3] What follows is Canon Rose's critique—in English translation—of the *French* versions of Sacred Scripture in liturgical use and of the liturgical texts of the *French* vernacular editions of the liturgical books. For an examination of this problem in the *English* translations in liturgical use, cf. E. Duffy, "Rewriting the Liturgy: The Theological Implications of Translation," in S. Caldecott, ed., *Beyond the Prosaic: Renewing the Liturgical Movement*, T&T Clark, Edinburgh 1998, pp. 97-126 [Ed.].

— *Et dederunt in escam meam fel*: "They gave me also gall for my meat" (Ps. 68: 22, quoted at Matt. 27:34 and parallels), becomes: "They gave me poison for food."

— *Pretiosa in conspectu Domini mors sanctorum eius*: "Precious in the sight of the Lord is the death of his saints" (Ps. 115:6), becomes: "It costs the Lord something to see his own people die." The very old application of the text to the death of the martyrs — made as early as Saint Cyprian — becomes impossible.

- The psalms that talk of the Lord coming "to judge the earth" — an allusion to the Parousia — are translated as "to govern the earth". Have we become millenarians?

— *Salus* is very often rendered as *victory*. Yet these psalms which are used at Christmas — "The Lord has made known his salvation" — point to the coming of Christ, who is bringing salvation.

2) A few other examples:

— On the Fourth Sunday of Advent in year A, we read the famous passage from Isaiah 7:14, *Ecce virgo concipiet* ("Behold, a virgin shall conceive"), translated as follows: "Behold, a young woman is pregnant," whereas in the Gospel which follows it, the text of Matthew 1:23 indeed offers us: "Behold, the *Virgin* shall conceive." The faithful are hearing the same text in different versions!

— Romans 4:16 (the 19th March: Saint Joseph), on salvation by faith, is translated: "Not only *because* they belong to the people of the Law, but *because* they share the faith of Abraham, the father of us all." Saint Paul is saying the opposite of that; he is talking about salvation by faith *in Christ*. The *because* distorts the whole conception: "The promise is guaranteed to all his descendants — not only *for* those who adhere to the Law, but also *for* those who share the faith of Abraham, the father of us all."

These few examples show how a more faithful and more consistent translation is required.

b) The Translations of Liturgical Texts

1) *In the Ordinary of the Mass*

— The invitation to penitential prayer runs: "Brethren, let us admit our sins, that we may prepare to celebrate the Holy Mysteries." The official translation: Let us prepare for the celebration of the Holy Eucharist, by admitting that we are sinners" (a somewhat saccharine version of the text...).

— The third formula of penitential prayer, "Lord Jesus, sent by the Father to save the broken-hearted," has been translated: "to save *all men*."

—The ending of the collects, in French, runs: "Through Jesus Christ…who reigns with you and the Holy Spirit"—instead of, "who *lives* and reigns with you *in the unity of the Holy Spirit*" (the authentic text).

—In the *Hanc igitur* of the First Eucharistic Prayer (the Roman Canon), the adjective "eternal" has been removed from the translation of *æterna damnatione*.

—In the Third Eucharistic Prayer, we find "You do not cease to gather together your people, that *throughout the world* [Fr. "partout dans le monde"] they may present to you a pure offering." Yet the text of Malachi 1:11 runs: "so that from the rising of the sun to its setting…a pure offering may be made to thee." This text, quoted by Saint Justin, disappears completely in the official French text. Monsignor Jenny[4] had protested about this at the time.

—It seems that Christ no longer gives us any command. Where the Latin text of the Third Eucharistic Prayer runs: *cuius mandato hæc mysteria celebramus*, the French translation makes do with the verb "say" [Fr. "dire"]: "As he told us to do," "As he said to us to do." In the same way, whilst the Latin collect for the Second Sunday in Lent has the expression: "God, who *commanded* us to listen to your Son" (that is an allusion to the story of the Transfiguration, read on that day: "Listen to him!"), the French version puts it thus: "You have told us ("dit"), Lord, to listen to your beloved Son."

—The embolic development of the last petition of the *Pater* actually runs: "in this life, in which we wait for the blessed hope," a reminiscence of Titus 2:13. The genuine text therefore runs: "awaiting the blessed hope." That becomes simply: "the happiness you have promised…" Why remove the mention of *hope* in the translation of this scriptural formula, not only in the text of the Ordinary of the Mass, but also in the version of Titus 2:13 for Christmas Night?

These few examples show that a complete revision of the French version is needed, done so that the faithful may be able to hear the texts and prayers in the genuine wording and meaning suggested by the Church.

I have only been talking about the texts of the Mass, but I should add that the liturgical Offices in French present some hymns quite different from those of the official Latin text. Father Ephrem Yon OSB writes, concerning these new compositions:

The 'transposition into French' which took place in the years around 1968 had the disadvantage that we were led to believe that this was just a matter of transposing into another language what already existed in Latin. The transformation actually performed was in fact far more significant that it

---

4 Archbishop of Cambrai.

seemed at first glance, for we moved from a mysterious and holy world into another which no longer was. And it no longer was, not through simple inadvertence or incompetence, but because amongst the liturgists who created this, it was thought that a different way of praying needed to be brought in, in the Church. There was introduced, in place of the range of perception traditional in the Liturgy, shot through with an awareness of the mystery of God and of his transcendence, the intention to encourage a liturgy of man and of his questionings. What was to be presented to God was man's anxiety as he confronted the needs of the world, and at the same time accompanied by the contradictions of a faith torn between the wish to believe and the difficulties and uncertainties of doing so. It was at that point that the questions appeared in the hymn and in the new songs: "Will he come back, to walk in our ways?" The *Credo* declares: he will come in glory. The song, for its part, will not make up its mind. He will come back, in the way that he might perhaps not come back. The question mark leaves us hovering in the hesitations of doubt.

In conclusion: this somewhat detailed investigation, at times a little tedious, and yet necessary, shows us an aberration which is a serious threat to the faith of believers, and we must hope for a complete revision of the reform, in faithfulness to the Faith of the Church and to its Tradition.

Translated by Henry Taylor

Towards a New Liturgical Movement

Intervention of Dom Charbel Pazat de Lys OSB[1]

1. Introduction

WE are being encouraged to re-create a new Liturgical Movement, not only by your Eminence in a private capacity, but also by the Magisterium of the Church as such: witness this passage from *Liturgiam Authenticam*, a recent Instruction from the Congregation for Divine Worship, which "envisions and seeks to prepare for a new era of liturgical renewal."[2] "New era of renewal" certainly asserts that there has been a first period—and that should not be denied—but implies that, in some respects, this did not achieve its purposes.[3] In what respects there has been a renewal,

---

[1] Father Charbel Pazat de Lys has been a monk of Barroux since 1985. At the request of his superiors, he has specialised in liturgical studies, and is pursuing higher studies at the Pontifical Institute of Liturgy in Rome.

[2] *Liturgiam Authenticam*: Fifth Instruction for the Right Implementation of the Constitution on the Sacred Liturgy of the Second Vatican Council: On the Use of Vernacular Languages in the Publication of the Books of the Roman Liturgy, para. 7.

[3] Romano Guardini pointed out that "What people referred to under the very approximate name of the Liturgical Movement never has been entirely homogenous" (*La Maison-Dieu*, no. 3, 1945, p. 8). See also Cardinal Ferdinando Antonelli's 'Journal,' no. 16, for 14 March 1962 (in Nicola Giamprietro, OFM Cap., *Il Cardinal Ferdinando Antonelli e gli sviluppi della riforma liturgica dal 1948 al 1970*, Studia Anselmiana, Analecta Liturgica 21, Rome, 1998): following his nomination as Pro-Secretary of the Congregation of Rites, "I replied merely that, with the experience I have of the Congregation, I would have in mind to take in hand the world-wide Liturgical Movement very quickly, not in order to put a stop to it, but to give it a *single direction*, and to disengage it from exaggerated stances." The Liturgical Movement was heterogeneous in character, not only as regards points of detail, but at the level of doctrine, philosophy, ideology, which determines the interpretation of the Liturgy. Waldemar Trapp, *Vorgeschichte und Ursprung der liturgischen Bewegung* [The Origins and the Prehistory of the Liturgical Movement] Regensburg, 1940, quoted by Father Aidan Nichols, OP in *Looking at the Liturgy: A Critical Review of its Contemporary Reform*, Ignatius Press, San Francisco 1996, has no hesitation in tracing its origins back to the period of the Enlightenment, when there was a conflict between the "Enlightenment radicals" who were trying to transform the life of the Church so as to put it at the service of a certain vision of the world, and the "Enlightenment moderates" who were trying to put at the service of the Church some elements of the outlook then current, which could be turned in a positive direction. On this basis, someone like B. Neunhauser could write that "it is increasingly obvious and indeed certain that the first impetus towards the programme of liturgical

and in what respects things have been lacking, that is what many people have devoted much effort to elucidating during these sessions, and we need not go over all that again. Facing resolutely toward the future, we will simply try to suggest some points around which our reflections may turn, so that at the end of these sessions we may be able to set down the basic outlines of a new Liturgical Movement. For there to be movement, there must be a magnet, and every magnet has a positive pole and a negative pole; these can be described in two words: breakdown and irruption.

2. The Negative Pole: Breakdown

It seems in fact that one can not, in all honesty, fail to recognise that in one way or another, the first Liturgical Movement has finished up, in practical terms, in three attitudes which represent a breakdown.[4] Among the ways in which this appears at present is, first, people who deliberately wish to make a break with the past, with history. And then there are two forms of "exaggerated conservatism,"[5] whose aims are opposed to each other but who work things out in similar fashion: those who hold that the old Roman Liturgy represents the culmination of liturgical progress, which can not be surpassed

---

reform, and the first attempts to put it into practice, are found — and in an astonishing durable and articulate form — in the Enlightenment period" (article, 'Movimiento Liturgico' in the 'Nuovo Dizionario di Liturgia' [New Dictionary of the Liturgy], D. Sartore – A.M. Triacca, 1988, p. 843). Fr. Jounel admits that "the new Missal would not have been what it is, if it had not drawn, especially for the sanctoral, upon a source which it would be unjust not to mention: that is to say, the eighteenth century French Missals" ('La Maison-Dieu' no. 103). Cf. Fr. Jean-Robert Armogathe, in Reconstruire la Liturgie [Reconstructing the Liturgy], ed. Father Claude Barthe (published F.-X. Guibert, 1997) p. 27: "You are talking about a crisis. For my part, I reckon that it started in the seventeenth century, and was no doubt at its height at the end of the nineteenth and the beginning of the twentieth centuries. This is not in fact a crisis in connection with the Second Vatican Council, even though some of conflicts it has caused became apparent at that particular moment."

[4] It is undeniable that the old Liturgy has profoundly affected everything that we mean by "western civilisation" — or what remains of it — since "the Liturgy itself generates cultures and shapes them" (Catechism of the Catholic Church, para. 1207). Only we can easily see that civilisation for its part, does not change either within a few years, nor through some meetings of commissions and some administrative work... "with the result that many of the faithful could not see the inner continuity with what had gone before...Today we might ask: Is there a Latin rite at all any more? Certainly there is no awareness of it;" (Cardinal Joseph Ratzinger, The Feast of Faith: Approaches to a Theology of the Liturgy, Ignatius Press, San Francisco 1986, p. 84). And Father Gelineau, who can hardly be regarded as an extremist, bears witness to that: "In fact it is a different Liturgy of the Mass. We must say it plainly: the Roman rite as we knew it exists no more. It has gone ["Il est détruit"]; The Liturgy Today and Tomorrow, Darton, Longman & Todd & Paulist Press, London & New York, Ramsey & Toronto 1978 & 1979, p. 11; French: Demain la liturgie: Essai, Cerf, Paris 1979. See also Paul VI's address of the 26th November 1969 [French trans. in Doc. Cath. for 1969, pp. 1102-1103]).

[5] This is one of the aberrations of the Liturgical Movement which Romano Guardini pointed out in his letter to the Archbishop of Mainz; cf. Herder Correspondence, August 1964, pp. 237-239.

and should remain untouched;[6] and those who think the same about the new postconciliar forms, as if any reform of the reform would necessarily represent a backward step. *In both cases*, it is assumed that there has been *a complete break*,[7] whereby those who hold these views are, without being aware of this,

---

[6] This is an attitude very strongly taken by members of the Society of Saint Pius X. Yet the liturgical tree can be neither rooted up, nor chopped-off at ground level, nor transformed into a Japanese "bonzai" by preventing its growth: it simply needs to be pruned, so that it may bear fruit. Monsignor Marcel Lefèbvre, the founder of this society, seemed nonetheless to be admitting this point, when he wrote: "Should we conclude that we ought to preserve all these things unchanged? The Council, in a prudent and measured fashion, has replied that we should not. There was something to be reformed, something to be rediscovered...It is clear that the first part of the Mass, designed for teaching the faithful and for bringing them to express their faith, needed to achieve these aims in a clearer and, to a certain extent, more intelligible fashion. In my humble opinion, two reforms with this aim seemed helpful: first, the rites of this first section and some translations in the vernacular language; to arrange things so that the priest come close to the faithful, communicates with them, prays and sings with them, stands at the lectern therefore, says the collect in their own language, and likewise the readings of the Epistle and Gospel; that the priest should sing the traditional sacred airs of the *Kyrie*, the *Gloria* and the *Credo* along with the faithful. These are felicitous reforms, by which this section of the Mass rediscovers its true purpose. For the sacraments and the sacramentals, it seems even more necessary to use the language of the faithful, since they concern them more directly and more personally;" *Un Évêque parle* [A Bishop Speaks Out], DMM 1974, pp. 57-58; reproduced from *Itinéraires* no. 95, July-August 1965, pp. 78-79. One ought also to read what Pius XII says: "As circumstances and the needs of Christians warrant, public worship is organised, developed and enriched by new rites, ceremonies and regulations...From time immemorial the ecclesiastical hierarchy has exercised this right in matters liturgical...it has not been slow—keeping the substance of the Mass and sacraments carefully intact—to modify...and to add...The Sacred Liturgy does, in fact, include divine as well as human elements...the human components admit of various modifications...The Church is without question a living organism, and as an organism, in respect of the Sacred Liturgy also, she grows, matures, develops, adapts and accommodates herself to temporal needs and circumstances, provided only that the integrity of her doctrine be safeguarded...The Liturgy of the early ages is most certainly worthy of all veneration. But...more recent liturgical rites likewise deserve reverence and respect. They, too, owe their inspiration to the Holy Spirit, who assists the Church in every age;" (*Mediator Dei*, part I) And again: "There are found in the Liturgy unchangeable elements, a sacred content which transcends time, but also elements which are variable and transitory, and sometimes even imperfect...On the part of the Church, the Liturgy today admits of a preoccupation with progress, but also of conservation and defence. She returns to the past without slavishly copying it, and creates anew it the ceremonies themselves, in the use of the vernacular, in the popular chant and in the building of churches..." (Address to the International Liturgical Congress, 22nd September 1956; *The Assisi Papers*, The Liturgical Press, Collegeville 1957, pp. 235-236.

[7] Cardinal Joseph Ratzinger: "The prohibition of the missal that was now decreed, a missal that had known continuous growth over the centuries, starting with the sacramentaries of the ancient Church, *introduced a breach* into the history of the Liturgy;" *Milestones: Memoirs 1927-1977*, Ignatius Press, San Francisco 1998, pp. 147-148. Some amongst the reformers already felt this, in the case of Fr Thierry Martens without being concerned by it: "'They're changing our religion:' this is a slogan widely heard amongst Christians...this witticism has at any rate something sound about it—the average believer judges religion not only on the

taking a view of history inherited from the Enlightenment, which sees it not as a chain, at the end of which we stand, but as a kind of display cabinet from the shelves of which we make our choice, a choice determined in the end by man and his rational thinking.[8]

We want to have nothing to do with any thinking which reckons with a break in tradition in any sense at all, for:

> When…the worldwide unity of the Church *and her history*, and the mystery of the living Christ are no longer visible in the Liturgy, where else, then, is the Church to become visible in her spiritual essence?…And because the ecclesial community can not have its origin from itself but emerges as a unity only from the Lord, through faith, such circumstances will inexorably result in a disintegration into sectarian parties of all kinds — partisan opposition within a Church tearing herself apart.[9]

Far be it from us to call into question here, either the good intentions of anyone at all in history or at the present time, nor the intrinsic value of the various statements of the Magisterium. But is it not permissible to remark that even these actions and statements[10] do not seem to have proved adequate[11] for

---

basis of teachings, but on that of worship. The defining of a new dogma would leave him cold, far more than would any possible compulsion to celebrate Mass 'facing the people.' That is, of course, a weakness, but we can not refuse to acknowledge it as a genuinely healthy attitude: it is in the Liturgy that dogma and moral teaching are experienced and tested for truth. Altering that does really amount to calling a great many things into question…Seeing again the reactions of our faithful…is enough to make us aware how widespread is an attitude of setting one's face against changes and taking refuge in a series of taboos…We may hope from the next Council for some important changes, and there is a danger that our faithful are not sufficiently open-minded for these;" (*Les risques de plafonnement du Mouvement Liturgique*, [The danger of the Liturgical Movement's reaching a "ceiling"] *Paroisse et Liturgie* no. 49, Bruges 1961, pp. 11-12.

[8] "It is the duty of the Church constantly to reflect upon its relation to the Tradition which comes to us from the Lord by way of the Apostles, in the form it has taken in the course of history" (John-Paul II, address to *Ecclesia Dei* pilgrims, 26 October 1998. This would make for a better understanding of the underlying significance of the fact that down through the centuries the Church has always favoured *renewal*, whilst frequently condemning *innovation*.

[9] Joseph Ratzinger, *Milestones: Memoirs 1927-1977*, p. 149.

[10] Including that of *Mediator Dei*, which nonetheless does give some benchmarks, as for example in part I.

[11] For example, *Sacrosanctum Concilium* several times refers to the "true and authentic spirit" of the Liturgy [Translator's note: The French: "les principes d'un véritable et authentique esprit liturgique" is a reasonably good translation of the original — "cum rationibus veri et authentici spiritus liturgici congruat" — but the English version is imprecise.], but nowhere does it seem to define this. See also Pius XII, Address to the International Liturgical Congress of the 22nd September 1956, in *The Assisi Papers*, pp. 224, 227, 234. In this address, in which he weighs up the essential elements of the Liturgical Movement, we are struck by the fact that, whilst addressing particular errors, and whilst admitting the existence within the Movement of differences of opinion and even of "erroneous tendencies," the Holy Father — at least in this text — does not seem to give full weight to the deep chasm separating

the purpose of marking-out, defining, and clearly and directly stigmatising, not *this* or *that* flagrant abuse,[12] but the general *attitude*[13] of promoting discontinuity which, taking its standpoint upon one or another criterion of reform approved by the Popes, and giving undue emphasis to this, has put them at the service of various ideologies?

For the difficulty does not in the first instance lie directly in the various motivating ideals which were at work throughout the life of the

---

the main lines of thought from each other, even at the level of the norms of interpretation. We quote here a few passages which demonstrate this lack (not that we are claiming that the Pope is saying anything wrong, but that in what he says there we do not find that distinction made, which we would *a posteriori* expect): "The Liturgical Movement is thus shown forth as a sign of the providential dispositions of God for the present time, of the movement of the Holy Ghost in the Church, to draw men more closely to the mysteries of the faith and the riches of grace which flow from the active participation in the liturgical life."…"Our encyclical *Mediator Dei* had already corrected certain erroneous assertions which were tending either to direct religious teaching and pastoral activity along an exclusively liturgical path or to raise obstacles to the Liturgical Movement which was not understood…There is a real diversity of opinions, but this does not present insurmountable obstacles."…"The question of how the tabernacle could be placed on the altar without interfering with celebration facing the people admits of several different solutions. On these the experts will give their opinion."

[12] They have certainly done that, right down to *Vicesimus Quintus* (John Paul II, Apostolic Letter *Vicesimus Quintus Annus*, on the occasion of the twenty-fifth anniversary of *Sacrosanctum Concilium*, 12th April 1988, published on 14th May 1989; right down to *Liturgiam Authenticam*: in paras. 3 and 32 there is reference to the existence of ideologies, but without tracing them back to their source (which is not the aim of that Instruction): "Liturgical books marked by sound doctrine, which are exact in wording, free from all ideological influence;" "To be avoided on this account are expressions characteristic of commercial publicity, political or ideological programs, passing fashions, and those which are subject to regional variations or ambiguities in meaning."

[13] "This session (of the *Consilium*) has been constructive. But I do not like the spirit of it. There is a spirit of criticism and of impatience towards the Holy See which can not bring any good in the end. And then a spirit of rationalism in the Liturgy, and no serious interest in true devotion" (Cardinal Antonelli, *Journal* for 19th April 1967, in Giamprietro, op. cit.) "What is really sad, is one basic element, a kind of spirit, a position taken up at the outset… and that is, that many of the people who have influenced the reform…have no love, no veneration for everything that has been handed down to us…A negative, unjust and destructive spirit" (Cardinal Antonelli, *Note sulla Riforma*, in Giamprietro, op. cit.) "What is for Us yet another still more serious cause of affliction," — *the reforming Pope complains* — "is the widespread inclination to desacralise (as they even dare to express it) the Liturgy (that is, if it ought even still to be called thus) and, with it, and in deadly fashion, Christianity. This new *mentality,* which it would not be difficult to trace back to its *murky origins,* which people are trying to use as the moral basis for the demolition of authentic Catholic worship, implies such a reversal of doctrine, discipline and pastoral method, that We have no hesitation in regarding it as an aberration." (Paul VI, Address to the *Consilium* on 19th April 1967, in Giamprietro, op. cit.) Whilst on the same day, Cardinal Antonelli noted: "And the Pope can not even see that all these difficulties arise from the *overall direction* which the *Consilium* has imparted to this reform;" (*Journal*, in Giamprietro, op. cit.).

Liturgical Movement:[14] simplicity, intelligibility, giving their full significance to all the rituals and formulas, active participation, turning back to the origins, the communal aspect, a greater wealth of biblical material, and so on. It lies in the fact that one and the same key concept may be used to open quite different doors, according to the manner in which it is applied, just as Dom Guéranger observes: "The ill-judged reintroduction of customs from the Early Church *is sometimes tantamount to innovation*, and might well have the same results."[15]

These results, as we have seen, are ways of making a break with the past. If, therefore, we would like to know what will ensure that there is, in one single rite, that "organic continuity" for which the Council expressed a desire, and which was recalled by the Congregation for Divine Worship,[16] then the question arises: what are the correct methods of applying the criteria of reform? That is a point on which any new Liturgical Movement can not dispense with the achieving of a sound and accurate discernment. To that end, it will not suffice to make an inventory of the damage wrought by misapplying the criteria, it will not suffice — although it would be useful — to take each of these motivating concepts, one by one, and explain how they may have been applied in faulty and decadent fashion: we have to discover why, and how, people came to choose mistaken methods of applying them. We have *above all* to explain — and the explanation must be logical and rational — how we should determine the genuine methods for applying the principles of reform. For in periods of disturbance the *sensus fidei*, the *sensus Ecclesiæ*, the *sensus pietatis* are of course still valid indicators of the right course, but are too

---

[14] Cf. Cardinal Antonelli: "We can see at this stage that the question concerning the Liturgy, even it has played a great part in developing this mindset, is nonetheless part of a far greater complex of difficulties, all of which is in essence doctrinal. That is why the great crisis is that of traditional teaching and of the Magisterium;" (*Journal* for 1st November 1967, in Giamprietro, op. cit.). The same Cardinal observes that "In the Liturgy, every word and every action transmits an idea, which is a theological idea. Given the fact that at the moment all theology is under discussion, the theories currently popular among advanced theologians affect liturgical formulas and rituals, with the very serious result that, whilst the theological discussion does not go beyond the higher level, that of educated men, once it has filtered down to the liturgical formulas and rituals, then it goes on be popularised among ordinary people. I could illustrate this way of seeing things with various points from last year's *Instructio de cultu mysterii eucharistici;*" (*Note sulla Riforma liturgica (1968-1971)*, S. Congregazione per le cause dei Santi, Città del Vaticano, pp. 1-3, in Giamprietro, op. cit.).

[15] *Institutions Liturgiques*, second edition in four volumes, Paris, 1878 onwards, vol. III p. 504. A completely new study ought to be made of the writings of Dom Guéranger (including letters and other unpublished documents) in order to get an accurate idea of what his reaction to the new Liturgy might have been. It is nonetheless probable that it would have been quite the opposite of regarding it as constituting a break with the past, and his reaction would have included great surprise at how this Movement, of which Paul spoke of him as being the Father, had ended up. (See the letter of Paul VI to Dom Jean Prou, on the occasion of the centenary of Dom Guéranger's death, on 20th January 1975, in *Doc. Cath.* for 1975, pp. 255-256).

[16] *Sacrosanctum Concilium*, para. 23; *Liturgiam Authenticam*, para. 4.

generalised in sense to enable us to achieve unanimity in making the choices which they imply.

If, for example, we take the criterion of "turning back to the Early Church," *Mediator Dei* explains both the possible benefits and the destructive possibilities of exaggeration.[17] Yet over and beyond the *extrinsic* and general principle of obedience to the Holy See, how can we discover the *immediate intrinsic* principle or principles which would allow us, whenever the question legitimately arises — and that could well be the case for a reform of the reform — to make a judgement: in this case, we ought not to revert to ancient practice, in that one, yes, we should — but to what extent? That is not all, for even after having answered this first question, there is at least a second which arises: *in concreto* should not our aim be, not just to *go back in abstracto*, on paper as it were, to this or that ancient practice, but rather to *take us back* there, that is to say, to rediscover *the entire matrix* of conditions which gave this practice its real value? But in that case, under what conditions — when, in what circumstances, by what means? The answers to these questions are what would produce for us the immediate intrinsic principles. That would require a great deal of time and work, but the work would be amongst the most valuable contributions to any future elucidations on the part of the Magisterium, as they would be to a *new* Liturgical Movement, if this could be freed of the ambiguities of the first one.

However, before any official answers can be given to all these questions, would it not be prerequisite to agree on one point, which can be established by everyone as a matter of history: we have been too hasty?[18] Even amongst many liturgists who are far from being suspected of undiluted traditionalism, this remark is made by almost everyone. Thus, a new Liturgical Movement should resolutely avoid any haste, and that means that it ought not to allow itself to be misled by the pretext that anything is urgent:

---

[17] Cf. Part I, no. V.

[18] "There is enormous pressure to go forward, and we are not being allowed time for reflection," admitted Cardinal Antonelli, yet again (*Note sulle adonanze*, in Giamprietro, op. cit., pp. 76-77); and yet he was far from applying any brake to this movement when he suggested to the Pope that he should "speed up the reform as much as possible," amongst other things "because if we don't get things done quickly, by the time we have finished it all, what we did to start with will already be no longer any use (we are already finding this out in practice);" Letter for the audience of the 15th July 1967, Arcivio la Verna, Fondo Antonelli, in Giamprietro, op. cit., pp. 1-5. In his diary entry for the 31st October 1969, he complains that the promulgation of the new rite "will come into effect on the 30th November, whereas the texts are not yet available, and whilst those very texts have been promised for the 15th November. How can it be possible to prepare for such a far-reaching transformation *in ten days*?" In order not just to be quoting this Italian cardinal, let us recall this answer from Father Jounel: "Have you sometimes felt yourself overwhelmed by this disordered creativity? — Certainly, things were moving very fast. I remember having seen, during the Council, a cover-photo from 'Paris-Match.' It showed a Dutch priest giving an adolescent Communion in the hand. I said to myself, 'It can't be true'...I felt things were getting beyond me" (in *Célébrer*, October 1995).

when time alone does the work, urgency simply prevents it.[19] "This is not something which can be done in a few months, nor even in a few years. When it is a matter of re-educating the masses, time is measured in units of generations."[20]

All these points are merely benchmarks, or factors to be considered in a generally negative sense: how to avoid making the same mistakes as the first Liturgical Movement. But for now, what can we get hold of so as to begin some positive work, the work of establishing "immediate intrinsic criteria"? Pius XII offers us a suggestion: "Three characteristics of which Our predecessor Pius X spoke should adorn all liturgical services: sacredness, which abhors any profane influence; nobility, which true and genuine arts should serve and foster; and universality, which, while safeguarding local and legitimate custom, reveals the Catholic unity of the Church."[21] This is the first subject to which we now wish to turn our attention.

3. The Positive Pole: Irruption

It is a mere commonplace, when we say that we need to get back to the sacred,[22] so we need not consider the need for this. We need rather to think about its nature, and its expression. It should be well understood that we lay

---

[19] We should well weigh these thoughts of Cardinal Y. Congar: "Reforms are difficult to carry through. *Impatient men*, with too little awareness of Tradition, putting their pet notion before all else, are liable to turn any reform into a sectarian movement. Certain conditions are necessary, in order that a reform may be effected without schism: putting charity and pastoral usefulness first, before the *systematising spirit* and pure intellectual deduction; a care for keeping communion with the whole, which means we are just as much obliged to seek the approval of central moderating organs, as perhaps to go beyond the positions occupied at present, which are not adequate in view of the demands of a full Catholic Tradition; *patience*, which avoids official notices and being in *a hurry to have everything done at once*; seeking to achieve a true renewal by a living application of principles in a new situation, and not the mechanical substitution of different ways of thinking or of doing things, for those which held sway hitherto; and common sense;" in *L'Église, une sainte…*, pp. 143-144 as quoted by Jean-Guy Pagé, Professor in the Theology Faculty of Laval University, in *Qui est l'Église?* vol. 2, *L'Église, corps du Christ et communion*, Bellarmin, 1985.

[20] Cardinal Antonelli, *Antecedenti, principi [etc.]*, Lezioni di Liturgia, 12 Jan. 1965, p. 6 in Giamprietro, op. cit.

[21] *Mediator Dei*, Part IV.

[22] We have already seen (above, note 13) how Paul VI, in his 1967 address, was complaining about the tendency to desacralising; now, in 1968, under one of the headings in his French presentation of the document *Tres abhinc annos* (Second Instruction for the correct application of the Constitution on the Sacred Liturgy, 4 May 1967), Fr Thierry Maertens talks about "a certain desacralisation," which in fact represents his interpretation. These interpretations are still in widespread existence today, but are perhaps losing a little of their influence. One recent example of a reaction in the opposite direction: the former pastor Michel Viot, a very recent convert to the Catholic Church, says: "We have to give people back a sense of the sacred, sermons will have to talk about the inner life, about the life of the invisible world" (In *La Croix* for Monday 16th July 2001; based on an interview with Jean-Marie Guénois).

no claim to be working out here a definition of the sacred, to which so many writers have made their contribution,[23] a definition which might well be the subject of extensive theoretical studies, nor to settle here and now such a very important question. We would simply like to suggest a direction in which we might work.

In such a perspective, we do not believe it to be over-bold to take a phenomenological approach to this: uniting our common sense with the ideas of one of my teachers,[24] we might set as our simple starting-point that something is sacred, when it shows the *irruption* of transcendence, of the supernatural. As far as concerns the Catholic Liturgy, then that is sacred which witnesses to the irruption into this world of the God who is Trinity.

But that alone has already taken us quite a long way. For to witness is to communicate: we would then have to define what it is that determines the conditions of the sacred, in each of the means of expression which are at man's disposal. And then we have been saying "irruption," a concept which implies quite a number of things.

It assumes first of all a distance, for nothing can irrupt which is already present, without any distance. Does this not require us resolutely to reject all those ways of thinking—whether of naturalism, realism, fideism, whatever...—which declare that distance between the natural and the supernatural to be either non-existent, a matter of indifference, beyond our knowledge, inexpressible, or unbridgeable? But in that case, that in itself ought to bring about a modification in our metaphysics, to a realist

---

[23] Just as an example, we give here the interesting definition given by Dom Robert Le Gall, OSB: "The Latin word *sacrum* signifies both a cultic object, and a religious action. Like the *sanctum*, the *sacrum* is something which is inviolable, in virtue of its connection with the divine. The Sanskrit root *sac* or *sak* is used to refer to everything which comes close to, or follows, the divinity. If sacredness is the character of what has been rendered inviolable in virtue of coming into contact with God, we may understand this in two complementary fashions: on the one hand, everything that is, as such, comes from God, and only exists through having received the divine 'touch;' and on the other, every being which has come from God tends back toward him. The first perspective, of descent, offers us an immanent conception of the sacred...The second perspective, of an ascent, places what is sacred beyond the limited beings which have a share in it, in the sphere of what is divine properly speaking, which can be reached only by a series of separations, of 'Easters:' here it is the note of transcendence which is emphasised. Whenever the divine takes hold of creatures in whatever way, this makes them sacred, but the sacredness of things or actions, to the extent to which it is perceived or experienced, directs us towards what is sacred *par excellence*, life in God in his sphere of transcendence. This double dimension of sacredness—God coming to his creatures, and they going towards Him—is the very structure of the Liturgy, brought to its perfection by the redeeming Incarnation: Jesus, God and man, is the sacred being (cf. Luke 1:35) who is completely endued with the divine life, and is capable of helping us to pass, following him, into the bosom of the Father. The Liturgy is the exercise of sacredness by the Church, thanks to the priesthood of Christ;" *Dictionnaire de Liturgie*, published C.L.D., 1982, p. 226.

[24] Prof. Heinrich Pfeiffer SJ, professor of Art and Liturgy at the Pontifical Institute of Liturgy and the Pontifical Gregorian University, at Rome.

metaphysics which includes our truly being able to know the essence of things:[25] in a world of pure concepts, or of pure relations, an "irruption" — if such a thing exists — must take place on the same plane, and therefore without any real distance, and thereby is no longer capable of expressing any transcendence.

And then, if the divine does irrupt, then it is not we who "make" this, nor who transport ourselves into its sphere: it is the divine which comes to us, which exerts its will upon us, which goes before us.[26] We will take this point as being settled, since Cardinal Ratzinger has so often emphasised it already. But let us take note that the concept of "irruption" is next-door-neighbour to "interruption," which is at any rate something quite different from separation: if we take this word in an analogical sense (dynamically, as a kind of stopping-point in the natural course of things; statically, as something in-between), this may offer a key which could subsequently be of help.

What we need to find, in fact, is the common denominator which enables various different means of expression capable of expressing an irruption of God. For the new Liturgical Movement, that is an essential subject for research. The theme for our work is as follows: this common denominator of sacredness, might it not be indeed a certain kind of "interruption," of "in-between"? Let us try to talk more clearly, to particularise something which might at first appear too abstract. We find many languages in the Sacred Liturgy: besides the verbal language which is declaimed or sung, there are the languages of gesture, of colour, of architecture, the language of art, those of

---

[25] *Fides et Ratio*, paras. 22 & 46: "This is to concede to human reason a capacity which seems almost to surpass its natural limitations. Not only is it not restricted to sensory knowledge, from the moment that it can reflect critically upon the data of the senses, but, by discoursing on the data provided by the senses, reason can reach the cause which lies at the origin of all perceptible reality. In philosophical terms, we could say that this important Pauline text [Romans 1:20] affirms the human capacity for metaphysical enquiry...In the field of scientific research, a positivistic mentality took hold which not only abandoned the Christian vision of the world, but more especially rejected every appeal to a metaphysical or moral vision."

[26] Let us take note that this applies even to the liturgical books themselves, which should be *accepted* as being *sacred*, in such a way as to make it impossible for them to be the subject of remarks such as these: "The new official books, however good they may be in many respects, have here and there too much the appearance of having been *deliberately planned-out by professors*, and reinforce the idea that a liturgical book can be 'made,' just like any other book;" Cardinal Joseph Ratzinger, *La Célébration de la Foi*, Téqui, Paris 1985, p. 92; cf. *A Feast of Faith*, pp. 86-87. Now, Dom Guéranger used to remark, on the subject of the Gallican Liturgies, that "discredited by their number, they lost their authority; they were very quickly considered as *private works;*" quoted after Dom Olivier Rousseau, OSB, *Histoire du Mouvement Liturgique*, Cerf, 1945, p. 30 [cf. ET: *The Progress of the Liturgy*, Newman Press, Maryland 1951]; whereas "one could sense" — he wrote, speaking about the Roman Liturgy — "that this had not been drawn up with the help of a concordance, as have the products of our modern liturgical authors. It was *not the result of trying to make a book*, of trying to say everything about everything" (*Institutions*, vol. II, p. 300, as quoted in Rousseau, op. cit.).

scents, of light, of the particular choice of liturgical objects and the materials from which they are made...and in all that, what might this "irruption" be?

Liturgiam Authenticam talks to us about translations, thus about language which is declaimed: "If indeed, in the liturgical texts, words or expressions are sometimes employed *which differ somewhat from usual and everyday speech*, it is often enough by virtue of this very fact that the texts become truly memorable and *capable of expressing heavenly realities*. Indeed, it will be seen that the observance of the principles set forth in this Instruction will contribute to the gradual *development*, in each vernacular, *of a sacred style* that will come to be recognised as proper to liturgical language. Thus it may happen that a certain manner of speech which has come to be considered somewhat obsolete in daily usage may continue to be maintained in the liturgical context."[27] Do we not find here all the elements we have mentioned? A certain stopping-point, in relation to ordinary language, a more effective expression of transcendence, and thereby in fact constituting a sacred style, which is peculiar to the Liturgy. When we express things thus, then the value of Latin as a sacred sign becomes readily comprehensible: "Consideration should also be given to including in the vernacular editions at least some texts in the Latin language."[28]

Yet if we turn to architecture, is not the same principle applicable there? For, to be brief, if we have a round church, which a more or less central altar, with a more or less lateral door, with circular seating, and even perhaps tiered, the way it is arranged in a cinema, then where is this "irruption" which takes account of a meeting, not a meeting with one's neighbour across the way, but with a marvellous being who comes from somewhere else, and who irrupts before us and within us? In the idea that some people have, of a *Domus Ecclesiæ* which would be as it were in counterpoint to the *Domus Dei*,[29] it is

---

[27] *Liturgiam Authenticam*, para. 27 emphases added.

[28] Ibid., para. 28. Considering the relation between this recent direction and the reality of the last thirty years, it seems that that is not consistent with the sense of the wish expressed by Archbishop Henri Jenny, that Latin should have only a "vestigial" importance ("vestige" was the term he used, in presenting the Constitution on the Sacred Liturgy, in the edition published by Centurion, 1963, p. 22). We should note that one of the difficulties in relation to Latin consists in not considering it as a liturgical language *except* as the vehicle for concepts (it is that, of course, but not only that), in such a way as to justify a historicist point of view. If, on the other hand, we consider it also as a *sacred sign* of the Liturgy, then that might offer us a key for establishing an organic continuity in the correct use of Latin.

[29] Jacob's dream and the act he performs afterwards are a perfect synthesis of the elements of sacredness: "Cumque evigilasset Iacob de somno ait: Vere Dominus est in loco isto et ego nesciebam, pavensque quam terribilis—inquit—est locus iste, non est hic aliud nisi domus Dei et porta cæli. Surgens ergo mane tulit lapidem quem subposuerat capiti suo et erexit in titulum, fundens oleum desuper, appellavitque nomen urbis Bethel quæ prius Luza vocabatur. Vovit etiam votum dicens: Si fuerit Deus mecum et custodierit me in via per quam ambulo, et dederit mihi panem ad vescendum et vestem ad induendum, reversusque fuero prospere ad domum patris mei, erit mihi Dominus in Deum et lapis iste quem erexi in titulum vocabitur Domus Dei;" (Gen. 28:16-22); "Venit igitur Iacob Luzam quæ est in terra

only the interrelating of the participants which counts; consequently, the priest is no longer anything more than one element in these relations, and the place of things around the altar scarcely has any importance any more. If, on the other hand, we have a church which, as in this one here, is directional from the great porch up to the apse, looking eastward, where the altar and its sanctuary so occur as to constitute a sort of interruption in that progress, then something is being said about the irruption of God into our world and into our life, something is being said about this meeting, and this wedding, which make of the Christian church a *Domus Thalami*.[30]

But is it not the same case, with colours (liturgical colours; gold), with ecclesiastical clothing, with ornamentation (signifying quality), with light and windows (stained glass), with gestures,[31] and so on? It is not their quality of being possibly exaggerated and precious that interests us in itself, but simply that quality of "irruption" which reveals something of God. Believing that these things were once current simply on account of pious custom mixed-up

---

Chanaan cognomento Bethel ipse et omnis populus cum eo, ædificavitque ibi altare et appellavit nomen loci Domus Dei: ibi enim apparuit ei Deus" (Gen. 35:6). Cf. also all the other passages in the Bible where *Domus Dei* or *Domus Domini* are mentioned; for example: "Non prævaluit David ire ad altare ut ibi obsecraret Deum, nimio enim fuerat timore perterritus videns gladium angeli Domini, dixitque David: Hæc est domus Dei et hoc altare in holocaustum Israhel;" (I Chron. 21:30 – 22:1). "O Israhel, quam magna est domus Dei et ingens locus possessionis eius" (Baruch 3:24), and many of the Psalms: "Alleluia, laudate nomen Domini, laudate servi Dominum qui statis in domo Domini, in atriis domus Dei nostri" (Ps. 134:1).

[30] See the Vespers hymn, in the Common of the Dedication of a church. Let us also take note that this same common denominator of "interruption" explains certain important and ever-present features of sacred art: the number three (or five, or seven); certain rules of symmetry or of proportion; the place of certain objects, and so on—all things which also, in their way, signify "interruption" and "in-between."

[31] Hence, for example, the problem with shaking hands with each other for the peace: there is no "interruption" in relation to the way this gesture is used in the world, in a formal manner even with enemies. If this had ever born a purely Christian significance, for the sake of which martyrs might have shed their blood, then we would easily be able to understand why this sign should be used as a kiss of peace between the faithful; it seems, however, that no-one died for that...And this is one of the reasons why the "peace," as it is actually exchanged in the course of present-day celebrations, has most of all the appearance of being a sign of natural mutual solidarity, and not of supernatural solidarity. On the other hand, how many martyrs have suffered for the sake of the sign of the cross, and how many instances of that sign have been done away with! See Father Jean-Robert Armogathe, in *Reconstruire la Liturgie*, ed. Father Claude Barthe, F.-X. Guibert, 1977, pp. 28-29: "Could we not then say that there is a crisis, when it is—on the contrary—religious ritual which is being shaped by secular ritual; to take an example, when the kiss of peace is replaced by a handshake?—*This is a very good example; a very interesting little thesis could be written about the development of the "peace," from the transmission of the peace to the faithful by giving them to kiss the* instrumentum pacis, *the instrument of peace, a lamb or a cross in metal, right up to the shaking of hands, the contemporary 'handshake.' This latter fashion is in fact a very western phenomenon: heaven be thanked, other episcopal conferences are suggesting different kinds of salutation."*

with a taste for luxury and for superstition—is that not to forget the signs that are communicated by these things?

For "The Sacred Liturgy engages not only man's intellect, but the whole person, who is the "subject" of full and conscious participation in the liturgical celebration. Translators should therefore allow the signs and images of the texts, as well as the ritual actions, to speak for themselves; they should not attempt to render too explicit that which is implicit in the original texts. For the same reason, the addition of explanatory texts not contained in the *editio typica* is to be prudently avoided."[32] In this paragraph of *Liturgiam Authenticam* it becomes quite clear, does it not, that none of these various liturgical languages we have mentioned is sufficient in itself: the fact that a language may be more explicit does not mean that it achieves better communication, since to describe the Infinite in detail is to reduce it in size. We believe that what most fully communicates sacredness, the divine irruption, what brings about the inter-ruption of a true supernatural encounter in a purely natural universe, is rather the whole interaction and balance of these various languages brought together.[33] And is it not at that point, that sacred silence has its place? Far from being an empty pause, it is more like an amplifier or, if you will, the "sound mixing" for all the other languages. Is it not silence which decodes, translates, and communicates to us, in the unique language of the impression we receive in our inner selves, all the data which are engrossed in encrypted form in the other modes?

Finally, let us say just one thing: for the purpose of rediscovering the spirit of sacredness, there is a model, and that is the old Roman Liturgy. We do not wish here to make a comparison with the new, nor to start again on the discussion as to the best opportunity, the time and the means for perfecting it. We will just say that it exists, that it is Latin and Roman. It is one of the paradoxes of the postconciliar period to have wanted—so it is said—to get back to "the pure Roman rite of the fifth century," whilst at the same time borrowing heavily from other liturgies, Latin or otherwise. At a time when thirst for the sacred is impelling so many souls towards the oriental forms, would it not be high time to offer once again this model—peculiar to our western tradition—of sacredness and continuity?

For a new Liturgical Movement, it would be necessary to look again, in depth, at all this, to reflect upon it in a manner both organic and practical, so as to provide, at all levels of the hierarchy, those means, and those practical

---

[32] *Liturgiam Authenticam*, para. 28.

[33] *Catechism of the Catholic Church*, 2655: "In the sacramental Liturgy of the Church, the mission of Christ and of the Holy Spirit proclaims, makes present and communicates the mystery of salvation, which is continued *in the heart that prays*. The spiritual writers sometimes compare the heart to an altar. Prayer internalises and assimilates the Liturgy during and after its celebration. Even when it is lived out 'in secret' (cf. Matt. 6:6), prayer is always prayer *of the Church*; it is a communion with the Holy Trinity (*General instruction on the Liturgy of Hours*, 9);" emphasis added.

directives, which would make it possible to regain possession, from the presbytery to the Curia, of the sacred, that unique style of the Unique Bridegroom.

4. Conclusion

Dealing with the Liturgy, is the same as dealing with Christ himself, and if we wished to summarise in a few words the balance to be achieved as between the two poles we suggested earlier, then we could do no better than to use once more the formula of Saint Leo concerning the hypostatic union: *Non commixtionem passus, neque divisionem.*[34] After that, our practical conclusion would be a call not only to courageous patience, but — more on our humble level — a call for much more study, for serious studies, so that we may be in a position to make our own the prayer of Saint Francis of Sales:[35]

> My God, grant me the serenity…to accept what I can not change.
> My God, grant me the courage…to change what can be changed.
> My God, grant me the wisdom…to know the difference.

APPENDIX 1: THE ESSENTIAL RÔLE OF THE CLASSICAL LITURGY

We would like here to point out the place of the traditional Liturgy within the perspective of a new Liturgical Movement.

In the first place, it must serve as a lighthouse and as a haven for those who feel they can sail no further amid the thousands of liturgies in present use; the faithful, whilst awaiting the results of the "reform of the reform," have the right to conserve or to rediscover their faith in contact with this age-old treasure, which must appear to them as a special demonstration of the fact that the Church is "holding on course."

In the second place, even for those who habitually attend the new Liturgy, it should serve as a point of reference. In fact — since God writes straight with crooked lines — the permanent place of the classic rite offers an irreplaceable witness to the continuity of the Church and of its Liturgy. For this rite has not suffered from the congenital ambiguity of the first Liturgical Movement and of what it produced "in the spirit of the Council;" and this means that in it we can find a guideline for making correct choices in practice, and a link with the period "before the break" which helps us to rediscover the true spirit of a Liturgy in "organic continuity" with its past.

In the third place, the traditional Liturgy represents a factor which is indispensable for a "reform of the reform." We have quite sufficiently demonstrated the existence of a break in development, and have emphasised the need for continuity, and the fact that this is required so as to respect the very nature of Liturgy. Now, as we have just said, this continuity is *fully visible*

---

[34] The Antiphon from Lauds for the Feast of the Circumcision.
[35] Quoted in *Una Voce*, no. 210, January/February 2000, p. 6, as being that of Chesterton.

today only in the classical Liturgy, which should henceforth, in our view, serve as a "matrix" for the future restoration of liturgical unity—if, and when, and in whatever manner, and by whatever means, the Magisterium may judge to be opportune. Some people might object that, since the classical Liturgy is in use only in a restricted number of places of worship, it is difficult to see how it could, in practice, serve as the "matrix" for a new Liturgical Movement and for a new reform. But one should bow to the inevitable and obvious.[36] Nor, in practice, is there right now a "rite of Paul VI," in the sense of a single rite celebrated everywhere[37] with a sufficient degree of uniformity for it to serve as a reference-point...It is therefore more appropriate to limit ourselves,

---

[36] And Denis Crouan himself, though he is most attached to the new Liturgy and to its original and official forms, honestly acknowledges this: "Since, in the parishes of my diocese, I am unable to find the current Liturgy celebrated with a strict respect for the rules (whether it be in Latin or in French), I go fairly often to a church where the Mass is celebrated—with the permission of the bishop—in its pre-conciliar form (the rite known as that 'of Saint Pius V'). There, I notice that the faithful—who on average are not very old— follow the Liturgy, which is entirely in Latin, with no difficulty, despite the 'fortunate absence' of a leader of worship...So, once again, we are bound to ask ourselves why it is, that what can be done with dignity for the old rite suddenly becomes brutally impossible for the current rite? We certainly have to give an answer to this question. If the Liturgy in its current form is being rejected, that is not because it can not be celebrated, but quite simply because people do not want to celebrate it. Everything is being done to ensure that that Liturgy, which is nonetheless the Liturgy called for by Vatican II, should disappear, or should be replaced by faked-up liturgies, reduced to the simplest possible forms of expression, with neither beauty nor dignity. And at present, in the majority of those seminaries which are still open, the future priests are neither taught to respect the rubrics of the Missal, nor to sing plainchant, nor to celebrate the Liturgy worthily;" *Bulletin Pro-Liturgia*, no. 110, February 1998.

[37] It is the case, that we would need to be able to take as our starting-point a *universal practice which is sufficiently uniform*, and not just a "laboratory version" of the Liturgy 'of Paul VI,' otherwise the difficulty of the continuity of the rite being *visible to everyone* would not have been resolved. Hence, all that would happen would be that we would meet with conservative reactions, whether in favour of pre-conciliar or of post-conciliar practice, and in that way all we would have succeeded in doing would be in creating a third Roman rite, no more faithfully celebrated than the second...It seems to us, that at present the classical rite, and that alone, offers the double (and irreplaceable) advantage, on the one hand of being practised in a sufficiently uniform manner, over several continents, and on the other hand of its indisputably clear connection with the age-old practice of the Church. In any case, even if we admitted that the new rite could in fact claim to be celebrated in a sufficiently uniform manner, everywhere, it can not claim the second of these advantages. And beyond that, in view of how little effect seems to be achieved in practice, by the Holy See's pronouncements and directives aimed at ensuring that the new rite is celebrated in a more regular fashion, it is becoming obvious that only the bringing about of a situation in which the two rites may be seen side-by-side in practice, *on the ground*, will mean that this solid model of comparison constituted by the classical rite may be able to lead pastors toward a better understanding and a greater vigilance. That can already be seen, in those places where the two rites are in fact being practised side-by-side. Hence the urgent need to give people *total* freedom to use the classical rite.

as a starting-point, to that one of the two rites whose continuity is more undisputed.

For all these reasons, it is becoming really urgently necessary to give complete freedom, to those priests and faithful who wish to do this, to use the classical rite.

When will there be achieved, by grafting the Roman rite back onto its original trunk, the liturgical unity (and not merely canonical unity)[38] of that Rite? We know not. On the other hand—as we have already said—we must not dream of a new form of clericalism which, in the course of five or six years, would brutally impose a new changeover, of whatever kind: the only result—as recent history clearly shows us—would be a third Roman rite...or, indeed, further schismatic movements! Everything leads us to believe that the immediate future will bring a live-and-let-live, side-by-side existence for many years yet.

APPENDIX 2: STUDIES NEEDING TO BE UNDERTAKEN AND/OR TO BE COLLATED[39]

1) A classified list of the criteria for liturgical reform, with their chronological relationships.
2) A list of erroneous liturgical practices denounced by the Magisterium.
3) A list of the cultural, theological or ideological conditions which may have brought about modifications in the Liturgy.
4) A discernment of the various currents and influences at the origin of the first modern Liturgical Movement.
5) A discernment of the enduring characteristics, of the roots and of the theological implications of what Dom Guéranger calls "the anti-liturgical heresy."
6) A discernment of the Catholic concept of Tradition and its application in the sphere of Liturgy, and of its social and anthropological impact.

---

[38] For at the present moment, we have a single canonical identity (like a shared passport or identity card) for two rites which are liturgically and historically different: "Roman junior" and "Roman senior."

[39] See the Constitution on the Sacred Liturgy, para. 23 [personal remarks are *italicised*]: "That sound tradition may be retained, and yet the way remain open to legitimate progress, careful investigation is always to be made into each part of the Liturgy which...should be theological, historical, and pastoral. [*That, if we may believe the remarks of Cardinal Antonelli, is what may have been lacking, particularly with respect to a theological awareness within the Consilium itself.*] Also the general laws governing the structure and meaning of the Liturgy [*laws which perhaps have not in fact been sufficiently clarified*] must be studied in conjunction with the experience derived from recent liturgical reforms [*nowadays, this would obviously refer to the post-conciliar reforms*] and from the indults conceded to various places [*and why not those indults concerning the old rite?*]. Finally, there must be no innovations unless the good of the Church genuinely and certainly requires them; and care must be taken that any new forms adopted should in some way grow organically from forms already existing [*amongst which must be numbered the rite "of Saint Pius V," a very stable form*].

7) A discernment of the concept of a 'sign' in the sphere of Liturgy, and its application there; its theological implications; its relation to Tradition and to cultural and historical data, both local and universal; its social and anthropological impact.

8) A discernment of the concept of organic continuity, and its application; discernment (and application) of its theological consequences and of its sociological and anthropological impact.

9) The relating to each other of the various general criteria for the reform or for the conservation of the Liturgy, as they have been presented in various texts of the Magisterium, in order to eliminate contradictory interpretations.

10) To put the question honestly, by means of a total comparative study (both of texts and of the rituals), as to whether the old rite, with some additions, with some improvements, and with an improvement in its practice, but without any radical alteration, could not correspond to the aspirations expressed in *Sacrosanctum Concilium*.[40]

Translated by Henry Taylor

---

[40] See, for example, the impartial witness, based on experience, of a diocesan priest from England who normally celebrates according to the new Liturgy: "I should like also to thank the Father Abbot of the community for having invited me to take part, in such an intimate fashion, in the *Triduum*, and thus to experience a Liturgy which is celebrated with such love, with such beauty and dignity. I had the impression that the way you have of celebrating the Liturgy was that which one would expect on the basis of the Council's Constitution *Sacrosanctum Concilium*" (Father Richard S. Aladics, in a personal letter to the author of May 3rd 2000). Our Abbey, in its conventual Mass, celebrates the old Liturgy with some modifications from 1965.

The Reform of the Reform
and the Old Roman Rite

Intervention of Professor Robert Spaemann[1]

IN making the following observations, I shall be speaking neither as a theologian — which I am not — nor with the authority of my understanding of philosophy, but as an ordinary Catholic layman with some common sense, or so I hope, and who has seventy years of experience of that *participatio actuosa* which Saint Pius X was asking for.[2] That was before the days of my youth. In all the parish churches and monastic churches where I worshipped in all those years, that kind of participation was all I knew. The climax of this participation, for me personally, was Easter Sunday in 1943 — I was fifteen years old then — when I had to substitute for the community of monks of Saint Joseph's Abbey at Gerleven in Westphalia (a foundation of Beuron), and sing the Easter Proper, starting with the *Resurrexi*. I had been baptised in that abbey church at the age of three. The monks had been expelled by the Nazis, but there was a Sunday Mass for the villagers, who used to sing the ordinary all together — especially the children, at the tops of their voices — not Mass I of the *Kyriale*, but the *Missa de Angelis*. The clergy had not yet told them that they were too stupid to learn Gregorian chant. Nowadays, they are thought to be equally incapable of understanding that it is truly the Body of Our Lord that we receive at Holy Communion. The children do not know that when they go to receive their First Holy Communion. That is the point at which an ordinary layman starts to think. And here are a few somewhat pragmatic remarks.

1. The point of view of someone taking part in the Sacred Liturgy is different from that of a specialist in the history of the Liturgy. The latter sees the rite of the Mass as a contingent stage in the course of a long and continuing

---

[1] Prof. Dr. Dr. (*honorum causa multorum*) Robert Spaemann formerly taught philosophy at the universities of Heidelberg, Salzburg and Munich. He is a life member of the Pontifical Academy. His books have been translated into thirteen languages. He is the founder, former vice-president, and currently honorary president of the association *Pro Missa Tridentina*.
[2] Cf. Motu Proprio *Tra le sollecitudini*, 22 November 1903; C. Braga & A. Bugnini, eds., *Documenta Ad Instaurationem Liturgicam Spectantia 1903-1963*, Centro Liturgico Vincenziano, Rome, 2000, pp. 12-27; ET: R. Kevin Seasolz, *The New Liturgy: A Documentation 1903-1965*, Herder, New York 1966, pp. 3-10.

evolution; whereas through this rite the former comes into contact, at every moment, with something eternal, the Paschal Mystery. And through this eternal element the form itself is consecrated and loses its radical contingency. That is why Cardinal Newman said, in one of his sermons, that the Church has never abolished such a rite, and that she could not do so without gravely endangering religion.[3]

That is why today we have two Roman rites: besides Paul VI's *Novus Ordo Missæ* there still remains the Roman missal in the *editio typica* of Blessed John XXIII. At the same time, we have two rites for the distribution of sacraments, the ordination of priests in either seven or two stages, the Baptism of children with an exorcism — as in the first century — and the answer "Faith" to the priest's question, "What do you ask of the Church of God?" or — for thirty years now — with no exorcism and without that reply (the new answer is Baptism"). There is no denying, it seems to me, that there are two rites. The Dominican rite, for example, or the Ambrosian rite at Milan, used to differ much less from the *Missale Romanum*, before the reform, than the *Novus Ordo* does now. They, nevertheless, were looked upon and recognised as rites differing from the Roman rite. And if, for example, a Dominican Father was saying Mass in a parish church, he had the right and the duty to celebrate according to his own rite. The little acolytes had to learn the different customs rapidly — something that used to take them ten minutes — and the parish congregation was happy to discover the wealth of the Church's Liturgy. The differences were small, but this was another rite. In my view there can be no doubt that a Liturgy of the Mass which has no offertory, with a multiplicity of Eucharistic Prayers and the almost complete abolition of use of the Roman canon, with a different calendar — with, for example, the abolition of the pre-Lenten period (from Septuagesima onward) — with a different set of readings from Sacred Scripture — that such a Liturgy, as I say, is a different rite; especially if we consider not only the origin but the appearance of the two liturgies: the orientation of the priest, the liturgical language, etc. An Orthodox friend told me that he finds more similarity between the old Roman Mass and his own Liturgy, than between that and the Masses usually celebrated today.

Given the fact of these two rites, then the abolition of the old Roman rite would, as a matter of course, be illegitimate even if not illegal. As Cardinal Ratzinger has shown us, in its whole history the Church has never abolished a legitimate rite which was hallowed by Tradition. The Second Vatican Council confirmed this respect for legitimate rites, seeing the plurality of rites not as an inevitable ill, but as a treasure of the Church.[4] And our Holy Father, in his well-known address to the monks of Barroux,[5] expressly applied this principle to the old Latin rite.

---

[3] Cf. Sermon on the Feast of the Circumcision of the Lord, January 1st 1831, *Parochial and Plain Sermons*, vol. II Longmans Green & Co, London 1898, pp. 69-78.

[4] Cf. *Sacrosanctum Concilium* nos. 4, 37, *Orientalium Ecclesiarum* no. 2.

[5] 28 September 1990.

Nor is the existence of two rites in the same canonical territory an evil to be averted. In the Ukraine, in the same area there are communities using the Latin and the Byzantine rites. And in Milan, where Mass is generally said in the Ambrosian rite, there are also Masses in the Roman rite, in the church of the Catholic university for example. That does not worry anyone. And if a priest of the Roman rite says Mass in a Milanese parish, no-one makes him use the Ambrosian rite. So where is the difficulty, except for ideological fanatics? A few years ago, I travelled from Rome to Milan on Ash Wednesday. My colleagues at the Catholic university invited me to dinner that evening. When they noticed that I was eating very little, they asked me whether that was on account of Lent. If that were so, I need have no scruples: at Milan, there is no such thing as Ash Wednesday; Lent does not start until the Sunday—which is in fact a more ancient custom than the Roman one. So why is it not possible for the Sundays from Septuagesima onward—for which Johann Sebastian Bach wrote some of his most wonderful cantatas to go on being kept in communities of the old Roman rite, whilst they have disappeared in other congregations?

This dualism of Roman rites could have been avoided, if the liturgical reform had been kept within the limits of the principles laid down by the constitution *Sacrosanctum Concilium*, as happened up to 1969. They preferred to have a new rite in place of the old. The fanatical preservation of the old one by a fairly considerable number of priests and laymen was the inevitable consequence.

Every Catholic Christian has the right to fight for a form of prayer hallowed by his ancestors, by many saints, and by the entire Church for centuries. This right would disappear only if the new rite were in every respect better than the old. That is almost impossible. And in the case of the last reform of the Roman Liturgy, there is no longer any doubt today that there have been painful losses, even if people can not agree as to whether the advantages outweigh the losses. Now, the Council was explicit that changes were permissible only where there was no doubt that they did outweigh them.[6] If we ignore this principle, that each innovation should have to be justified, then we can hardly complain of the problems which arise from this. Those taking part in this colloquium are—so I suppose—all of the opinion that the quality of the *Novus Ordo Missæ*—even if one rates it very highly—does not justify the abolition of the old *Missale Romanum*. The hostility of some of the advocates of the new rite towards the old is the strongest argument in favour of maintaining it. Only a bad conscience in respect of their parents can explain someone's refusal to obey the commandment to honour them. A respect for those who continue to be loyal to the old Roman rite, something the Pope has clearly requested, is—in my opinion—a necessary presupposition for the legitimacy of the new rite.

---

[6] Cf. *Sacrosanctum Concilium* no. 23.

2. Now if there are genuinely some difficulties in the coexistence of two rites in the same territory, these are usually exaggerated. People talk about every Catholic having to worship in his own parish on a Sunday. Well, that has never been the case. In the time of my childhood, there were always some of the faithful who found their spiritual home in a monastery church, even if it were a Dominican priory with a different rite. Maybe the parish priest was not too happy about it, but nobody criticised these Catholics. *Salus animarum suprema lex.* My parents, for example, regularly went to a different parish church from our own, for the sake of the *actuosa participatio* to be found there. But we live in a climate of intolerance, and the question is, how to overcome the difficulties arising from the coexistence of two rites in the same territory. It is possible, it seems to me, to imagine three solutions, of which only two are realistic. For the straightforward disappearance of one of the two rites, leaving only the other, is just Utopian. That goes without saying for the new rite. As for the old, it is kept going by a schismatic community, just as the Byzantine rite is; the Pope could do away with it only within the Catholic Church.

There remains: either, the peaceful and fraternal coexistence, for an indefinite period, of the two rites; or, the union of the two rites by changing them both — that is to say, on one hand a cautious attempt at a sensible reform of the old rite, an attempt which would keep strictly to the limits laid down by the Second Vatican Council; on the other, the reform of the reform, that is to say the abolition of the *Novus Ordo Missæ* and its replacement by a missal similar to that of 1965.[7]

I will make just a few remarks on this last possibility, which seems to me for the moment to be no more realistic than the first.

3. Whether a general return to the missal of 1965 is desirable or not is the question which separates people. At the time, in a letter to the monks of Beuron which served as a preface to the "Schott" (peoples' missal) of 1965, the Cardinal Secretary of State officially declared that this Missal was the definitive realisation of the Council's commands.[8] Today, a return to that Missal would encounter insuperable resistance in areas of great influence. It would already be something, if the Eucharist was everywhere celebrated according to the Church's books, if the Roman Canon was used as often as the

---

[7] Professor Spaemann refers to the "missal of 1965" a number of times in this intervention. In fact, there was no 1965 *editio typica* of the *Missale Romanum* between those of 1962 and 1970. That to which he is in fact referring is the *Ordo Missæ* of 1965 which was incorporated into various editions of missals — both for the people and for the altar — published in different countries following the release of the *Ordo Missæ* of 1965; cf. *Ordo Missæ, Ritus Servandus in Celebratione Missæ et De Defectibus in Celebratione Missæ Occurrentibus*, Typis Polyglottis Vaticanis 1965; J.B. O'Connell, *The Order to be Observed in the Celebration of Mass: A Translation of the New 'Ordo Missæ,'* Burns & Oates, London 1965. [Ed.]

[8] Cf. Anselm Schott OSB, *Das Messbuch der Heiligen Kirche*, Herder, Frieburg, Baselm Vienna, 1966.

other Eucharistic Prayers, if the custom of the priest's being turned *versus orientem resp. versus crucem* was not falling into complete disuse, as likewise the use of Latin from the Preface onwards, and if the universal Church clearly favoured the distribution of Holy Communion upon the tongue. There is yet another point worth mentioning: the *Confiteor*. I can not see the "undoubted spiritual advantage"[9] in the omission from it of the names of Saint Michael, Saint John Baptist, and Saints Peter and Paul. Well, even if there is such an advantage, the fact of the *Confiteor* being said by the priest and the people together is a nonsense. It is psychologically impossible to accept the request of my brother to pray for him, whilst I am speaking and asking the same thing of him. Either listen or speak. In the new rite, the *Vobis fratres* is no longer really addressed to anyone. It seems to me that those who, for ideological reasons, introduced a single *Confiteor*, have never truly turned and asked their brothers to pray for them, otherwise they would not have had that absurd idea.

The achievement of these six *desiderata* would make sure of a visible link between the tradition of the Latin rites and the *Novus Ordo Missæ*, and would leave the door open for a future reunion of the rites.

4. It would, in principle, be much easier to adapt the old Roman rite in accordance with the Council's wishes. In abbeys such as Fontgombault and Barroux, for several years now, experiments have been made in this direction, in the hope of preparing the way for something of importance to the whole Latin Church. Now, we need to be quite clear what is being prepared. This is certainly not a preparation for the reform of the reform, since the reform of the reform concerns the reformed Liturgy and not the old Liturgy. If a reunion of the rites was the order of the day, then both would have to undergo changes, which would be much more radical in the case of the reformed Liturgy; whereas, for the moment, it is only in the old rite that movement is expected — which is not reasonable. It should be for the traditional rite, in this view, to draw closer to the new, whereas it is the latter which is further from the intentions of the Council than the former. No, it seems to me that any reforms of the old Roman rite should be free of any kind of tactical or strategic consideration with a view to a future reunion of the rites, and should be motivated solely by intrinsic spiritual or pastoral considerations — in the true sense of the word! And we should always be aware of that common-sense principle — which was recalled in the constitution *Sacrosanctum Concilium*, and is nowadays systematically ignored — that the burden of justification is never on the side of tradition, but always on that of change.

---

[9] Cf. *Sacrosanctum Concilium* no. 23.

5. Considered in itself, the classic Roman rite, if it is to remain living and vital, must develop, as it always has done. It would otherwise become petrified, like a museum-piece. It should, for example, always be open to new saints.

Those persons present here know better than I do, the problems which arise in this regard. I just want to formulate one *desideratum*, that is not generally mentioned, whereas, in my opinion, it is the only thing which is truly worth while restoring: this is Communion under both species, on certain important occasions in the life of a congregation or one of the faithful. Nowadays, such a wish is not inspired by any doubt as to the validity of the sacrament, but by a desire for the fullness of the Sign instituted by the Lord. Some other changes are sometimes suggested to us, for no good reason. Thus, for instance, singing the *Pater* together. This is clearly contrary to the Roman tradition: Saint Gregory was already defending the Latin custom of its being sung by the priest alone, and Saint Augustine himself knew no other usage. On that point, the custom of the Latin rite is better founded than that of the Greeks. For the *Pater* is neither an acclamation, nor a hymn, it is a prayer. It is not the prayer of the priest alone, but that of the whole congregation. Now, it is a serious mistake to think that the congregation's prayer ought to be sung together, like a hymn. Even from the psychological point of view, it is easier to share personally in a prayer by following the singing of a single voice, than by all singing together. Singing together has an altogether different significance; it is appropriate for acclamations or for hymns. Note that Pius XII, when he introduced the saying together by the congregation of the *Pater* on Good Friday, did not have it sung, but simply said together—and that, on this occasion only. It is deeply moving to hear the voice of Father Abbot, at the end of Vespers, singing the *Pater* in the silence of the great abbey church. Everyone can join in this prayer—provided that it is not distorted by a sound-system. Happily, that is not done at this office, whereas yesterday, during the Mass, I heard—for the first time in my life, in the old Liturgy—the *Per Ipsum* and the Preface not from the altar, but through loudspeakers, with the voice changed and rendered unnatural by technology. For about a thousand years, the Liturgy was celebrated in this abbey church without such artificial aids. Yes, the priest is a long way away, and his voice is weak. But he also looks small, as seen from where the faithful are, and you can not see the host at the moment of elevation: why not set up, in the middle of the church, a screen on which we could see a magnified priest and host, rather than just a little real priest at the real altar? The microphone distorts real space and takes us into a virtual world, where we are taken every day these days by the media. Reverend Fathers, I hope I can persuade you, I ask of you: do away with the microphone in the Liturgy, and just keep it for the homily. Do not encourage people to confuse prayer with the sermon. The bride does not speak to her divine spouse with a microphone.

Given that there are two Roman rites today, there is no good reason for introducing into the old rite any of the new elements which are in the new rite. That would only be justified, if a reunion of the rites was on the order of the day—which is not the case. A shared penitential rite at the beginning of the Mass has, for example, a certain spiritual interest. But you can not collect together all the best possible elements in a single rite. For the plurality of rites would then no longer be this ecclesial treasure that the Council talks about, and we would have to construct an altogether artificial rite, which would be a mixture of all the various traditional rites—a monstrosity.

6. And so I come to my last point. The development of the old Roman rite is carried on today under unfavourable conditions. And I would emphasise the need for the greatest caution in this business, especially in non-monastic congregations. Pius XII may have accomplished liturgical reforms—in Holy Week, for example—which were pretty radical. But everyone accepted them, often gratefully. For there was no doubt about the intention of these reforms, nor any suspicion that the reform might lead towards goals one could not foresee.

The 1965 Missal itself was accepted without a murmur of complaint, insofar as it was considered definitive. And it was declared to be definitive by the Cardinal Secretary of State. Yet today, that Missal appears to many of the faithful as one stage in a revolution. Just as the reform of 1789 appears in retrospect as a transitory stage in the revolution which showed its true face in 1792. Today any innovation, any reform of the rite is met with suspicion and mistrust on the part of the friends of the old Roman rite. And with good reason. We feel we're being treated like children. "Where are they taking us? One time already we've been taken where we did not want to go." One of the most disturbing things about the new Mass is the fact that ordinary laymen are treated like children. They no longer know, for instance, whether the Eucharistic Prayer the priest says is one of the Canons approved by the Church, or just one he has made up. The layman has to accept everything put before him. If he has taken refuge in the old Liturgy, he does not want to be once more degraded to the status of a minor again, and left at the mercy of just anyone, at any price. Hence the sensitivity, and sometimes extreme mistrust, of "traditionalists" towards the least innovation. How should we respond? First by respecting them. The mistrust is not without its basis in painful experience. It thus seems to me that we should not introduce into non-monastic congregations, little by little, any innovation without people knowing what its *telos* is—a word that means both "end" and "purpose." If we believe that the old Roman rite should be reformed in the direction of the Missal of 1965, the faithful have the right of having that done in the form of a new *editio typica* of the Roman Missal. And they should know that this edition is not just a temporary step towards a new *experimentum*. They have the right to be sure that their children, if they have been estranged from the Church for years, will recognise their Father's house when they return, and will not have to say: *Tulerunt Dominum meum et nescio ubi posuerunt eum* (John 20:13).

Personally, I am convinced that the old Roman rite does have the strength and the vitality to absorb just a very few innovations, as for example Communion in both kinds on certain occasions, omitting the recitation by the priest of doublets of texts sung by the people—that is, supposing that the people do not sing paraphrases of those texts. Yet many of my friends can not stand such thoughts so much as being uttered. And the dreadful thing is, that I understand their attitude. In view of the hostility they so often encounter in the Church, there is a not unfounded suspicion that a good few bishops and priests see in the disappearance of the old Roman rite the simplest solution to all these problems. And the friends of the old rite are afraid that any change approved by the authorities is nothing more than a further step towards its definitive abolition. This fear is reinforced if changes are introduced without the existence of a Missal, approved by the Church, including these innovations. If the faithful ask the priest why he is reading a different gospel from the gospel of that day according to the Roman Missal, and if the priest replies that he has heard from someone that a letter was sent to this or that community giving permission for this change of readings, the faithful have every right to feel worried. They wanted to escape the domination of arbitrary change in going to the "old Mass," and they did not want to meet with it even there. In one diocese, the bishop strictly proscribes any mixing of the old and new rites, in another the bishop insists on it.

In such a situation as that, a new *editio typica* of the *Missale Romanum*, bearing the name of the Pope, could dissipate fear and suspicion. Once they had been definitively recognised as a community with its own rite in the Latin Church, no doubt the hearts of the "traditionalists" would be open to a few cautious reforms of this rite so dear to them. They are in principle more ready to submit to legitimate authority than other groups within the Church. Now, I should add this: authority has a duty not to disavow those who obey—as it did in the case of altar girls—and it ought not to give way to the blackmail of the *fait accompli*—as happened with Communion in the hand.

A word, in this context, on the form of Holy Communion. In the Masses of the *Novus Ordo*, there is no longer a single, shared rite for Communion. The faithful are divided at this moment of unity, and each is obliged to visibly align themselves with one of the two groups. This is unique in the history of the Liturgy, and is, truth to tell, a scandal. And now there is a rumour that they are preparing to permit Communion in the hand for the old Roman rite as well. Why quite needlessly introduce this anomaly of two different forms for receiving the Body of the Lord, into a Liturgy which was free of this up to now? Is there some secret envy here, of a liturgical world which had hitherto remained intact? There are no pastoral reasons for this. In the rare cases when one of the faithful asks for Communion in the hand, the priest will always deal with this prudently. He has, after all, read and assimilated the treatise on *epikeia*. We should not follow the favourite method of subversion: changing the rules for the sake of rare exceptional cases.

One solution of the problems posed by the two rites is certainly possible, if we grasp that the value for the universal Church of the permanence of the old Roman rite is inestimable. In a period of great confusion, it upholds the norm, presents the criteria for what each Catholic Liturgy worthy of the name ought to be like. It is a kind of lighthouse.

Each celebration of the Holy Mass should be able to stand up by this standard. And I dream of the day when every bishop will make his seminarians go to a Mass of the old Roman rite several times. We are not vagabonds. We should know where we have come from. It is those people who know and love the old Liturgy, who offer a guarantee that the new will be celebrated worthily and with dignity. It is a fact that you best learn what the Eucharist is, by studying the traditional rite. It seems to me that the destiny of the Liturgy in the Latin Church depends on respecting this commandment, on which God has made all earthly life depend: "Thou shalt honour thy father and thy mother."

Translated by Henry Taylor

Raising Questions About the Liturgical Reform

Intervention of Professor Miguel Ayuso-Torres[1]

Introduction

L ET me start by explaining to you the reasons for the content of my paper, and why it is so brief. These are the limitations of my French, and the fact that I am not a liturgist, but a modest scholar in the spheres of law and of politics (even though I feel very attached to the intellectual tradition of the Church, and to its traditional practices, notably in the Liturgy). I also bear in mind the placing of this paper — to which I have not given any title — at the end of this meeting, which reflects its nature as a personal witness.

It is not, therefore, that I am not interested in the matter, nor that I have insufficient respect for the people here present; quite the contrary, I intend to concentrate my entire attention upon the very serious question with which we are concerned, and am thus obliged to omit any apodictic assertions, and any attempt at originality. In the simplest manner, I shall deal with a few questions about the liturgical reform, often using the words of other writers, and with a properly "philosophical" attitude, that is to say, one which deals with the "problematics"[2] here, although this applies to a question with multiple facets: aesthetic, educative, moral, theological, religious...

2. Towards a Conceptualisation of the Liturgical Reform

A first methodological requirement is that of locating the liturgical reform within a particular doctrinal and historical context, which is certainly that of the spiritual and intellectual atmosphere surrounding the Council which produced it. Let us imagine, simply for the purpose of argument — since, as the Italians say, *con si e con fa, la storia non se fa* (history is not made with 'ifs' and with 'buts') — let us imagine that Pope Paul VI had not promulgated his new Missal, and that he had made do with a limited reform, like those made earlier by Pius X (1911), Pius XII (1955), or John XXIII (1962).

---

[1] Professor Miguel Ayuso-Torres lectures in political science and public law at the Comillas Pontifical University in Madrid. He is chief editor of the review *Verbo*, which is concerned with civic education and cultural activities from the point of view of Christianity and of Natural Law.

[2] Cf. Marino Gentile, *"La filosofia come intelligenza della esperienza"* [Philosophy as the Understanding of Experience], in *Filosofia Oggi* (Genova), no. 3 (1985) pp. 449 ff.

Let us then suppose that he had restricted himself to a few discreet little re-adjustments, just touching-up the ancient edifice: readings in the vernacular, a few simplifications, introducing concelebration on exceptional occasions, and so on.

In a certain sense, this is what would seem the natural result of the conciliar Constitution dealing with the Liturgy:

> The rite of the Mass is to be revised in such a way that the intrinsic nature and purpose of its several parts, as also the connection between them, may be more clearly manifested, and that devout and active participation by the faithful may be more easily achieved. For this purpose the rites are to be simplified, due care being taken to preserve their substance; elements which, with the passage of time, came to be duplicated, or were added with but little advantage, are now to be discarded; other elements which have suffered injury through accidents of history are now to be restored to the vigour which they had in the days of the holy Fathers, as may seem useful or necessary.[3]

From this point of view, one could imagine parishes with the altar "turned towards the Lord,"[4] where the offertory and the Canon would always be recited in Latin, and where on Sundays the great pieces of the 'Common' would be sung in plainchant: the *Kyrie, Gloria, Credo, Sanctus,* and *Agnus Dei.* On this hypothesis, it seems probable that the reactions of rejection of the broad lines of the Council, a rejection which ran fairly deep, would not have occurred on the scale, nor with the strength of determination, that has actually been the case. Amongst the reasons for these reactions having been less widespread in the Spanish and Italian-speaking worlds, we can not disregard the way in which the *novus ordo* was put into effect with more discretion there. And the Council would have been widely and peacefully accepted…

Nevertheless, such a dream, though it may be seductive, is no more than an absurd hypothesis:

> For not only was it the case that the breathtaking revolution desired by Vatican II could only be effected through an unprecedented modification of the rules governing worship (the *lex orandi*), but furthermore because this liturgical metamorphosis formed an integral part of the sweeping change that was brought about. In response to that—and this is true far beyond the milieu of 'traditionalism'—any criticism, even the most moderate, of the new Liturgy of the Mass has served to express a more generalised scepticism concerning the novelties introduced by the Council. And that is also the reason why any attempt to realise 'after the fact' the dream I have just evoked, to which some people hold fast, imagining that it would be

---

[3] Constitution *Sacrosanctum Concilium*, para. 50.

[4] Cf. Klaus Gamber, *The Reform of the Roman Liturgy: Its Problems and Background*, Una Voce Press & Foundation for Catholic Reform, San Juan Capistrano & Harrison NY 1993, part II: "Facing the Lord: On the Building of Churches and Facing East in Prayer."

possible to reintegrate the reform of the Liturgy into a visible continuity with previously existing tradition, would not only rob it of all significance, but besides that would spring a fatal leak in the hull of the conciliar bark. That is demonstrated by the cries of fury aroused by the criticism with respect to this reform expressed by Cardinal Ratzinger, in his recent autobiography. Getting at the new Liturgy is necessarily getting at the Council.[5]

That same author from whom we have just quoted very modestly adds that he may be mistaken. But if we were to look at a fair number of opinions on this matter, we should find that, more or less explicitly, they incline towards one or the other of two analyses: according to the one, the liturgical reform is the bad fruit by which we can recognise the evil nature of the tree; according to the other, the reform is sound, but it has in general been misinterpreted and wrongly applied in the atmosphere of crisis at the end of the nineteen-sixties, which was not what the Council had in mind at all. In any case, one conclusion emerges: "the dissatisfaction is more or less general."[6] Thus, it seems that one can not abstract the question from its context, in any examination of the reform and its results.

3. A Context of Dissolution

The connection between the context of a general attack on society's traditional view of the world, and the liturgical reform, which is implicit in the attitudes and stances which are called "traditionalist,"[7] has in our own day been given a strange and "heterodox" explanation — if you will excuse the paradox — in the school of thought known as *Radical Orthodoxy*. Catherine Pickstock, for example, has been sufficiently lucid as to re-establish the connection which links Liturgy with philosophy, by approaching the question of truth, truth as professed and as actually experienced, whether individual or collective truth, in relation to the Liturgy. This Cambridge researcher was thus able to emphasise how "being 'modern' is characterised above all by the rejection of Liturgy," that — in practical terms — "public space in America (that

---

[5] Claude Barthe, *Reconstruire la liturgie*, Paris, 1997, pp. 4-5. The reference to the autobiography of Cardinal Ratzinger, *Milestones: Memoirs 1927-1977*, Ignatius Press, San Francisco 1998, could now be complemented with his recent book, *The Spirit of the Liturgy*, Ignatius Press, San Francisco 2000.

[6] Claude Barthe, op. cit., p. 5.

[7] I am not, in the first instance, referring to an intellectual connection. A distinguished Spanish writer has written a most illuminating passage about the doctrinal essence of traditionalism: "Stability in life creates solid commitment, full involvement in the Church, which gives birth to gentle feelings and a healthy, moral way of life. These take the concrete form of benevolent institutions, which in turn preserve and strengthen the good moral behaviour" (cf. Miguel Ayuso, *Koinós: El pensamiento político de Rafael Gambra* [Koinós: the Political Thought of Rafael Gambra], Madrid, 1998).

is, the U.S.A.) is the most a-liturgical," that "publicity and advertisement is the only form of official liturgy,"[8] etc.

This is not the point at which to draw up a balance-sheet of the inspirations, and the errors, of the exaggerations and of the omissions of this strange intellectual movement, which we shall meet again in the course of this paper. The writer is far from being in the best position to draw up a summary of its achievements. But that should be enough to show how the awareness – which we simply could not have had in the past – is spreading, from one person to another, of how it is impossible to incorporate Christianity into the culture of modern civilisation and its present-day forms, whether we are concerned with its "hard" technocratic and promethean form (which we would have to call hyper-modern), or with its "weak" deconstructionist and nihilist form (which we may quite properly call post-modern).[9]

In that sense, the privatising of faith is one of the great tendencies to be observed in this panorama of many and varied versions of being "modern" which weave in and out of one another. And it has, in any case, an important bearing upon the Liturgy.[10]

First of all, since we are now talking about the privatisation of faith, we should take note that this is more closely connected with the *Contrat social*, than with a freedom to reflect and to choose. And it is not the case, that the de-dogmatisation of Catholicism has nothing in common with the Protestant crisis of the sixteenth century (Luther transferred the Pope's function, of discerning Revelation, to each baptised person); but, with the Kantian insistence upon the independence of reason, the interpretation of Revelation is not merely being carried out by someone else, but it takes on a different meaning: that is the kind of subjectivism we may call "do-it-yourself"...

From the point of view of Liturgy, we may observe how the easy-going attitude of *laissez faire, laisser passer*, which becomes a new principle of liturgical development, overlaps with the application of this principle in the parishes, which makes anarchy into a point of principle: "All in all, we find two kinds of privatisation have taken place. On the pretext that the public worship of the Church ought to 'bring community into existence' – something most praiseworthy in itself – ritualism has been exploded, likewise the sacred language which is held to be incomprehensible, the mystery of symbols, and the succession of memories which constitute tradition. With the result that there is not only a kind of explosion into a "multi-community," but beyond that we see the self-celebration of the community by means of a rite which is

---

[8] Cf. Catherine Pickstock, *After Writing: On the Liturgical Consummation of Philosophy*, Blackwell, Oxford 1998. [It would appear that Professor Ayuso-Torres is not quoting directly here, but is referring to chapter two (pp. 47-100) of *After Writing*; Ed.]

[9] Cf. Miguel Ayuso, "*Un orden social católico, todavia?*"[A Catholic Social Order, by all means?], in *Verbo* (Madrid), no. 371/72 (1999), pp. 9ff.

[10] Cf. Claude Barthe: "*À chacun son Credo*" [To each his own creed] in *Catholica* (Paris), no. 64 (1999), pp. 19ff.

personalised as much as possible. The other aspect of liturgical privatisation, in one sense worse, is that the reaction against this fragmentation of the rite, following on from the reform of Vatican II, itself for the most part takes the form of a demand for privatisation: that people with a particular religious sensibility be allowed the freedom to practise the Liturgy which suits them! In that respect, Danièle Hervieu-Léger is right in saying that the circle of modernity encloses even anti-modern demands. It is appropriate to add, that this is because the people making these demands give in to the easy way of consenting, in order to be able to make themselves heard."[11]

4. The "Difficulties" of the Counter-Reform

These last few lines raise a new and important question, by emphasising the influence of this dissolving context, not only on the diffusion of the new Liturgy and the way it was imposed, but also on those people who believe they are standing aside from it. Yet more, they also show us some of the difficulties facing the "reform of the reform," or if you prefer to speak more clearly, the "counter-reform." Even so, it is not easy to suggest any other way than the simple retrieval of the tradition.

Let us take one example. The *Radical Orthodoxy* of which we were speaking above is seeking — and again, it is Catherine Pickstock who says it — to work out a systematic criticism of the secularist claims, with the aim of rediscovering the tradition, but without this process being simply one of nostalgia or melancholy. That is why she resolutely affirms: "Seeking simply to recover the tradition exactly as it was, taking no account of the changed circumstances of our world, would in fact be a modern and entirely secular way of doing things; we are proposing to make a 'non-identical' approach to this."[12] Nonetheless, when another distinguished representative of the same tendency, likewise a lecturer at Cambridge, the Dominican Aidan Nichols, wishes to suggest a practical response, following an interesting and serious historical survey (which is for that reason more critical of the new rite), he suggests nothing less than a return to the Tridentine rite, though with the introduction of a few reforms.[13] At a stroke, the problem of two rites reappears, but now reversed: what would become of the rite of Paul VI? And the British friar replies that its use would be tolerated in certain cases: for example, it could be used as a transitional rite for convert Protestants. He even supposes that it would continue to be used, in those parishes and religious

---

[11] Barthe, loc. cit., pp.21-22. The reference to Hervieu-Léger seems to be to his book, *Le pèlerin et le converti: La religion en mouvement*. [The Pilgrim and the Convert: Religion on the Move] Paris 1999.

[12] Catherine Pickstock: "*L'Amérique, terre profane*" a conversation with Hugues Duchamp, in *Catholica* (Paris) no. 64 (1999), p. 35.

[13] Cf. Aidan Nichols OP, *Looking at the Liturgy: A Critical View of its Contemporary Form*, Ignatius, San Francisco 1996.

*Left, the Abbot of Fontgombault,
Dom Antoine Forgeot opening the
conference.*

*Below, Cardinal Joseph Ratzinger
during a lecture.*

Below, the intervention by Msgr Léonard, Bishop of Namur.

Abbot Clément

Dom Cassian Folsom OSB

Dom Daniel Field, OSB
monk of N.D. de Randol

Canon Rose

Above, Professor Robert Spaemann

Above, Dom Charbel Pazat de Lys OSB, monk of Barroux

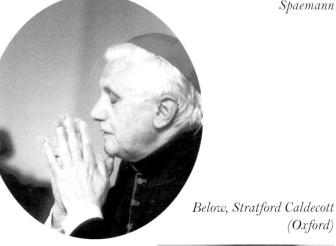

Below, Professor Miguel Ayuso-Torres (Madrid)

Below, Stratford Caldecott (Oxford)

Right, an intervention by Father Bonino, OP (Toulouse)

Below, the Abbot of Triors, Dom Hervé Courau, chairing the discussions.

Above, the Cardinal with Msgr Aumonier, Bishop of Versailles.

Above, the Conference Hall during the intervention of Professor Spaemann

*Right, facing,
Dom Gérard Calvet,
Abbot de Barroux*

*Right,
the Abbots of
Kerganon and de
Randol*

Above, Msgr Léonard, Cardinal Ratzinger and the Abbot of Triors, Dom Hervé Courau

Below, left-right, Philippe Maxence (Homme Nouveau), Christophe Geffroy (La Nef) and Loïc Mérian (CIEL)

Above, Professor Roberto de Mattei (Rome)

Right, Professor Miguel Ayuso-Torres

Right, the Cardinal in the company of Father Koster (AED)

Below, Msgr Clemens, secretary to the Cardinal

Below, Canon Rose and Professor Spaemann

Left, the Cardinal and Msgr Camille Perl (Ecclesia Dei commision)

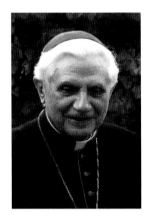

Above, the Cardinal during
his closing speech

Above, Professor Roberto
de Mattei (Rome)

Right, the Cardinal giving his blessing
at the close of the conference

communities of the Latin Church who would not wish to recover the historical and spiritual heritage of the Latin rite in its full, undiluted form. As has been remarked, not without a certain irony, Father Nichols does not envisage, in his hypothesis, that those faithful and priests who might remain sentimentally attached to the Mass of Paul VI would have to ask permission of their bishop, nor to celebrate it in chapels and at times determined by him, since he assumes that this concession will be applied in a broad and generous fashion.[14]

Translated by Henry Taylor

---

[14] Cf. Claude Barthe, *"Liturgie réformée ou liturgie traditionnelle: Difficulté des justifications respectives"* in *Catholica* (Paris), no. 61 (1998), pp. 26ff.

Reflections on the Liturgical Reform

Intervention of Professor Roberto de Mattei[1]

MY paper, as you can well imagine, will not be that of a liturgist nor of a theologian, but that of a man of culture, of an historian, of a Catholic layman who is trying to locate the problems of the Church within the horizon of his own time.

From this perspective, I propose to follow-up certain reflections about the cultural and historical roots of the post-conciliar liturgical reform. I am in fact convinced that the clearer our picture of this, the easier it will be to understand and to resolve the complex problems before us.

To grasp the crux of any problem, and the Liturgy is no exception here, it has to be seen in a wider context. Anyone wishing to study gothic architecture, for example, could not afford to neglect its connection with mediaeval scholasticism, so brilliantly illustrated by Erwin Panofski,[2] just as if you wish to understand the figurative art of the nineteenth and twentieth centuries, you would have to consult the studies by Hans Siedelmayr,[3] which set down their deeper ideological dimension.

I am trying to say that, just as a talk about art should go beyond the art, not contenting itself with a technical and aesthetic verdict, equally a talk about the Liturgy should go beyond the Liturgy itself, looking for its ultimate significance.

---

[1] Professor Roberto de Mattei holds the chair of Modern History in the Faculty of Letters and Philosophy of the University of Cassino, where he teaches. He founded the *Lepanto Cultural Centre at Rome* in 1982, which he continues to direct, the aim of which is the defence of the principles and institutions of Christian civilisation. In 1997 he founded the *Institut Européen de Recherches, Études et Formation*, at Brussels which publishes the French language current affairs report *Correspondance européenne*. Amongst his most recent books are a biography of Blessed Pius IX (Piemme, 2000) which has been translated into Portuguese with a preface by Cardinal Saraiva Martins, Prefect of the Congregation for the Causes of Saints, and a book about Necessary Sovereignty, published in France by Xavier de Guibert and in Italy by le Minotauro (2001).

[2] Erwin Panowski, *Architecture gothique et pensée scolastique* [Gothic Architecture and Scholastic Thought], French trans. and afterword by Pierre Bordieu, Éditions de Minuit, Paris 1967.

[3] Hans Siedselmayr, *Perdita del centro: Le arti figurative del XIX e XX secolo come sintomo e simbolo di un'epoca* [Losing the Centre: Nineteenth and Twentieth Century Figurative Art as Symptom and Symbol of an Age], (Italian trans.) Borla, Turin 1967.

The Liturgy, in any case, is not just the whole collection of rules which govern its rituals. These rituals, in all their variety, refer us to the unity of a faith. Without this content, Christian worship would be an external activity, empty and valueless, not a sacred but a "magical" activity, as is typical for some gnostic or pantheist views of the world. In that sense it has been well said that "...worship, seen in its true breadth and depth, goes beyond the action of the Liturgy."[4]

In its wording, in its rituals, in its symbols, the Catholic Liturgy should reflect the dogma. The dogma, it has been said, is for the Liturgy what the soul is for the body, the thought for the words.[5] The relationship between Liturgy and belief should therefore be made intimate and profound, as traditionally expressed in the saying, *lex orandi, lex credendi*.[6] We may find in this axiom a key to understanding the present crisis.

1. The Axiom: "Lex orandi, lex credendi" in the Theology of the Twentieth Century.

At the beginning of the twentieth century, the Modernist theologians reinterpreted the axiom *lex orandi, lex credendi* in accordance with their own categories of thought, which were influenced by the ideologies then dominant, and hence drew upon an evolutionism which was the matrix for ideas which were both positivist and irrationalist.

George Tyrell in particular, who is considered by Ernesto Bonaiuti as the person "most deeply filled with faith and enthusiasm for the Modernist cause,"[7] identified revelation with direct experience ("religious experience"), which has its place in each individual's consciousness. It was thus the *lex orandi* which ought to dictate the norms for the *lex credendi*, and not vice versa, seeing that "the Credo is implicitly comprehended in prayer, and should be

---

[4] Joseph Ratzinger, *The Spirit of the Liturgy*, Ignatius Press, San Francisco 2000, p. 20. This recent book by Cardinal Ratzinger should be read together with *The Feast of Faith: Approaches to a Theology of the Liturgy*, Ignatius Press, San Francisco 1986.

[5] Mgr. Mario Righetti, *Manuale di storia liturgica*, Editrice Ancora, Milan 1964, vol. I, p. 30. The Congregation for the Doctrine of the Faith has recently reaffirmed that "Defined teaching has compulsive force for all Liturgy, for interpretation, and for new forms of Liturgy" from 'Notification concerning certain publications of Professor Dr. Reinhard Meßner,' Rome December 2000.

[6] This aphorism, also expressed in the formula *legem credendi statuat lex supplicandi*, is taken from the *Capitula Celestini* of 431, which should perhaps be attributed not to Pope Celestine I, but to Prosper of Aquitaine (cf. MPL 50, 535; and now in Heinrich Denzinger, *Enchiridion Symbolorum*, re-edited by Peter Huenemann, EDB, Bologna 1995, no. 246). Paul De Clerck, in his '*Lex orandi, lex credendi:' Sens originel et avatars historiques d'un adage équivoque*, [The Original Meaning and the Historical Manifestations of an Equivocal Saying] in *Questions liturgiques* no. 4 (Sept.-Dec. 1978), tries to make the meaning of this adage even more equivocal than it actually is.

[7] Ernesto Bonaiuti, *Storia del Cristianismo*, Dall'Oglio, Milan 1943, vol. III, p. 652.

very carefully extricated from it; and every formulation should be tested and explicated by the religious practice which it is formulating."[8]

The history of Modernism after its condemnation still needs to be written; but it is certain that several of these attitudes worked their way into the "Liturgical Movement,"[9] to such an extent that Pius XII found himself obliged to intervene, with his substantial encyclical *Mediator Dei*, of the 20th November 1947, to correct the errors concerned.

The pope condemned, in particular, "the error and fallacious reasoning of those who have claimed that the Sacred Liturgy is a kind of proving ground for the truths to be held of faith," basing their claim on a mistaken understanding of the adage *lex orandi, lex credendi*. "But this is not," affirms Pius XII, "what the Church teaches and enjoins...if one desires to differentiate and describe the relationship between faith and the Sacred Liturgy in absolute and general terms, it is perfectly correct to say...let the rule of belief determine the rule of prayer."[10]

Pius XII thus reaffirms the primacy of faith as an objective entity over the Liturgy insofar as it is understood as subjective "religious experience," in opposition to those who seemed to be pointing to "liturgical practice" as the new norm for the Catholic faith.

After the Constitution *Sacrosanctum Concilium* of the 4th December 1963,[11] the liturgical reform which was undertaken by Paul VI as an application of the conciliar decrees, which resulted in the Apostolic Constitution *Missale Romanum*, of the 3rd April 1969,[12] once more brought to

---

[8] George Tyrell, *Through Scylla and Charydbis*, London (Green & Co.) 1907, p. 104. The problem of the relationship between dogma and practice constitutes the *leitmotiv* for the entire Modernist movement. Cf. for example Rudolf Michael Schmitz, *Dogma und Praxis: Der Dogmenbegriff des Modernisten Edouard Le Roy kritisch dargestellt*, Libreria Editrice Vaticana 1993.

[9] Concerning the Liturgical Movement, see the overall synthesis in the article by Burkhard Neunheuser OSB, in the *Nuovo dizionario di liturgia*, edited by Domenico Sartore and Achille Maria Triacca, San Paulo, Roma 2001, pp. 1279-1293; and, for a critical attitude, Didier Bonneterre, *The Liturgical Movement*, Angelus Press, Kansas City 2002.

[10] *Mediator Dei*, Part I.

[11] The Constitution on the Sacred Liturgy, *Sacrosanctum Concilium*, 4th December 1963, in *A Pope and a Council on the Sacred Liturgy*, St Michael's Abbey Press, Farnborough 2002. Cf. Manlio Sodi, *Vent'anni di studi e commenti sulla "Sacrosanctum Concilium"* [Twenty years of study and comment on *Sacrosanctum Concilium*], in the edition provided by the Congregation for Divine Worship: *Constituzione liturgica "Sacrosanctum Concilium:" Studi*, (BELS 38) Rome 1986. "There is just a little crack," says don Gianni Baget Bozzo, "between the last great encyclical of Pius XII, and *Sacrosanctum Concilium*. Through this crack crept in the self-destruction of the Church; that was the way that the 'smoke of Satan in the Temple of God,' to which Paul VI referred in a moment of the fullness of papal charism, came in;" in *L'anticristo*, Mondadori, Milan 2001, p. 51.

[12] The Congregation for Divine Worship, *Missale romanum ex decreto sacrosancti Œcumenici Concilii Vatican II instauratum auctoritate Pauli PP VI promulgatum*, Vatican City 1970, 1975.

light the problem of the relationship between the *lex orandi* and the *lex credendi*.[13]

The first and most influential critics of the liturgical reform, Cardinals Ottaviani and Bacci, when they presented a *Brief Critical Examination of the Novus Ordo Missæ*,[14] defined the new rite as "an impressive distancing from the Catholic theology of the Holy Mass, as it was formulated in the Twentieth Session of the Council of Trent." That session, as we have seen, had defined the Mass as a truly propitiatory sacrifice, in which "Jesus Christ himself is present and is sacrificed in unbloody fashion."[15] The criticisms of Cardinals Ottaviani and Bacci, and of other authors following them,[16] emphasised how the new *lex orandi* of Paul VI did not, on this point, reflect in an adequate

[13] The memoirs of Mgr. Annibale Bugnini (1912-1982), *La riforma liturgica (1948-1975)*, new ed. Rome (Edizioni Liturgiche) 1997 [ET of the first Italian Edition: *The Reform of the Liturgy 1948-1975*, Liturgical Press, Collegeville 1990], and of Cardinal Ferdinando Antonelli (1896-1993), ed. Nicola Giampietro OFM Cap., *Il Cardinale Ferdinando Antonelli e gli sdviluppi della riforma liturgica dal 1948 al 1970* [Cardinal Ferdinando Antonelli and the Development of the Liturgical Reform from 1948 to 1970] (*Analecta Liturgica* 21), Pontificio Ateneo Sant'Anselmo, Rome 1998, are of great importance, on account of their responsibilities in the *Consilium ex Exsequendam Constitutionem de Sacra Liturgia*, and in the Sacred Congregation for Divine Worship. See also Emil Joseph Lengeling, *Liturgie-Reform 1948-1975: Zu einem aufschlussreichen Rechenschaftsbericht* [Liturgical Reform 1948-1975: an Informative Report], in Theologische Revue 80 (1984), pp. 265-284.

[14] This study, sponsored by "Una Voce–Italia," has been republished by the same association, together with a *New Critical Examination of the Novus Ordo Missæ*, which is the work of a French liturgist and theologian (*Il Novus Ordo Missæ: due esamine critici*, "Una Voce," supplement to nos. 48-49 of their bulletin, January-July 1979). ET: *The Ottaviani Intervention: Short Critical Study of the New Order of Mass*, Tan, Rockford 1992.

[15] Cf. Concilium Tridentinum, Sessio XXII, 17th Sept. 1562, *Doctrina et canones de ss. Missæ sacrificio*, in Denzinger-Huenemann, nos. 1738-1759. "Si quis dixerit, Missæ sacrificium tantum esse laudis et gratiarum actis, aut nudem commemorationem sacrificii in cruce peracti, non autem propitiatorium; vel soli prodesse sumenti; neque pro vivis et defunctis, pro peccatis, pœnis, satisfactionibus et aliis necessitatibus offerri debere: anathema sit" (no. 1753, cap. 9, canon 3).

[16] The fundamental critical works are those of Louis Salleron, *La Nouvelle Messe*, Paris (Nouvelles Éditions Latines) 1970, 2nd ed., revised with additions, Paris 1981; Arnaldo Xavier da Silveira, *La nouvelle Messe de Paul VI: Qu'en penser?* [Paul VI's New Mass: what should we think of it?] Chiré-en-Montreuil (Diffusion de la Pensée Française) 1975; Michael Davies, *Pope Paul's new Mass*, Angelus Press Dickinson, Texas 1980; Klaus Gamber, *The Reform of the Roman Liturgy: Its Problems and Background*, Una Voce Press & Foundation for Catholic Reform, San Juan Capistrano & Harrison NY 1993. See also the volumes of the reports of colloquia and studies of historical, theological and canonical aspects of the Roman Catholic rite, sponsored by the *Centre International d'Études Liturgiques* (CIEL); Christophe Geoffroy/Philippe Maxence, *Enquête sur la Messe traditionelle, 1988-1998* on the tenth anniversary of the Motu Proprio *Ecclesia Dei*, La Nef 1998; Franz Breid, ed., *Die heilige Liturgie*, papers from the "Internationale Theologische Sommerakademie 1997" of the Priests' Circle of Linz, Ennsthaler Verlag, Steyr 1997. This volume includes significant contributions from Cardinal Alfons Maria Stickler and from Leo Scheffczyk, Robert Spaemann, Egon Kapellari, Wolfgang Waldstein, Erwin Keller, Brian W. Harrison, Robert Prantner, Anton Ziegenaus, Gerhard Wagner.

fashion the traditional *lex credendi* of the Church.[17] A discussion then started, which has not yet been concluded, which led to individual crises of conscience and splits within the Church. The *Novus Ordo Missæ*, which came into being, as well as for other reasons, as a concrete form of liturgical encounter with non-Catholics, finished by producing, on the contrary, a period of liturgical disunity amongst Catholics.

The basic thesis which I am going to try to expound amounts to this: the *lex credendi* — *lex orandi* relationship, which is implicit in the liturgical reform, should be viewed in the light of the new theology which prepared the way for the Second Vatican Council, and which above all tried to give direction to what developed from it. In this sense, the *lex credendi* expressed by the *Novus Ordo* appears as a revision of the Catholic faith by refraction through the anthropological and secularist "turn" of the new theology; a theology, it must be emphasised, which not merely re-presents the themes of Modernism, but appropriates these themes in a marxist sense, that is to say, by way of a system of thought which offers itself as a radical "philosophy of practice."

That means that an overall verdict on the reform, above all thirty years afterwards, can not be limited to a technical analysis of the new rite promulgated by Paul VI, but ought necessarily to be extended to the "liturgical practice" which followed on its being instituted.[18] The liturgical reform today can no longer be considered as a static entity, in its foundational documents, but should be seen in its dynamic aspect, paying attention to a multiplicity of factors which, although they were not foreseen in the *Novus Ordo*, have become part and parcel of what one could describe as the liturgical *praxis* of the present day.

---

[17] The Apostolic Constitution *Missale Romanum* was made up of two documents: a presentation of the new rite (*Institutio Generalis*), and the *Ordo Missæ* properly speaking. The criticisms of Cardinals Ottaviani and Bacci, and others which were added to theirs, resulted in the *editio typica* of the Roman Missal, promulgated on March 26th 1970, having been modified at certain points, and especially that the definition of the Mass offered by article 7 of the *Institutio* ("A Holy Synaxis or gathering of the people of God, which has come together to celebrate, under the presidency of the priest, the memorial of the Lord") was changed. People noted however that although the presentation of the new rite had been corrected, the rite itself remained the same in its structure and was thus full of the ambiguities outlined by the *Institutio*.

[18] The main limitation of a recent study circulated by the Priestly Fraternity of Saint Pius X, in which the doctrinal principle of the new Liturgy is discerned as being the new "theology of the Paschal Mystery," is the deliberate refusal to consider the "praxis" of the Church over the last thirty years: cf. The Society of Saint Pius X, *The Problem of the Liturgical Reform*, Angelus Press, Kansas City 2001.

2. The Secularisation of the Liturgy

The Mass, which is the sacred action *par excellence*,[19] has always been governed by a rite, that is to say, by its *ordo*, in the words of Saint Augustine: *"totum agendi ordinem, quem universa per orbem servat Ecclesia."* [20] The essence of the Sacrament, which remained valid[21] and retained its entire efficacity, did not change with the liturgical reform, but—to use the expression of Cardinal Ratzinger[22]—a rite was "manufactured" *ex novo*.

The rite, the classic definition of which was first given by Servio (*Mos institutus religiosis cæremoniis consecratus*[23]), is not in fact the sacred action itself, but the norm which guides the way in which this action is performed. It may be defined as the entirety of the formulations and the practical norms which have to be observed in the accomplishing of a given liturgical function, even if sometimes the term has a wider meaning, and means a family of rites (Roman, Greek, Ambrosian). That is why the sacraments are unchangeable in their essence, whereas the rites can change according to people and epoch.

In theory, the *Novus Ordo* of Paul VI establishes a whole collection of Norms and prayers which governed the celebration of the Holy Sacrifice of the Mass in place of the old Roman rite; in fact, the liturgical practice showed us that we were faced with a new and protean, many-formed rite. In the course of the reform, a whole series of novelties and variants were in fact introduced, a certain number of which had been foreseen neither by the Council, nor by Paul VI's Constitution *Missale Romanum*.

The *quid novum* certainly did not consist merely in the substitution of vernacular languages for the Latin used in worship; but in the altar being conceived as being a "table," so as to emphasise the aspect of the feast, in place of that of sacrifice; in the *celebratio versus populum* being substituted for that *versus Deum*—with, as a consequence, the abandonment of celebrating facing East, that is, towards Christ as symbolised by the rising sun; in the absence of silence and recollection during the ceremony, and in the theatrical

---

[19] See for example H. Leclercq's article *Messe*, in the *Dictionnaire d'Archéologie chrétienne et de Liturgie*, Letouzey et Ané, Paris 1933, vol. XI, cols. 513-774; and the synthesis of Mgr. Antonio Piolanti, *Teologia sacramentaria*, Librertia Editrice Vaticana 1997, pp. 210-230.

[20] See for example St Augustine, *Epistula* 54, 68.

[21] That was the position taken by Mgr. Lefèbvre. See *Mgr. Lefèbvre et le Saint Office*, in *Itinéraires* no. 233 (1979), p. 146. The position of Fr. M.L. Guérard des Lauriers OP, one of the theologians who had contributed to the *Brief Critical Examination*, remained isolated. He had finished up by asserting the invalidity of this rite, and the illegitimacy of the authorities which had sponsored it (cf. *Le Siège Apostolique est-il vacant?* (lex orandi, lex credendi), in *Cahiers de Cassiciacum*, no. 1 (1979), pp. 5-99).

[22] "In the place of the Liturgy as the fruit of organic development came fabricated liturgy;" Cardinal Joseph Ratzinger, *Klaus Gamber, l'intrépidité d'un vrai témoin* [Klaus Gamber: the Boldness of a True Witness], introduction to *La réforme liturgique en question*, Éditions Sainte-Madeleine, Le Barroux 1992, p. 8.

[23] Servius, *Commentary on the Aeneid*, 12, 836a.

quality of the celebration, often accompanied by songs which tended to desacralise the Mass, with the priest often being reduced to being the "president of the assembly;" in the exaggerated development of the Liturgy of the Word, as against the eucharistic Liturgy; in the "sign" of the Peace, which replaced the genuflections made by priest and faithful, as an action symbolising the change from the vertical to the horizontal dimension in the liturgical action; in Communion being received by the faithful standing, and in the hand; in women being allowed to approach the altar; in concelebration, which tended towards the "collectivisation" of the rite. Finally, and above all, it consists in the changing and replacing of the Offertory prayers and of the Canon. The elimination of the words *Mysterium Fidei* from the words of consecration, in particular, can be considered, as Cardinal Stickler has remarked, as a symbol of the demythologising, and thus of the humanising, of the central core of the Holy Mass.[24]

The consistent strand running through all these innovations may be expressed as the theory according to which, if we wish to make faith in Jesus Christ accessible to present-day man, then we must live this faith, and present it, within modern thought and the modern mentality. The traditional Liturgy, it is held, by its incapacity to be adapted to the mentality of the present day, estranges man from God, and thus becomes responsible for the loss of God in our society. The reform was meant to adapt the rite, without affecting the essence of the Sacrament, so as to make it possible for the Christian community to "share in what is holy" in this way, which was unable to be achieved by means of the traditional Liturgy.

Through the principle of *participatio actuosa*, the community as a whole becomes the agent in the Liturgy, and carries the action forward. "The expression of 'full, active, and conscious participation,' which so modestly makes its appearance, reveals an unexpected background,"[24] as Father

---

[24] "That is also why the removal of the *Mysterium fidei* from the form of consecration becomes the symbol of the demythologising, and thereby the humanising, of the central element of worship in the Holy Mass;" (Cardinal Alfons Stickler, *Erinnerungen und Erfahrungen eines Konzilperitus der Liturgiekommission* [Recollections and Experiences of an Advisor to the Council in the Commission for the Liturgy], in *Die heilige Liturgie*, op. cit., p. 176). Cardinal Stickler recalls that the *Sacramentarium Gelasianum*, that is to say the oldest Missal of the Roman Church, clearly contains in the original text (in the *Codex Vaticanus Reg. Lat. 316*, folio 181 verso) the *mysterium fidei* (op. cit., p. 174). It is in any case Saint Thomas himself who affirms that these words derive from the apostolic tradition (*Summa Theologica*, III, qu. 78, art. 3).

[24] "Es muß doch wundern, daß die Kritiker der Liturgiereform noch nicht darauf hingewiesen haben, wie sehr das Liturgieprüfende Kriterium der 'Teilnahme' jenen Vorgang in der Liturgie einführt, der in der Theologie als die 'anthropologische Wende' markiert wurde, die aber auch wieder nur der Ausdruck einer Wende im neuzeitlichen Bewußtsein vom Bereich des Göttlichen weg zum Lebensraum des Menschen hin darstellt, von der numinosen 'kosmichen dimension' zur entsakralisierten 'gesellschaftlichen Wirklichkeit'. Die Liturgiereform des Zweiten Vatikanischen Konzils nimmt damit einen tiefgreifenden Paradigmenwechsel der Neuzeit auf und versucht, ihm gerecht zu werden.

Angelus Häussling observes, underlining the relation between the *participatio actuosa* of the liturgical reform and what, following the example of Karl Rahner, has been called the "anthropological turnaround" (*anthropologische Wende*) of theology.[25]

It does not seem exaggerated to assert that the *participatio actuosa* of the community seems to be the ultimate and basic criterion for the liturgical reform, within the perspective of a radical secularisation of the Liturgy.[26] Such a process of secularisation includes the extinction of sacrifice, the sacred action *par excellence*, for which is substituted the profane activity of the community which glorifies itself, or — to use the words of Hans Urs von Balthasar — is inclined to respond to the praise of the grace of God with a purely human "counter-glory."[27]

The agent here is not so much the priest *in persona Christi*, that is, God himself, as the community of the faithful, *in persona hominis*, so as to represent the exigencies of that modern world which a disciple of Rahner defined as "as if holy and sanctified in its profanity, that is, holy in an anonymous form."[28]

Das so bescheiden daherkommende Wort von der 'tätigen, vollen und bewussten Teilnahme' legt einen unerwarteten Hintergrund frei" (Angrelus A. Häußling OSB, 'Liturgiereform. *Materialen zu einem neuen Thema der Liturgiewissenschaft*', in *Archiv für Liturgiewissenschaft*, XXXI (1989), pp. 1-32; p. 29) [It must surprise us that the critics of the liturgical reform have not yet pointed to the great extent to which the criterion of 'participation' for judging liturgy introduces into the Liturgy the same process which was singled-out in Theology as marking the 'anthropological turnaround,' but which in its turn merely represents the expression of a turning-around of modern consciousness, away from the sphere of the divine and towards the sphere of human life, away from the numinous 'cosmic dimension' and towards the de-sacralised 'social reality.' The liturgical reform of the Second Vatican Council is thereby taking up a far-reaching modern change in the model of reality, and attempting to live up to it. The expression of 'full, active, and conscious participation,' which so modestly makes its appearance, reveals an unexpected background.]

[25] Amongst the many works of Karl Rahner, see in particular the study on the nature of the Liturgy, published in the fourteenth volume of his *Shriften zur Theologie* in 1980: Italian trans. *Sulla teologia del culto divino*, in *Sollecitudine per la Chiesa*, nuovi saggi, VIII, Edizione Paoline, Roma 1982, pp. 271-283. For a criticism of this, see the fundamental studies of Fr. Cornelio Fabro, *La svolta antropologica di Karl Rahner* [Karl Rahner's Anthropological Turnaround] Rusconi, Milan 1974, and *L'avventura della teologia progressista* [The Gamble of Progressive Theology], Rusconi, Milan 1974.

[26] Cf. Michael Kunzler, *La liturgia all'inizio del terzo millennio*, in *Il Concilio Vaticano II: Recezione e attualità alla luce del Giubileo*, Rino Fisichella, ed., San Paolo, Cinisello Balsamo, Rome 2000, pp. 217-231.

[27] Hans Urs von Balthasar, "The Grandeur of the Liturgy," in *Communio* vol. V no. 4 (1978), pp. 344-351.

[28] Cf. Luis de Maldonado, (Italian trans.) *Secolarizzazione della liturgia*, Edizioni Paoline, Rome 1972, p. 473. "L'uomo è un 'essere del mondo', un 'essere mondano;' e così lo ha voluto e redento Dio. Questa è la radice ultima della secolarità e del suo valore teologico" [Man is a "being of the world", a "profane being", that is how God willed him to be, and how God saved him. This is the ultimate reason for secularity, and for its theological value.] (ibid., p. 478).

To a "divine Word, sacral and multi-secular." the consequence of which is "a sacralised Liturgy, separated from life,"[29] a Word of God is opposed which "is not pure revelation, but also action; realising in practice what it signifies;" this is "the absolute self-realisation of the Church."[30]

The distinction suggested by Rahner, between "secularisation" which should be positively received, as being an inevitable phenomenon, and anti-Christian "secularism," which would in his view constitute a deviant form of secularisation, is clearly specious. For all that it has a number of differing meanings,[31] the word secularisation is nonetheless generally understood, in the same way as secularism, as an irreversible process of "mondanisation," of reality's "becoming worldly," as it has progressively freed itself from having any transcendental or metaphysical aspect.

Secularisation offers itself in fact not merely as the *de facto* acceptance of an ever-greater secularisation of the present-day world, but as the idea that this process is irreversible and, inasmuch as it is irreversible, true. Secularisation is "true" because truth is, come what may, immanent in history; the sacred is "false" on account of its illusion of transcending history and of affirming a qualitative distinction between faith and the world, between what is transcendent and what is transcendental. Faith in the power of history thus takes the place of faith in the providence and the power of God.

This philosophy of history is based on the myth, characteristic of Enlightenment thought, of the world which is becoming "adult," and which has to free itself from the values of the past, which belong to the childhood of humanity, to as to attain to a fully rational level of existence. This kind of vision has been rigorously expressed in Protestant thought, especially in the theory of Bonhoeffer about the so-called "maturity of the world" (*Mündigkeit der Welt*),[32] a maturity which is attained through the expulsion from life of the sacred, in all its dimensions. Yet this idea of "maturity" has been carried to its final degree of coherence by Gramsci's version of marxism, which represents the most coherent development, in the twentieth century, of Enlightenment thought, and represents the point at which secularism becomes a radical immanentism. Progressive theology, especially since the Council, has tried to replace traditional philosophy with "modern" philosophy, inevitably subordinating itself to marxism, which appeared to the progressive tendency in Catholicism as the first system of thought which had transferred its

---

[29] Maldonado, op. cit., p. 478.

[30] Ibid., op. cit., pp. 474-475.

[31] Amongst the many texts on secularisation, see Augusto Del Noce, *L'epoca della secolarizzazione*, Giuffré, Milan 1970; Émile Poulat, *Chiesa contro borghesia: Introduzione al divenire del cattolicesimo contemporaneo*, (Italian trans.) Casale Monferrato (Marietti) 1984, pp. 227-254; Massimo Introvigne, *Il sacro postmoderno: Chiesa, relativismo e nuova religiosità*, Gribaudi, Milan 1996; René Rémond, *La secolarizzazione: Religione e società nell'Europa contemporanea* (Italian trans.) Laterza, Rome/Bari 1999.

[32] See especially Dietrich Bonhoeffer, *Letters and Papers from Prison*, SCM, London 1971.

criterion of truth into the realm of practice, and which — in the success of its practice — seemed to be demonstrating the truth of its thought.[33]

We have noticed the affinity between the vision of Tyrell, based on the primacy of *lex orandi* over *lex credendi*, and Karl Rahner's concept of the "self-realisation" of the Church in its pastoral and liturgical activities.[34] But the things the first modernism was seeking were however developed by progressive Theology within a horizon of thought which was not simply positivist, but marxist. This was because within this horizon there was united to the ultimate result a process which was judged necessary: a process whose roots plunged into Enlightenment philosophy and into Protestantism, and more distantly, into the intellectual movement which brought about the end of mediaeval society.[35] "The philosophy of *praxis*" — according to Gramsci — "is the crowning achievement of this whole movement of intellectual and moral reform;...it corresponds to the nexus of Protestant Reform + French Revolution."[36]

Gramsci's philosophy of praxis, rewritten in theological terms, leads to the requirement for a new *praxis orandi*. The liturgical reform thus appears as the Word of a new theology making itself flesh, that is to say, practice, "self-realising" the Church through the medium of the new secularised Liturgy.

---

[33] We can not omit the reference to Marx's *Theses on Feuerbach*, as interpreted by Gramsci. Augusto Del Noce is the thinker who has made the most profound analysis of this fundamental aspect of Marxism (see his *I caratteri generali del pensiero politico contemporaneo. Lezioni sul marxismo*, Giuffré, Milan 1972, pp. 38-64).

[34] "Sembra che Rahner abbia voluto accettare la sfida di Tyrell quando questi diceva che il suo compito, pienamente realizzato, è stato quello di formulare una domanda alla quale altri avrebbero potuto dare una risposta, visto che egli non ne era stato capace" [It seems that Rahner had wanted to accept Tyrell's challenge, when the latter said that his task, which he had fully realised, had been that of formulating a demand to which others would have been able to make a response, seeing that he had not been able to do that]; Stefano Visintin, OSB, *Rivelazione divina ed esperienza umana: La proposta di George Tyrell e la risposta di Karl Rahner* [Divine Revelation and Human Experience: George Tyrell's proposition and Karl Rahner's response], thesis for a doctorate in Theology, Rome (Peter Lang) 1999, p. 251.

[35] By widening the historical context, it can easily be seen how the principle by which faith is measured not according to the doctrine which is believed, but in "life," and in the actions of the believer, had already been clearly formulated by Anabaptism and the radical sects in the Protestant reformation (cf. R. de Mattei, *A sinstra de Lutero: Sette e movimenti religiosi nell'Europa del '500'* [To the Left of Luther: Religious Sects and Movements in Fifteenth Century Europe], Città Nuova, Rome 2001, pp. 105-125). Even a Protestant scholar like Vittorio Subilia has remarked that, long before Karl Marx declared that "Man must demonstrate the truth in his practical actions," and the theologians of revolution and of liberation elevated practice to be the necessary premise and the interpretative norm of the Gospel, "The Pietist J.K. Dippel (1673-1743) rejected the entire dogmatic system of Christianity, by setting orthopraxy against orthodoxy" (*Solus Christus*, Claudiana, Turin 1985, p. 55).

[36] Antonio Gramsci, *Quaderni dal carcere*, edited Valentino Gerratana, Einaudi, Turin 1975, vol. III, p. 1860; ET: *Prison Notebooks*, 2 vols., Columbia University Press, 1992 & 1996.

3. New Liturgy and Post-Modernity

The problem, as we have been able to see, goes far beyond the Liturgy itself: it involves a judgement on the whole area of the relations between the Church and modern civilisation; it refers us to the need for a theology of history. Above all, it can not be resolved in the abstract, but has to take account of what has happened in the Church in the last thirty years.

It is through the liturgical reform that the secularist theology has been looking for the confirmation of its own truth in practice; the truth which has sprung from this practice has not been the bringing together of Church and world, but on the contrary an increasing alienation of the Church from the world, culminating in the crisis of faith which is nowadays recognised by everyone.

The new theology has been seeking an encounter with the modern world, right on the eve of the *débacle* of that world.[37] In 1989, in fact, along with the so-called "real socialism," all the myths of modernity and of the irreversibility of history which represented the fundamental postulates of secularism and of the "anthropological turnaround" have collapsed. The paradigm of modernity has been followed today by that of post-modernity, of "chaos" or of "complexity," the basis of which is the negation of the principle of identity/causality in all aspects of reality.[38] The new theology, which is subordinating itself to this post-modernist cultural project, has in view the "deconstruction" of everything which it had itself "manufactured" in the past thirty years, starting with a liturgical reform which nowadays is reckoned to have been constructed according to an abstract and "bureaucratic" model. As against the "modern monocultural" scheme of the new *Ordo Missæ*, is thus set the post-modern "inculturation" of the Liturgy, which is left to the "creativity" of the local Churches.[39] This distancing from the Roman Liturgy has been described by Anscar J. Chupungo in terms of the phases of "acculturation," of "inculturation," and of "liturgical creativity," passing through a dynamic process which, from the point *a quo* of the traditional Roman rite, arrives, as the point *ad quem*, at "values, rituals and traditions" which belong to the local Church.[40]

---

[37] On the *débacle* of the twentieth century, see for example Robert Conquest, *Reflections on a Ravaged Century*, W.W. Norton, New York 2001.

[38] For a critical exposition of this thought, see R. de Mattei, *De l'utopie du progrès au règne du chaos* [From the Progressive Utopia to the Reign of Chaos], L'Age d'Homme, Lausanne 1993. For a apologetic presentation of this theory, see for example Fritjof Capra, *Le temps du changemènt*, Éditions du Rocher, Monaco 1983; H.P. Prandstaller, *L'uomo senza certezze e le sue qualità* [The Man with No Certainties and his Characteristics], Laterza, Rome/Bari 1991.

[39] See for example Gerard M. Lukken, *Inculturation de la liturgie: Théorie et pratique*, in *Questions liturgiques* 77 (1996) 1-2, pp. 10-39.

[40] Ascar J. Chupungo OSB, *Liturgies of the Future*, Paulist Press, Mawah 1989, pp. 23-4. Chupungo defines liturgical acculturation as "the interaction between the Roman Liturgy and the local culture;" inculturation "as the process through which the texts and customary

Within this horizon of "liturgical tribalism" there could equally be contemplated the creation of a traditionalist "ghetto," canonically recognised, and understood as the "local Church" of those who wish to remain inculturated in the past. Yet this post-modern "multi-ritualism" has nothing to do with the plurality of rites traditionally acceptable to the Church within the unity of the same faith and of a single *lex credendi*, of which the various rites are the expression. Today, the fragmentation of rites threatens to result in a parcelling-out of theological and ecclesiological visions, which are bound to come into conflict with each other. The liturgical chaos appears as the reflection of the institutional disorder which people want to introduce into the Church so as to transform its divine constitution.

How can I do otherwise than share with you these words of Cardinal Ratzinger?

> What we previously knew only in theory has become for us a practical experience: the Church stands and falls with the Liturgy. When the adoration of the divine Trinity declines, when the faith no longer appears in its fullness in the Liturgy of the Church, when man's words, his thoughts, his intentions are suffocating him, then faith will have lost the place where it is expressed and where it dwells. For that reason, the true celebration of the Sacred Liturgy is the centre of any renewal of the Church whatever.[41]

4. Suggested Solutions

From these considerations which I have expounded, there are some conclusions of a practical nature to be drawn, which I venture to put forward in a spirit of love for the Church and for truth.

1) From the point of view of Catholics faithful to Tradition, both priests and lay people, the solution to any problem, in the short term, is to be sought in my opinion within two "invariables:" on the one hand, the "traditionalist" faithful must recognise, not only in theory, but also in all its practical consequences, the fullness of jurisdiction appertaining to ecclesiastical authority from its legitimacy. On the other hand, it is clear that ecclesiastical authority can not legitimately demand of priests and faithful any positive

---

rites of the worship of the local Church are inserted into the framework of the culture, in such a way as to absorb the thought, the language, the ritual models;" "by liturgical creativity is meant the composition of new liturgical texts, independently of the structure of the Roman Euchologion" (ibid.). The Congregation for Sacred Rites and the Discipline of the Sacraments has devoted an Instruction to *The Roman Liturgy and Inculturation*, Libreria Editrice Vaticana 1994.

[41] Cardinal Joseph Ratzinger, preface to *Die heilige Liturgie* (see above, note 16). The liturgical reform has turned out to be "not a revival, but a devastation," writes Cardinal Ratzinger in his preface to the book in which Monsignor Klaus Gamber describes it as "a liturgical devastation of frightful proportions" *La réforme liturgique en question*, p. 15.

action which runs counter to their own conscience. Cardinal Ratzinger has written some very penetrating pages concerning the inviolability of the conscience, whose essential force derives from the right to believe, and to live as Christian believers.[42] "The fundamental right of the Christian," he has written, "is the right to the whole faith"[43]—and, we might add, to the whole Liturgy. It will not be difficult to deduce the canonical and moral consequences of these clear principles.

2) Looking at things not from the point of view of Catholics faithful to the Tradition, but *sub specie Ecclesiæ*, it seems to me that the only path which the ecclesiastical authorities can reasonably follow, in the medium term, is that referred to in the formula "reform of the liturgical reform."[44]

This path arouses perplexity and scepticism in some traditionalists, in as much as the "reform of the reform" will not constitute a true and entire "restoration" of the traditional rite. Yet if it is true, as those same traditionalists maintain, that the liturgical reform brought about a real and genuine "revolution," whilst indeed it was asserting its continuity with Tradition, then how can one deny that a reform in the opposite direction, opposite in spirit, would have the possibility of achieving, albeit gradually, a return to the Tradition?

It should be clear, on the other hand, that the "reform of the reform" would have no point if it was "offered," or rather imposed, on the "traditionalists" in order to demand that they give up a rite which they, in conscience, feel they can not renounce; it would on the contrary have a point, if it were offered to the universal Church so as to correct, even in part, the liturgical deviations currently at work. The "reform of the reform" makes sense as a "transition" towards the Tradition, and not as a pretext for abandoning it.

---

[42] Cardinal Joseph Ratzinger, *Church, Ecumenism and Politics,* St Paul's, Slough 1988, pp. 165-199. This does not, of course, refer to any subjective vision of the conscience, but to the traditional concept of it, as expressed for example by Ramon Garcia de Haro, in *La vita cristiana: Corso de teologia morale fondamentale,* Ares, Milan 1995.

[43] Cardinal Joseph Ratzinger, ibid., p. 202.

[44] Cardinal Joseph Ratzinger, *The Spirit of the Liturgy,* p. 67 of the Italian trans; Brian W. Harrison, "The Postconciliar Eucharistic Liturgy: Planning a 'Reform of the Reform,'" in Thomas M. Kocik ed., *The Reform of the Reform? A Liturgical Debate — Reform or Return,* Ignatius Press, San Francisco 2003. For Dom Gérard Calvet, it would seem necessary to reintroduce these elements, at least: "1) turn the altar round; 2) return to a silent Canon and to Latin for the great sung communal prayers; 3) give domicile again to gestures of adoration: kneeling, genuflecting to the altar, receiving Communion on the tongue, and re-establishing an offertory in a traditional form, not one made up, and which recalls the expiatory character of the Mass;" "*La liturgie est la richesse des pauvres,*" in C. Geffroy/P. Maxence, *Enquête sur la Messe traditionelle,* p. 114). For Jean de Viguerie, the elements would be: "the Roman Canon, celebrating turned towards God, and receiving Communion kneeling in the mouth" ("*Attendre la réforme de l'Église,*" in Geffroy/Maxence, p. 330).

3) These measures, though necessary, will not however resolve the basic problem. In a phase which some people may consider rather long, but which is in reality merely urgent, because it will not admit of short-cuts, it will be necessary to recover a theological, ecclesiological and sociological vision founded on the dimension of the sacred, that is to say, based on a project of re-sacralising society which is diametrically opposed to the project of secularisation and of de-christianisation of which we are presently suffering the dramatic consequences.

That means that it is impossible to imagine a liturgical reform or restoration trying to be effected whilst prescinding from a reform or restoration in the spheres of theology, ecclesiology and culture. The action taken at the level of *lex orandi* will have to be in parallel with that taken at the level of *lex credendi*, recuperating the fundamental principles of Catholic theology, beginning with that of a precise theological conception of the holy Sacrifice of the Mass.

Today secularism is in crisis; but the new forms of the sacred, whether we are dealing with *New Age* religion or with the spread of Islam in the West, eliminate the Sacrifice of Jesus Christ, and thus the idea that man can be saved only by the gratuitous Love of God, through his Sacrifice, and that man should respond to such a gift by himself embracing the redemptive cross.

We ought then to draw near with love to the mystery of the sublime Cross, and to the idea of sacrifice which springs from it. Sacrifice, of which martyrdom is the model, and the expression of which is the Christian struggle, is above all the renunciation of a good which is nonetheless legitimate, in the name of a higher good. Sacrifice presupposes the idea of truth and of good, and is incompatible with contemporary religious and cultural relativism. It presupposes a mortification of the intelligence, which bows before the truth, in a direction exactly contrary to that of the self-glorification of human thought which has characterised the last few centuries.

Yet how can a recuperation of the idea of sacrifice be thought possible, that idea which is at the heart of the Catholic vision of history and of society, unless that idea be above all experienced? It seems to me necessary for the idea of sacrifice to permeate society in the form, very largely abandoned today, of the spirit of sacrifice and of penitence. This, and not other forms, is the "experience of the sacred" of which our society stands in urgent need.

Against the principle of hedonism and of the self-celebration of the ego which constitutes the core of the centuries-old revolutionary process which is attacking our society, we need to set the lived-out principle of sacrifice. Without the spirit of penitence and of sacrifice, a Catholic reconquest of society is not possible, and without this recovery of Christian principles and institutions it is difficult to imagine a return to the authentic Liturgy and to its heart: the adoration due to the one true God.

The call to penitence, and above all the example of penitence, may be worth more than many theories. That is perhaps why at Fatima the Madonna points to the way of penitence as the only one by which the contemporary world can be saved. The triple call to penitence given by the angel in the third secret of Fatima[45] is a manifesto of doctrine and of life which points us the way for any possible restoration, even that of Liturgy.

Translated by Henry Taylor

---

[45] Congregation for the Doctrine of the Faith, *The Message of Fatima*, Libreria Editrice Vaticana 2000.

Assessment and Future Prospects

Paper by His Eminence, Joseph Cardinal Ratzinger
Prefect of the Congregation for the Doctrine of the Faith

I do not venture to suggest any conclusions; I have not had the time, the intellectual capability, nor the physical strength to prepare anything of the kind. I can simply offer you a few remarks. But above all I would like to offer my deepest thanks to you, Father Abbot, for the spirit within this monastery, which has inspired us with the peace of the Church, the peace of our Lord, and which thus helps us to seek together that Catholic Ecumenism within which there can be a reconciliation within the Church, in the midst of these differences which are both deep and hurtful.

What is it I want to say? I had been thinking of talking about four points: a first point, a further remark about the intellectual and spiritual make-up of the Liturgical Movement as I have known it; next, a word about the suggestions of Father Folsom and Professor Spaemann as to pluriformity within the Roman rite, about Roman rites within the Roman rite; a word about the "reform of the reform;" and also a word, in the discussion with my friend Professor Spaemann, about the future of the 1962 Missal.

1. The Spiritual and Historical Components of the Liturgical Movement

Yesterday, I talked about the origins of the academic discipline of liturgical studies (liturgiology), saying that on one hand it had developed from historical studies, and on the other from pastoral work; that was about academic liturgical studies, not about the Liturgical Movement. In Germany the Liturgical Movement developed from a number of roots, about which Father Koster spoke to us very well;[1] I should like to emphasise that it seems to me that the great Benedictine monasteries — Beuron most of all — were the true birthplace of the authentic Liturgical Movement. Beuron, a daughter-house of Solesmes, because the two Wolter brothers had been trained in the Benedictine life at Solesmes and had founded the Benedictine renewal first of all at Beuron, and then at Maria Laach, a daughter-house of Beuron, and in the other abbeys. It is interesting to read, in the *Memoirs* of Guardini, that he himself had discovered the Liturgy while taking part in the canonical hours at

---

[1] Cf. "Summary of the Discussions" below.

Beuron, sharing in the liturgical life experienced in the spirit of Solesmes, thus in the spirit of the Fathers, and how for him this was the discovery of a new world, of Liturgy proper; that, it seems to me, offers a key to understanding what the fathers of this Movement were thinking in Germany—even if Father Anselm Schott did have a different idea, as likewise Father Odo Casel, and so on. It was in fact the discovery of the Liturgy as a symbolical world filled with reality, full of meaning. In the context on the one hand of neo-scholastic theology which was for the most part pretty dry, and on the other of rationalism and modernism—Guardini studied at Tübingen, at a time when modernism was rampant there—this movement offered a new vision of Christian reality, on the basis of the Liturgy.

For a certain kind of textbook-theology, what mattered in the sacraments, and likewise in the Eucharist, was essentially their validity, and therefore the moment of consecration. Eucharistic theology had been reduced to an ontological and juridical problem, everything else being considered as beautiful ceremonies, interesting, and which might or might not be capable of interpretation in an allegorical sense, but not as the reality in which the Eucharist has its concrete existence. It was thus necessary to discover anew that the Liturgy is not just a collection of ceremonies which aim to give length and solemnity to the consecration, but that this is the sphere of the sacrament as such. This was a new vision, and in that sense they went beyond a narrow kind of theology and discovered a more profound vision not only of theology, but of the whole Christian life. We can grasp the stature of the Liturgical Movement only in the historical context of an understanding of the Liturgy which was severely lacking. For example, from the time of Leo XIII on, we used to recite the Rosary during the Mass all through October—and that was still the custom when I was young. The Mass was thus truly, as I wrote in the preface to my book, like a painted-over fresco. Thus, to rediscover that the Liturgy in itself is living, and is a reality experienced by the Church as such, was a development which considerably enriched the Church. We have therefore left far behind those misunderstandings, those inadequate conceptions and deficient visions of the Liturgy and of theology. I even think that, equally, the explosive outbreak of the Reformation in the sixteenth century was possible because there was no longer any real understanding of the Liturgy. For Luther, all that remained of the Mass was the consecration and the distribution of Holy Communion.

Yet in this genuine progress which the Liturgical Movement brought—which led us toward Vatican II, toward *Sacrosanctum Concilium*— there lay also a danger: that of despising the Middle Ages as such, and scholastic theology as such. It was from that point onward that there was a parting of the ways: Dom Casel showed himself as an exclusive advocate of patristic theology as he saw it, and of liturgical platonism as he conceived it. These one-sided ideas were then popularised with slogans which were most unfortunate and very dangerous; thus, it already used to be said—I can quite well recall—"The consecrated bread is not there to be looked at, but to be eaten." That was a slogan directed against eucharistic adoration; people thought that the whole business, the whole development in the course of the Middle Ages, was mistaken. There was thus a liturgical rigorism, and a tendency to archaeological liturgy, which in the end became very dangerous. People could no longer grasp that even the innovations of the Middle Ages— eucharistic adoration, and popular piety, and all that—were genuinely legitimate developments. Above all, a synthesis between the two currents of opinion was then no longer possible: Guardini split off from Maria Laach because he defended the Rosary, the Way of the Cross, eucharistic adoration, whilst the others had taken up a purist position which no longer allowed room for these later developments.

This question, therefore—which we discussed yesterday—remains open: what synthesis is possible between mediaeval theology and the Fathers, and what deeper vision do they share? I think that Saint Thomas Aquinas is both a theologian who opens the door to a new vision of theology, with the integration of aristotelian thought, and at the same time a perfectly patristic theologian: taking him as our starting-point, it ought to be possible to discover this synthesis. At the beginning of the twenties, Guardini wrote a very interesting dialogue between an exegete who was a university professor, rationalist but orthodox—of the kind there were in German universities at that time—a liturgical rigorist, and a director of *Caritas*, representing popular piety, especially keen on the Sacred Heart; in this *trialogue*, he was looking for a synthesis, and that still remains to be found.

It seems to me, that as early as the nineteen-fifties, and certainly after the Council, the latent and, likewise, the patent risks in the Liturgical Movement constituted a great temptation, a serious danger for the Church. After the Council there was a new situation, because the liturgists had acquired a *de facto* authority: all the time, the authority of the Church was accorded less recognition, and it was now the expert who became the authority. This transfer of authority to the experts transformed everything, and these experts in turn were the victims of an exegesis profoundly influenced by the opinions of Protestantism, that is to say, that the New Testament was against the category of sacredness, against cult and priesthood, and thus at the opposite pole to the great tradition, above all that of the Council of Trent. The view was maintained that the New Testament was against the cult because it separated itself from the Old Testament, from the Temple. The cult was now, it was said, reality as it was lived, as it was suffered by Christ who was crucified outside the walls of the city. That meant that it was now in the realm of the *profane* that we should see the true cult, and that the break with the levitical priesthood should be seen as a break with sacral priesthood as such: the presbyterate, it was said, was not a sacral priesthood; sacral priesthood was something belonging to the old Testament, or to paganism, not something belonging to Christianity. This interpretation of the New Testament by a point of view—a hermeneutic system—fundamentally Protestant and secularising has become ever stronger with time.

Finally, it seems to me that the transition from the universal Church to the local Church, and from the local Church to the local congregation—as Professor de Mattei has said to us—has been, and at present still is, one of our greatest difficulties. People say nowadays that the Liturgy reflects the religious experience of the congregation, and that the congregation is the only real agent in the Liturgy; that leads in fact not only in the direction of a complete fragmentation of the Liturgy, but in that of the destruction of the Liturgy as such, for if the Liturgy merely reflects the religious experiences of the congregation, it no longer involves the presence of mystery. This is therefore the point at which we have to stand firm; we must rediscover the Church—the Body of Christ—as the true agent in the Liturgy. Thus, we have to be aware that with a secularised exegesis, and with a hermeneutic system profoundly Protestant and secularised, we can not find the basis of our faith in the New Testament; and that with the fragmentation of the Liturgy, when it is considered as being the particular action of the local congregations, then we lose sight of the Church and, with the Church, of faith and of mystery. What we need, in contrast to this, is to return to an exegesis rooted in the living reality of the Church, of the Church of all the ages—especially of the Church of the Fathers—but of the Church of *all* the ages: even of the Church of the Middle Ages. We need also, therefore, to rediscover cultic reality and the sacral priesthood in the New Testament, and to win back the essentials for the Liturgy; in that sense, I was wanting to say that, within the limitations which are certainly to be found in the texts of Trent, Trent remains the norm, as re-read with our greater knowledge and deeper understanding of the Fathers and of the New Testament, as read with the Fathers and with the Church of all the ages.

2. The Problem of Roman rites within the Roman rite

The fact of this co-existence of rites is obvious, as Father Folsom has shown us clearly, and in convincing fashion, and likewise Professor Spaemann. Father Folsom made explicit two consequences of this: there are no liturgical arguments against the plurality of rites, but there is a difficulty with canonical criteria, and—as he remarked—with political criteria; I should say rather, with pastoral criteria. And that is really the problem facing the authority of the Church: what are the criteria?

Personally, I was from the beginning in favour of the freedom to continue using the old Missal, for a very simple reason: people were already beginning to talk about making a break with the pre-conciliar Church, and of developing various models of Church—a preconciliar and obsolete type of Church, and a new and conciliar type of Church. This is at any rate nowadays the slogan of the Lefebvrists, insisting that there are two Churches, and for them the great rupture becomes visible in the existence of two Missals, which are said to be irreconcilable with each other. It seems to me essential, the basic step, to recognise that both Missals are Missals of the Church, and belong to the Church which remains the same as ever. The preface of Paul VI's Missal says explicitly that it is a Missal of the same Church, and acknowledges its continuity. And in order to emphasise that there is no essential break, that there is continuity in the Church, which retains its identity, it seems to me indispensable to continue to offer the opportunity to celebrate according to the old Missal, as a sign of the enduring identity of the Church. This is for me the basic reason: what was up until 1969 *the* Liturgy of the Church, for all of us the most holy thing there was, can not become after 1969 — with incredibly positivistic decision — the most unacceptable thing. If we want to be credible, even with being modern as a slogan, we absolutely have to recognise that what was fundamental before 1969 remains fundamental afterwards: the realm of the sacral is the same, the Liturgy is the same.

Observing the developments in how the new Missal was applied, I very quickly found a second reason, one which Professor Spaemann has also mentioned: the old Missal is a point of reference, a criterion — as he said, a semaphore signal. It seems to me most important for everyone, that by its presence — which is a sign of the basic identity of the two Missals, even if they have differing modes of expression in ritual — this Missal of the Church should offer a point of reference, and should become a refuge for those faithful who, in their own parish, no longer find a Liturgy genuinely celebrated in accordance with the texts authorised by the Church. There is no doubt, on the one hand, that a venerable rite such as the Roman rite in use up to 1969 is a rite of the Church, it belongs to the Church, is one of the treasures of the Church, and ought therefore to be preserved in the Church.

One problem, on the other hand, does remain: how are we to regulate the use of the two rites? It seems to me clear that, in law, the Missal of Paul VI is the Missal in current use, and that using it is normal. We should therefore consider how to permit the use of the old Missal, and to preserve this treasure for the Church. I have often spoken along the same lines as our friend Professor Spaemann: if there used to be the Dominican rite, if there used to be — and, in fact, there still is — the Milanese rite, then why not likewise the rite, shall we say, "of Saint Pius V"? Yet there is a very real problem here: if the *ecclesial community* becomes a matter of free choice, if there are, within the Church, churches of ritual, chosen according to subjective criteria, that does create a problem. The Church is built, in the form of local Churches, on the existence of bishops in succession to the apostles, and thus presenting an objective criterion. I am in *this* local Church, and I don't look for my friends there, I find my brothers and my sisters; and these brothers and sisters are not people we look for, we just find them there. This situation, in which the Church in which I find myself is in no way *arbitrary*, in that it is not the

Church of my choosing but simply the Church which presents itself to me, is a very important principle. It seems to me that the letters of Saint Ignatius run very strongly along these lines: that this bishop is the Church; this is not my choice, as if I were to go with this or that group of friends; I am in the common Church, along with the poor, the wealthy, with people I like and people I don't like, with intellectuals and uneducated people; I am in the Church, which was there before me. Opening up the opportunity of choosing one's Church "à la carte," is something which could genuinely damage the structure of the Church.

One ought therefore — it seems to me — to look for a non-subjective criterion, with which to open-up the opportunity of using the old Missal. That seems to me very simple, in the case of abbeys: this is a good thing; likewise, it corresponds to the tradition by which there used to be orders with their own rite, for example the Dominicans. Thus, abbeys which ensure the continuing presence of this rite, and likewise religious communities such as the Dominicans of Saint Vincent Ferrer, or other religious communities, or fraternities — they seem to me to offer an objective criterion. Naturally, the problem becomes more complicated with the fraternities, which are not religious orders but communities of non-diocesan priests who are active in parishes. Perhaps the "personal parish" might be a solution, but that is not without difficulty either. In any case, the Holy See should open-up this opportunity, and preserve this treasure, for all the faithful; yet on the other hand, it must also preserve and respect the episcopal structure of the Church.

3. The "Reform of the Reform"

Professor Spaemann is right: the "reform of the reform" refers of course to the reformed Missal, not to the Missal in previous use. What can we do, given that the goal we are all aiming for in the end — it seems to me — is liturgical reconciliation, and not *uniformity*? I am not in favour of *uniformity*; but we should of course be opposed to *chaos*, to the fragmentation of the Liturgy, and in that sense we should also be in favour of observing unity in the use of Paul VI's Missal. That seems to me a problem to be faced as a priority: how can we return to a *common* rite, reformed (if you like) but not fragmented, nor left to the arbitrary devices of local congregations, nor that of a few commissions, or groups of experts? Thus, the "reform of the reform" is something which concerns the Missal of Paul VI, always with this aim of achieving reconciliation within the Church, since for the moment there exists rather a painful opposition, and we are still a long way from reconciliation, even if these days we have shared together here are an important step towards that reconciliation.

As concerns the Missal in current use, the first point, in my opinion, would be to reject the false creativity which is not a category of the Liturgy. We have more than once recalled what the Council actually said on this subject: it is only ecclesiastical authority which makes decisions, neither the priest, nor any small group of people, has the right to change the Liturgy. But in the new Missal we quite often find formulae such as: *sacerdos dicit sic vel simili modo...* or, *Hic sacerdos potest dicere...* These formulae of the Missal in fact give official sanction to creativity; the priest feels almost obliged to change the wording, to show that he is creative, that he is giving this Liturgy immediacy, making it present for his congregation; and with this false creativity, which transforms the Liturgy into a catechetical exercise for *this* congregation, the liturgical unity and the *ecclesiality* of the Liturgy is being destroyed. Therefore, it seems to me, it would be an important step towards reconciliation, simply if the Missal were freed from these areas of creativity, which do not correspond to the deepest level of reality, to the spirit, of the Liturgy. If, by means of such a "reform of the reform," we could get back to a faithful, ecclesial celebration of the Liturgy, then this would in my opinion be itself an important step, because the *ecclesial dimension* of the Liturgy would once more be clearly apparent.

The second point about which we have spoken is that of the translations: Canon Rose said some important things to us; the crisis is almost more serious in the United States, in the English-speaking world, with permanent changes in the language, with the problem of what is *politically correct* and that of "inclusive language." There are some congregations in the United States where, in the name of inclusive language, they no longer dare to say, "In the name of the Father, and of the Son, and of the Holy Spirit," because that is "male chauvinism" – the Father and the Son: two men. They then say, "In the name of the Creator, of the Redeemer, and of the Holy Spirit." That is just one example to show the seriousness of the problem, and there is the insistence of some bishops (not of the Bishops' Conference as such) on using what they call "real language" – according to them, the other kind is no longer real language. The use of inclusive language involves the disappearance of essential things, such as for example, in the Psalms, the whole christological dimension, because masculine words are forbidden. Thus the problem of translations is a serious one. There is a new document from the Holy See on this problem which constitutes, it seems to me, genuine progress.[2] I would just add this: we ought also to preserve some elements of Latin in the Liturgy in ordinary use; the presence of a certain amount of Latin seems to me important, as constituting a bond of ecclesial fellowship and communion.

The third problem is the celebration *versus populum*. As I have written in my books, I think that celebration turned towards the east, towards the Christ who is coming, is an apostolic tradition. I am not however in favour of forever changing churches around completely; so many churches have now been restructured, that starting all over again right now does not seem to me at all a good idea. But if there were always, on every altar, a cross, a quite

---

[2] Cf. Congregation for Divine Worship and the Discipline of the Sacraments, *Liturgicam Authenticam*, 28 March 2001.

visible cross, as a point of reference for *everyone*, for the priest and for the faithful, then we would have our east, because in the end the Crucified Christ is the Christian east; and we could, it seems to me, without any violence do as follows: we could offer the Crucified one, the Cross, as a point of reference, and thus give the Liturgy a new orientation. I think this is not a purely exterior thing: if the Liturgy is celebrated within a closed circle, if there is only the dialogue between priest and people, that constitutes a false clericalisation, and there is an absence of a common path towards the Lord, towards which we all turn together. Thus, having the Lord as a point of reference for everyone, priest and people, seems to me something important which can perfectly well be put into practice.

4. The Future of the Missal of Saint Pius V

I well know the sensibilities of those faithful who love this Liturgy — these are, to some extent, my own sensibilities. And in that sense, I can well understand what Professor Spaemann was saying when he asserted that if you do not know the aim of a reform, however small it may be, if you are left to suppose that this is just an intermediate step towards a complete revolution, then people feel sensitive about it. And in that sense we have to be very careful about any possible changes. However, he did also say — and I emphasise this — it would be fatal for the old Liturgy to be, as it were, placed in a deep-freeze, left like a national park, a park protected for the sake of a certain kind of people, for whom one leaves available these relics of the past. This would be — as Professor de Mattei said to us — a kind of inculturation: "There are also the conservationists, let that group have their own cultural version!" If it were to be reduced to the past in that way, we would not be preserving this treasure for the Church of today, and that of tomorrow. It seems to me that we should avoid, come what may, having this Liturgy frozen, as if in a deep-freeze, just for a certain type of people.

It must also be a Liturgy *of the Church*, and under the authority of the Church; and only within this *ecclesial dimension*, in a *fundamental* relationship with the authority of the Church, can it give all that it has to offer. Naturally, one can say, 'We no longer have any confidence in the authority of the Church, after all we have been through in the past thirty years.' It is nevertheless a basic Catholic principle to trust in the authority of the Church. I have always been much impressed by something Harnack said in a discussion with Peterson, a Protestant theologian who at that time was moving towards converting to Catholicism; Harnack answered the questions of his younger colleague by saying: it is obvious that the Catholic principle of *Scripture and Tradition* is better, and that it is the correct principle, and that it implies the existence of a given authority in the Church; but even if the principle in itself, the Catholic principle, is correct, we are better off living without an authority and without the actions such an authority might take. He had confidence that the free use of reason in studying the Scriptures would bring men to the truth, and that this was better than being subject to some authority which could equally make mistakes. That is true, authority can make mistakes, but being obedient to that authority is for us the guarantee of our being obedient to the Lord. That is certainly a very strong admonition to those people who are exercising authority, not to exercise it in the way you exercise power. Having authority in the Church is always an exercise in obedience. When the Holy Father decided that the Church does not have the power to ordain women, this was an exercise in obedience towards the great Tradition of the Church and towards the Holy Spirit. For me, it is always most interesting to see the keenest progressives and the fiercest opponents of the Church's Magisterium saying to us, "Why, no, of course the Church can perfectly well do that! You ought to make use of the powers you have available!" — No, the Church can not do everything, the Pope can not do everything. It seems to me that, towards an authority which in the present situation is becoming more than ever a conscious exercise in obedience, everyone can have, *must* have such confidence.

To speak more in concrete, practical terms, I am not going to do anything in this sphere for the moment—that is clear. But, for the future, we ought to think—it seems to me—in terms of enriching the Missal of 1962 by introducing some new saints; there are now some important figures amongst the saints—I am thinking, for example, of Maximilian Kolbe, Edith Stein, the martyrs of Spain, the martyrs of Ukraine, and so many others—but also thinking of that little Bakita in the Sudan, who came from slavery and came to freedom in her faith in the Lord; there are many really lovely figures whom we all *need*. Thus, opening-up the calendar of the old Missal to new saints, making a well thought-out choice of these, that seems to me something which would be appropriate at present, and would not have any destructive effect on the fabric of the Liturgy. We might also think about the Prefaces, which also come from the storehouse of wealth in the Church Fathers, for Advent, for example, and then others; why not insert those Prefaces into the old Missal?

Thus, with great sensitivity, and by showing a great deal of understanding for people's fears and preoccupations, maintaining contact with their leaders, we should be able to understand that this Missal is also a Missal *of the Church*, and under the authority of the Church, that it is not an object preserved from the past, but a living reality within the Church, *very much* respected in its particular identity and for its historical stature, but equally considered as something which is living, and not as a dead thing, a relic of the past. All the Liturgy of the Church is always a living thing, a reality which is higher than us, and is not subject to our decisions and our arbitrary intentions. Those are the few remarks that I wanted to make.

Translated by Henry Taylor

Summary of the Discussions

T HE discussions centred around the two themes associated with the papers given on Sunday 22nd and Monday 23rd of July: the theology of the Liturgy (whether considered in itself, or in respect of its anthropological presuppositions), and the development of the Liturgical Movement. In the third place—and especially on Tuesday morning, during the final and less formal round of discussions—particular and practical problems were raised. These will be the three headings under which this outline account is given.

1. The Questions Raised in the Discussions on the Theology of the Liturgy

1) Saint Thomas has given a most precise analysis of the rôle and the place of the moral virtue of religious practice, besides (and subordinated to) the theological virtues: in order to define and locate the specific characteristics of the liturgical and sacramental facts, we have to call upon this virtue of religious practice, since this is what enables us to think accurately and in a balanced way about the collaboration of God and man in the work of salvation. Sacrifice only becomes intelligible, if we take into account the fact that this is the action peculiar to the practice of religious virtue.

2) Luther had wanted to abolish the sacrifice of the Mass, in order to leave to the one sole sacrifice of Christ its proper place: it was on account of not knowing about the premises subsumed in the previous point, that the reform ended up in fact with the contrary result, by too often weakening people's sense of the presence of the Cross, now that it was no longer a part of the Liturgy of the Mass—which is in fact the only means whereby we can come in contact with the Cross itself, via the celestial Liturgy which acts as intermediary for us, in the manner portrayed in the Book of Revelation.

3) The cultural ambience of today creates difficulties for the proper development of the true spirit of the Liturgy. The rationalism of the Enlightenment and the Romanticism of the nineteenth century have in fact made it impossible for modern man to perceive the truth of anything which is neither purely rational and objective (as in the Enlightenment), nor a purely subjective approach (as in Romanticism). We have to transcend the opposition

between these two ways of apprehending the Liturgy, especially in order to become able to perceive the realities of this world as being symbolical of the realities of God. Symbolical knowledge, imparted by signs, is the type of knowledge most suited to the very nature of man: it is in this way that God teaches us in Holy Scripture, and in this way that the Liturgy expresses things. Thus it is, that Saint Thomas applies the same hermeneutical principles when he expounds the meaning of the rites of the Mass, as when interpreting Holy Scripture.

2. The History and the Development of the Liturgical Movement:

1) In the German-speaking world, it was Anselm Schott of Beuron who started the Liturgical Movement. The influence of Dom Guéranger can be seen here, as transmitted by the Abbey of Beuron, which had been given a very "solesmian" spirit by its founders, the Wolter brothers; but beyond that we should note the particular interest in Patristics and the Early Church, especially the eastern Churches (even before the advent of Baumstark in the twentieth century).

2) Dom Lambert Beauduin gave the Liturgical Movement a new direction, or rather, he gave it a second start, but in a quite different direction, which is described as being *pastoral*, and this is what characterises the Belgian Movement (the Abbeys of Louvain, Maredsous and Bruges). It was this *new* Movement which would be taken up by the Abbey of Maria Laach (somewhat in competition with its mother-house of Beuron), and then also Pius Parsch, an Austin canon of Klosterneuburg, who started up a popular movement for rediscovering the Bible; the latter would insist on a Liturgy in the vernacular and an altar facing the people. The various youth movements in Germany were used for trying out this or that person's ideas in practice: community spirit, songs in German (and there was, in this area, an old tradition going back before the advent of Protestantism, of singing in people's native language — but in the eighteenth century it was made compulsory by bishops who were influenced by *Enlightenment* ideas), an altar in a central position. The church was conceived of as being above all the *domus ecclesiæ*, rather than the *domus Dei*: and there, too, can be seen certain basic assumptions of the eighteenth century *Enlightenment*. Nonetheless, the great liturgist of Maria Laach, Dom Odo Casel, is more of a theoretician than a pastor, with his *Theology of Mysteries*, despite which his Masses, which were called *Community Masses*, were very influential.

3) Josef Andreas Jungmann SJ, is often considered to be one of the fathers of the 1969 reform, and to have written the Council's Constitution *Sacrosanctum Concilium*. In fact, in his book *The Early Liturgy to the Time of Gregory the Great*, he takes a purely historical approach to the Liturgy, and his *Missarum*

Sollemnia is rather concerned to promote a greater diversity within the interior unity of the Roman rite.

We can see that, above and beyond the historical vicissitudes of the Liturgical Movement, Dom Guéranger stands as a pioneering figure. The present-day results, however, do not seem really to correspond to the level of his ideals. Thus, on the sidelines of this discussion, it will be right to reproduce in their entirety the two papers about him which come from his own monastic family, that of Dom Hervé Courau, Abbott of Triors, and that of Dom Robert Le Gall, Abbott of Kergonan:

Dom Courau: In a monastic house which belongs to the same family as that of Dom Guéranger, it is appropriate to emphasise the critical place he occupies as the founder of the *first Liturgical Movement*, before the time when this followed its course without him, more or less divided, I think one can fairly say, into two branches which, to be as brief and as clear as I can, I shall call that of *liturgical mystery* (Odo Casel, Beuron) and that of *pastoral Liturgy* (Dom Lambert Beauduin).

The founding father of the Liturgical Movement often cuts a controversial figure, and is associated with the criticism inspired by *liturgical romanticism*. Isn't this being somewhat hasty? In view of our present difficulties, should we not reconsider this judgement? A more considered and balanced judgement is necessary, I believe, and it would be intellectual laziness to be content with this label of *Romanticism*. Whatever might be the intrinsic limits of this or that point of view which he defended, both our experience and our understanding suggest that his particular genius, this gift more or less recognised by the Church,[1] resides in *the balance he established between erudition, a spirit of synthesis, and culture, on one hand*, and what I should like to call *the family spirit as a characteristic of the Liturgy*: Mother Church gets her children to pray. The children are at one with the customs and usages, the furniture they inherit, without asking questions about it, it is all part of the well-loved scene, we accept it without knowing the details of the story of each separate piece, because it all inspires us with trust and filial obedience.

We know that in 1947 Pius XII's encyclical *Mediator Dei* (a statement of the Magisterium) denounced certain points about the Liturgical Movement of that time, with a view to reworking it upon a sounder basis. A paper was given on this at the CIEL colloquium at Laus in 1996.[2] Father Gy, a Dominican, gave a single-sentence answer: straight after publishing the encyclical, Pius XII appointed as members of the commission entrusted with applying the new guidelines the very persons who had been criticised by the encyclical. If such a measure had been taken with respect to Dom Guéranger, it is certain that his

---

[1] Cf. Paul VI, on the centenary of his death: *Doctor liturgicus.*

[2] Cf. Wolfgang Graf, "The Encyclical *Mediator Dei* and Eucharistic Doctrine" in *The Veneration and Administration of the Eucharist*, St Austin Press, Southampton 1997, pp. 112-145.

loyalty and his submission to the Magisterium would have been whole-hearted. The 1947 commission, on the other hand, merely treated the criticisms voiced by the encyclical as if they were non-existent. This is the origin of that impression of lack of loyalty to the Magisterium, which hangs over the liturgical reform, to far too great an extent, both before and during the Council.

In comparison with that, what one admires in Dom Guéranger (and whatever may be, once again, his alleged or possible limitations) is the inter-relation between *intelligence* (the ability for constructive thinking), *piety*, and *docility*. It is this *working combination* which has probably been lacking since then, and this which should characterise any future effort made to restart the Movement. In this sense, Dom Guéranger could breathe new life into the Movement, provided that we look at him afresh, that we make a new approach to studying him. He is often hoisted like a banner, but with contradictory meanings: either people string together quotations which seem to flay the new Liturgy, like shying at an aunt sally, or, on the contrary, other moderating passages are offered us, which would appear as the first springs of all that has happened further on downstream, in the past thirty years. Father Frénaud, Prior of Solesmes at the beginning of the sixties, conducted an exchange of letters with Father Bouyer, with a view to contradicting the caricature the latter had drawn. The study of Dom Cuthbert Johnson on the liturgical reform and Dom Guéranger (1970)[3] was perhaps written too soon, in the heat of the moment. The thirty years' distancing might allow of better handling of this theme in depth.

For the occasion of the initiation of the cause of his beatification in the diocesan tribunal, Solesmes has just published a new life of Dom Guéranger (by Dom Oury). This is well-written study, which would only require to be a little more precise and systematic in its details in the liturgical sphere, which is what interests us. *Dom Guéranger, the Unrivalled Liturgist*, that is a phrase of Dom Lambert Beauduin, who nonetheless took a very different path. No-one can speak to us in place of him, but there is no doubt, either, that he still has something to say to us, in our present difficulties. At this distance in time, one would love to bring Dom Guéranger into co-operation with others, with Newman for example (but the latter was the friend of Lacordaire, who opposed Dom Guéranger, whilst he himself was the friend of Faber, who was in opposition to Newman within the English Oratory...). We can not rewrite history, but we can read it wisely, and bring together, beyond the limits of time, things and people who would thus become more rounded.

---

[3] [sic]. Cf. *Prosper Guéranger (1805-1875): A Liturgical Theologian: An Introduction to his liturgical writings and work*, Studia Anselmiana 89, P. Ateneo S. Anselmo, Rome 1984 [Ed.].

Dom Le Gall: Adolf Adam criticised Dom Guéranger, asserting that he was not an advocate of liturgical participation. I have recently tried to show, in an article in *La Maison-Dieu*, that the opposite is the case.[4]

It was the Romantics who brought Dom Guéranger to read Holy Scripture. Next he discovered the Church Fathers. And on discovering the Roman Liturgy, at the Convent of the Visitation at Le Mans, he was struck by the unity which existed between this Liturgy and the Fathers.

Dom Guéranger's genius enabled him to talk about the Liturgy as a mystery of the bridegroom and the bride. And if he was granted such an understanding of the Liturgy, this was thanks to his docility in following where the Holy Spirit led; that was what enabled him to grasp the unity between priest and people in the Liturgy: those are the three factors which endow the Liturgy with a trinitarian dimension: Bridegroom, Bride, Holy Spirit.

In his paper, Cardinal Ratzinger emphasised that it is God who acts through the Liturgy. That is in line with Saint Benedict's interest in the *Opus Dei*, the Work of God, a key concept where the Liturgy is concerned.[5]

3. Particular Current Problems in Respect of Liturgical Celebration

1) In the current difficulties, what particular action could the *bishops* take? To give an example in the liturgical celebrations at which they preside, and to lose no opportunity of teaching the faithful how they can take part. As well as this, there is the problem of *teachers of Liturgy* in the seminaries and universities: the future of the Liturgy depends on the way in which future priests are going to understand it. There is a movement towards uniting the teachers of Liturgy with those who teach sacramental theology. This development seems encouraging.

2) Difficulties in connection with *liturgical singing* are numerous and serious. In France, the standard repertory has been reduced to a few popular pieces which you come across at no matter what season of the liturgical year, and indeed at no matter what place in the Mass.

In Germany, by contrast, there is a more well-established tradition, that of the *Deutsches Hochamt* (German High Mass) or *Choralamt* (Choral Sung Mass): with singing in the vernacular (for the Proper as well as for the Ordinary), and with a text differing from that of the Liturgy. The German episcopate, however, has just authorised the use of equivalent paraphrases in place of the Ordinary, and this measure strikes a blow at the Latin repertory, which had otherwise fortunately endured; this is so much so, that Masses are coming into general use, in which the authentic text is becoming a dead letter.

---

[4] *À l'unisson des Pères: L'influence durable de Dom Guéranger sur la réforme liturgique*, La Maison-Dieu no. 219, (1999), pp. 141-186.

[5] See the study by Father Hausherr on *Opus Dei* in the Benedictine Rule, *Opus Dei facientis.*

The wish has been expressed, that the celebrant should revive the usage from before 1969, of speaking the official liturgical text apart from the singing, as a kind of doublet, in just the way this had been done since the eighteenth century.

3) When one is trying to "bring back" a parish on which all the innovations have been inflicted, it is necessary, of course, to go at it very gently, so as not to come into direct conflict with the new habits of the parishioners. When the priest sets himself to this task in a spirit of faith, however, and with a coherent idea of the Liturgy, then the faithful are soon aware of this coherence, and of· the quality of the things being aimed at, and respect them: the opposition collapses of its own accord, the customs which lack any basis in tradition disintegrate. Yet the difficulties are significantly greater, whenever there are lay liturgical teams in existence, as an institution in competition with the authority of the pastor.

The Benedictine Abbey
of Saint Michael at Farnborough
was founded from the French
Abbey of Solesmes in 1895. The monks live
a traditional life of prayer, work and study
in accordance with the ancient
Rule of Saint Benedict.
At the heart of their life is the praise of God
expressed through the solemn
celebration of the Sacred Liturgy,
and supported through their work,
of which this publication is an example.